Best Wishes

[signature]

BILL BEAUMONT'S SPORTING YEAR

Looking in on the best of British sport

Stanley Paul
London Melbourne Sydney Auckland Johannesburg

Stanley Paul & Co. Ltd

An imprint of the Hutchinson Publishing Group

17–21 Conway Street, London WIP 6JD

Hutchinson Publishing Group (Australia) Pty Ltd
16–22 Church Street, Hawthorn, Melbourne, Victoria 3122

Hutchinson Group (NZ) Ltd
32 – 34 View Road, PO Box 40-086, Glenfield, Auckland 10

Hutchinson Group (SA) Pty Ltd
PO Box 337, Bergvlei 2012, South Africa

First published 1984

© Bill Beaumont 1984

Designed by Grub Street Design, London.
Set in Garamond by Margaret Spooner Typesetting, Dorset
Printed and bound in Great Britain by Anchor Brendon Ltd,
Tiptree, Essex

British Library Cataloguing in Publication Data
Beaumont, Bill, *1952*–
Bill Beaumont's sporting year 1984.
I. Sports—Great Britain
I. Title
796'.0941   GV605

ISBN 0–09–158440–X

CONTENTS

ACKNOWLEDGEMENTS

I would like to thank Ian Robertson, BBC rugby correspondent, for all his help in the preparation and editing of this book and for accompanying me on our far-flung tour of great sporting events, which included the length and breadth of Britain and places as far away as Hong Kong. I would also like to thank most sincerely BAT Stores and, in particular, their Chairman, Joe Phillips, for the very generous financial involvement they have had in the whole project. Without this sponsorship I would have had to lower my sights and would have been unable to attack the exciting venture in the way I had intended. I hope Joe and his company feel it has all been worthwhile and I am grateful for their support. I covered over 20,000 miles in six months and I would like to express my gratitude and appreciation to David Lyon at Dutton Forshaw garages, especially for generously providing me with a luxurious Rover throughout this period. The car has been well run in! It would have been quite impossible to capture the special flavour of each event without the cooperation of all the famous sporting personalities who gave so freely of their time to talk to me before and after the action, and I would wish to emphasize that I am indebted to all of them.

I am delighted to say that once again the book is greatly enhanced by the quality of photographs and the credit is largely due to Colin Elsey and his colleagues at Colorsport, who provided the vast majority from Sarajevo in February to Los Angeles in August. As always I would wish to express my thanks to the posse of half a dozen typists who wrought miracles to have the quarter of a million words transcribed from countless taped interviews to produce the finished script on the publisher's desk about six hours before the deadline. The secretarial pool was headed by Mandy Easterbrook and I am grateful to her for her tremendous dedication and speed and also to Dominique Shead, Caroline Burns, Elaine Stewart, Annette Kristensen, Barbara Moller and the others for their great efforts. I would like to thank Jo Edwards for the excellent job she has done with the copy editing, and Angela Patmore for helping with the introductory pieces. Thanks also to Len Matthews for his cooperation in dealing with a handful of important video tapes, and my secretary Evelyn Birchall for somehow managing to coordinate hundreds of phone calls and messages so efficiently during the busiest and hairiest and most enjoyable few months of my life. Finally, I would like to put on record the fantastic help and encouragement I received throughout the writing of the book from my very understanding wife, Hilary, and from Roddy Bloomfield who kept me on the right side of sanity when the going got tough.

PHOTOGRAPHIC ACKNOWLEDGEMENT

For permission to reproduce copyright photographs, the publishers would like to thank Colorsport, Patrick Eagar, Steve Yarnell, David Hastings, Selwyn Photos, Peter Dazeley Photography, *Boxing News*, Tommy Hindley and the *Guardian*.

FOREWORD

I am delighted to have the opportunity to introduce *Bill Beaumont's Sporting Year* — looking at the best of British sport in 1984.

Over the past few years, our companies have backed many sporting activities ranging from tennis to hockey to rugby and have derived much pleasure from being able to support many local activities and national sportsmen and women. Having personally been involved in the Olympic Fund Raising and the Sports Aid Foundation, I have grown to respect the influence that Bill Beaumont has had — not only in rugby, but over a much wider sporting field.

It is significant, therefore, that he has now chosen to examine no fewer than 18 sports and the peaks of achievement recorded both by individuals and teams during the last 12 months.

I also feel that it is appropriate that the BAT Stores retailing group should be involved in this exciting publishing venture, in view of our commitment to creating training facilities for young people.

In this Olympic year of 1984, we have again witnessed some outstanding personal achievements leading to the setting of new world and Olympic records. BAT Stores is itself 'going for gold' in British retailing and particularly in our new chain, 'The Jewellers Guild'.

I wish Bill Beaumont and our sports people every success in the future.

Joe Phillips
Chief Executive, BAT Stores, PLC

BAT Stores PLC is one of Britain's largest multiple retailers. The group comprises the Argos Distributors catalogue showrooms, International Stores supermarkets and the Jewellers Guild, a chain of jewellery shops.

THE CHELTENHAM GOLD CUP

Ironically for the achnowledged mecca of steeplechasing, Cheltenham's first races, at the beginning of the ninteenth century, were on the flat. Since then, with its prestige and choice of 'old' and 'new' courses, Cheltenham's three-day National Hunt Festival meeting in March has attracted the finest horses in the land, and so have Cheltenham's other fixtures during the jumping season.

Prestbury Park was first used in 1902, though there have been three different steeplechasing tracks in the Cotswold district. In 1964 the course was taken over by the Racecourse Holdings Trust, a non-profitmaking organization, and they reportedly bid almost a quarter of a million pounds for it. The famous Festival meeting includes, apart from the Cheltenham Gold Cup itself and the aptly-named Champions' Hurdle Challenge Cup, the so-called 'amateurs' Grand National – the four-mile National Hunt Chase. 'Hurdles' are built in sections which fall down when knocked by a horse; 'steeplechasing' is over solid obstacles, so that the horse falls rather than the jumps.

The first Gold Cup in 1924 was a memorable affair with a three-horse neck-and-neck finish. The winner, a five-year-old called Red Splash, held on by his whiskers from Conjuror II to take the £685 first prize, having run the original race distance of 3 miles, 3 furlongs. The distance has varied slightly over the years, and is now 3 miles, 2 furlongs, 76 yards: the supreme test of a horse's courage, stamina and precision over the sticks. The race is for five-year-olds and upwards, with the youngest horses carrying 11 stone 4 pounds and the others 12 stone.

There have been several Gold Cup superstars, beginning with Easter Hero, a stout-hearted beast who came second in the Grand National carrying under 12 stone 7 pounds just a fortnight after storming the 1929 Gold Cup by 20 lengths. He retained the Cup the following year, streaking home again by 20 lengths, but was lame for the National. Nothing but the weather could stop the illustrious Golden Miller from winning half a dozen Gold Cups from 1932 to 1937, whisking four different jockeys past the post. In 1934 this indomitable horse won both the Cup and the Grand National, previously considered an impossible feat.

Two of the greatest post-War horses who still live in the minds of racegoers were the Vincent O'Brien-trained Cottage Rake, ridden by Aubrey Brabazon to a Gold Cup hat-trick in 1948–1950, and the heroic Arkle, who won by contemptuous margins. Arkle strolled home by five lengths from Mill House in 1964, by 20 lengths from Mill House in 1965, and by 30 lengths in 1966, leaving second-placed Dormant dormant.

Armed with all this background material on the Cheltenham National Hunt Festival and with memories of the great Arkle fresh on my mind, I set off in high spirits for the 1984 Gold Cup. The racing cognoscenti insisted that to understand fully the unique atmosphere of the Festival it was essential to soak up the peripheral activities on the Wednesday evening, and it was generally agreed that there would be few better watering holes to soak up the ambience than chez Terry . . . Biddlecombe.

Terry Biddlecombe was one of the really outstanding national hunt jockeys of the last 20 years and living near Cheltenham he is still deeply interested and involved in the sport. Great jockeys, as I was soon to learn, do not usually make great tipsters but invariably they have a wealth of good yarns to spin and they are often outstanding raconteurs. In his own earthy, worldly-wise way Terry is quite capable of captivating an audience and, on the Wednesday evening, he had a most interesting and interested audience.

The whole town and surrounding area are all throbbing and buzzing on big race nights and there were parties galore within a radius of 20 miles from the winning post on the racecourse. I ventured tentatively into a couple of the big hotels to see if it were really true that compulsive gamblers would indeed be compulsively gambling right through the night, winning and losing considerable sums of money at cards or backgammon. It was true. Everyone seemed keen to tell me how they had very nearly won a fortune on the opening day of the meeting and how, but for unconscionable bad luck, they would definitely have had the bookies screaming for mercy from the highest roof tops in

Gloucestershire on Wednesday, the middle day of the three-day meeting.

I was impressed by the remarkably resilient optimism sustaining the keen punter at times when I would be tempted to slip quietly into the nearest hole in the ground and cower till the urge to thrust more money at the bookmakers had passed. At any rate, I noted that money was changing hands at a fair lick that evening. There was a cacophony of cosmopolitan voices in all the major public meeting places drowning my thoughts but I could detect an inordinate number of Irish accents. There was a general consensus that tomorrow, for sure, the bookies would be skinned and that, on a very lively night, people were happy and enjoying life.

In the belief that all big rugby players need a couple of barrels of beer as a nightcap before they can even contemplate sleep, I found Terry to be an extremely friendly and generous host and after a quick gargle at his house we departed for a nearby party at the imposing mansion of a well-known, American amateur jockey: George Sloan. There, I stumbled into rather august company including the Queen's racehorse trainer Ian Balding, leading national-hunt trainer Josh Gifford, well-known showjumping stars Ted and Liz Edgar, Dougie Bunn, the man who runs Hickstead, and Robin Gray, racing writer and broadcaster and a genuine racing expert. I relaxed in the safe knowledge that if this gathering failed to give me six winners for the next day then there would be very few noses pushed up against the glass of the pay-out window in any bookmaker's shop in Britain.

It was with this new-found confidence that I had a few drinks and agreed to play a couple of hands of cards back at Terry's house acknowledging that if, perchance, I lost around £15, I was guaranteed to recoup it all and a lot more on the racecourse. Three or four hours passed quickly and, after listening to our admirable host, George Sloan, relate a series of delightfully delivered jokes which would have gone down well at any rugby-club dinner, we adjourned to the Biddlecombes in the very early hours of Thursday morning. My intention to play

A spectacular shot of Fifty Dollars More leading Observe (no. 9) and the eventual winner of the Cheltenham Gold Cup, Burrough Hill Lad (no. 4), over a fence on the far side at Cheltenham

cards briefly got a little out of hand and, for three hours until six in the morning, I sat transfixed by the dining-room table leaving on only three occasions – once to get more money from my jacket, once to get more money from my suitcase, and lastly to dig into the reserve fund in my car. Someone left that table and staggered up to bed £60 better off, balancing my loss, but there was no time to lose sleep over it and, furthermore, I had the day's six winners written down and my wallet would soon be replenished.

Three hours later, at nine o'clock, we were all up, swallowing strong coffee and studying *The Sporting Life*, the punter's bible. All the house guests chipped in with a mass of conflicting advice for every race and I became a shade anxious that my first fully fledged fling at the bookies might not necessarily end in total triumph.

At mid-morning we set off in convoy to Cheltenham and sat down, a trifle gingerly, to an early lunch. As with the Derby and the Grand National, the build-up to the Gold Cup lasts approximately 12 months from the moment the previous year's winner passes the line. The talk over lunch was mainly about the Gold Cup and I knew, depending on which group of people I placed the greatest credence, that Wayward Lad was unbeatable, Bregawn had done it last year and was even better this year, Brown Chamberlain would pulverize the whole field on the uphill run-in and Burrough Hill Lad was unquestionably the class horse of the race.

I finished lunch in time to seek two more pieces to fit the apparently hopeless jigsaw puzzle, but I was encouraged by the fact that I was about to be entertained and informed by two unsurpassable, unimpeachable racing experts – Julian Wilson of the BBC and Mick Cuddy, the Irish international Rugby Union selector and owner of Drumlargan, fifth favourite for the Gold Cup. I approached Julian Wilson and received a tremendous boost to my confidence when he told me there was one certain way of being able to leave Cheltenham with a small fortune – to turn up initially with a large fortune. However, if pushed to give a selection in the opening race of the day, the

very competitive *Daily Express* Triumph Hurdle, he would plump for the favourite, See You Then, with Tom Sharpe the best outsider.

I thought it would be expedient to double check this advice, so I wandered up to the box which housed the amiable figure of Mick Cuddy. He said that if the ground had been a bit softer he would have had huge confidence in Drumlargan in the Gold Cup, but on ground too fast, he was just hoping to run into a place. What about the first race, I inquired somewhat tentatively. Mick quickly introduced me to his trainer, Eddie O'Grady, who was about to go to the paddock to saddle Northern Game, but I gathered from the massive shaking of heads and shrugging of shoulders that this four-year-old chestnut colt was not considered the outstanding bet of 1984. Eddie was hopeful that the horse might run quite well but he could hardly be expected to actually win the most prestigious four-year-old hurdle race in Europe because, like Drumlargan, he needed softer ground to show his best form. Mick suggested that if I was determined to throw greenbacks in the bookies' direction I could probably do a lot worse than invest in Childown, the stable companion of the favourite. There had been some inspired rumblings about this horse and, after a couple of nudges and winks from my Irish friends, I headed towards the bookmakers.

I was not the only lemming eagerly rushing to be parted from my money. It seemed that half of Ireland were at Cheltenham and a handful of loyal Irish rugby supporters joined me as we scrummaged our way to the betting area. I was able to assure the Irish that Northern Game had no chance and I thought the race was between See You Then, Tom Sharpe and Childown. It is odd how people suddenly become experts after only an hour on a racecourse but there I was, freely offering tips.

My bank balance had been dented by the card school in the early hours of the morning and I decided to ignore the favourite and just have £10 to win on the other two. I was concerned that, up to that point, the only evidence I had about Mick Cuddy's expertise

as a selector was the fact that he had helped to pick the Irish rugby team in 1984 and they had a playing record of four defeats in four matches to finish anchored at the wrong end of the Five Nations Championship. Perhaps he was better at selecting horses. The answer was not long delayed.

The 30-runner stampede was a most impressive sight and I was struck by the picturesque setting of the racecourse. Sadly, the worst fate of all befell Childown: he came a cropper at the second flight of hurdles, broke a leg and had to be destroyed. It was a tragic sight and it must have been a dreadful, depressing moment for everyone connected with the horse, especially the joint owners Dick Clifford-Turner and the former Hampshire county cricketer, Colin Ingleby-Mackenzie. Colin, by all accounts, has never been backward about coming forward to have a tilt at the ring and I expect he had a good bet on his horse. However, losing a bet pales into insignificance at the sight of half a ton of thoroughbred lying motionless on the ground, moments after it had been thundering along in perfect rhythm, an athletic and aesthetic model.

The race proceeded apace and the other horse I had backed, Tom Sharpe, was right up with the leaders. Unfortunately, at the fifth of the eight hurdles, he fell. By this point, I had more or less lost interest in the race but I stayed in the stands to watch the finish in case See You Then won. This horse hit the front coming to the last hurdle and looked as if it was going to win – to complete a disastrous opening race for me and my bank manager – when I spotted a jockey in blue and white silks and a blue and white cap storming up the nearside stand rails to cruise past the favourite and bolt home by two lengths. I checked the colours and the number on the racecard to discover that the winner, at the rewarding odds of 20 to 1, was Northern Game, trained by Eddie O'Grady. *C'est la vie.*

In the second race, the Foxhunters' Challenge Cup, I restricted myself to one bet of £10 on the 7 to 2 favourite Earls Brig, who had made the long journey from Hawick in Scotland. Hawick is better known for producing top-class rugby players than racehorses but Earls Brig was undefeated in 1984, so I felt he was guaranteed to give me a great run for my money. Wrong again. He was neatly tucked in behind the leaders as they sped off on the second circuit and he took the lead at the twelfth fence. However, he began to lose ground after that and at the seventeenth fence he fell.

Although I was fast running out of money the stage was now set for the *pièce de résistance*, the blue-riband event of the National Hunt calendar, the Cheltenham Gold Cup, with 13 of the best steeplechasers in Europe going to post to face the testing 3 miles 2 furlongs which culminates in a stiff uphill finish. I had placed £20 on Wayward Lad, the short-priced favourite on the good advice of comedian Lennie Bennett who has followed the career of the horse intimately. Several stars from the world of show business have recently become involved in horses and the huge cross-section of society owning shares in a racehorse is often amazing. In the Wayward Lad syndicate, the major shareholder is Mrs Shirley Thewlis, and the other two shareholders are Les Abbott and John Garner. John is an old friend of mine from Fylde Rugby Club. Les lives in Poulton-le-Fylde and earns his living selling Blackpool rock from a stall on the Golden Mile in the shadow of the Blackpool Tower. This is their latest and most successful venture into the ownership, and they have had enormous fun with one of the most brilliant chasers of the last three or four years.

I learned from chatting to Lennie Bennett, the most devoted supporter of Wayward Lad and a close friend of Les Abbott and John Garner, that the syndicate is indebted to the horse not only for his heroic exploits on the racecourse, but also for the peripheral benefits which can come from owning the best steeplechaser in Britain. The best of his four wins this season was at Kempton Park on Boxing Day when he strode away from a high-class field to land the valuable King George VI Chase for the second year in succession. The thrill of victory was, as it turned out, only to be a small part of a truly memorable day. After the race the co-owners were invited up to the royal box to meet Her Majesty Queen Elizabeth, the Queen Mother. She chatted to Ellen Abbott and Brenda Garner about how thrilled they must have been with the performance of Wayward Lad that day, and Her Majesty asked Ellen to point out her husband as she would like to meet him. Ellen pointed out Les who was almost hiding in a corner of the room; Ellen said he was too embarrassed to meet the Queen Mother because he had such a strong north-country accent and was perfectly happy minding his own business because he was sure Queen Elizabeth would not want to meet him. On hearing this, Her Majesty crossed the box and chatted to Les at length, talking knowledgeably about some of the great performances of Wayward Lad and saying what a thrill it must be owning such a good horse. Les Abbott was put quickly at ease and, completely relaxed, he enjoyed a long conversation with the Queen Mother to cap a wonderful day and to prove that the impossible is possible after all. He left the box walking on air.

But racing, like life, often gives with one hand while taking away with the other. History did not repeat itself at Cheltenham in 1984 and leading trainer, Michael Dickinson, who had the unique distinction of saddling the first five home in the 1983 Gold Cup (a record unlikely ever to be equalled), saw his two runners perform disappointingly this year. Bregawn looked disenchanted with the effort required to repeat his 1983 victory and he eventually finished sixth, about 27 lengths behind the winner. Wayward Lad ran a most uncharacteristic race; his normally bold, accurate jumping deserted him. He made a bad mistake at the seventh fence; he was pushed along to track the leaders in the middle of the race but made another mistake at the seventeenth fence; he blundered again at the nineteenth and, as he began to weaken and drop out of contention, his jockey Robert Earnshaw pulled him up.

Meanwhile the race was turning into a dream come true for the bookies and also for Jenny Pitman, the trainer responsible for Corbiere winning the 1983 Grand National and the lady in charge of the second favourite and ultimate winner, Burrough

Burrough Hill Lad (no. 4) leads Brown Chamberlain over the last en route to winning the Cheltenham Gold Cup

Hill Lad. Jenny has performed miracles to win the two best races in England in the space of 12 months from a relatively small stable, and she was most deservedly voted trainer of the month on each occasion. It was a magnificent achievement and I just wished I had had the foresight to discuss the race with her beforehand.

Nonetheless, I learned from her afterwards exactly why she had been so confident of winning the Gold Cup. Two years previously she ran Burrough Hill Lad as a six-year-old against Silver Buck at Haydock and, though her horse was receiving a stone and a half, he finished a good second. He would have done even better but he finished that race with a sprained check ligament. He had had leg trouble before and Jenny Pitman, knowing she had a top-class horse, resisted the temptation to try to patch the leg up temporarily in an endeavour to cash in on his current excellent form; she opted for a long-

term cure. The bad leg was line-fired and the horse was off the racecourse for 20 months.

In December, after his convalescence, he began his build-up to the 1984 Gold Cup with a race over hurdles at Nottingham, in which he finished third behind Queen's Ride. The jockey Ben de Haan said that if he had not ploughed straight through the third last flight of hurdles, knocking the stuffing out of himself in the process, he would have won. Burrough Hill Lad was on his way back. Jenny recalled that she then had a dilemma. Her horse was entered in the King George VI Chase on Boxing Day and also in the Welsh Grand National at Chepstow the following day. She regarded Burrough Hill Lad with 10 stone 3 pounds at Chepstow as a raging certainty, whereas the King George would prove vastly more difficult to win. It was, however, worth a great deal more. The horse was routed to Chepstow where he won comfortably and convincingly. In the winner's

enclosure Jenny said she had asked the jockey, John Francome, if the horse was good enough to run in the Gold Cup, and he had said there was no reason why not, as long as the ground was soft. That reply encouraged Jenny. 'I knew the horse was every bit as good on good ground as he was on the soft and, at that moment, I was certain I had a horse that had a great chance in the Gold Cup. We then went to Sandown on faster ground and I dispelled all Francome's doubts about the ability of the horse to act on any going, and Burrough Hill Lad won again, beating some very useful horses in the process.'

Another impressive triumph followed at Sandown, the horse spreadeagling a good-class field by 15 lengths before his final warm-up race at Wincanton at the end of February. That day Jenny walked the course and found that the better ground was on the stand side. It was less cut up and, being a true

professional, she advised John Francome to stick to that ground. In the event this proved shrewd advice because the enigmatic Bregawn, who set off in front, suddenly applied the brakes with a vengeance halfway down the far side of the track and he refused to race any further. Fortunately, Burrough Hill Lad was well wide of him at the time and he was not interfered with. He went on to win unchallenged by more than a fence.

By this stage, several of Jenny Pitman's owners had backed Burrough Hill Lad for the Gold Cup. One intrepid soul had initiated his plunge on the advice of the trainer immediately after the horse won the Welsh Grand National. He helped himself to 25 to 1 that afternoon and, after a couple more nibbles later on at shorter odds, he eventually won over £100,000. The hardy individuals who took advantage of the generous ante-post odds had a few anxious moments before collecting their winnings because, in the fortnight leading up to Cheltenham, there were persistent rumours that the horse had broken blood vessels and also injured his back.

It all started at Windsor 10 days before the Gold Cup where Jenny was nearly swamped by an avalanche of pressmen wanting to know exactly what was wrong. 'I told them that I had no idea what they were talking about and that to the best of my knowledge the horse was 100 per cent and would run a great race at Cheltenham.' The press, Jenny recalled, told her that they had received the information from a reliable source; they were more or less calling the trainer a liar. Jenny was upset and hurt and told the journalists that they could write whatever they liked but it would not stop the horse from winning. In retrospect she admits that her approach to the press resulted in more pressure being put on her and Burrough Hill Lad, and it became almost a matter of pride and honour that the horse either won or ran a great race.

Meanwhile, the bookmakers ignored the trainer's advice and instead heeded the rumours and the general scaremongering; they eased the odds on Burrough Hill Lad, almost doubling them in the final week. Jenny, quite rightly, stuck rigidly to her story right through the build-up, and had the courage to appear on 'Pebble Mill' the day before the Gold Cup and tell all the television viewers that in her opinion the horse had never been better, he would win the big race and a couple of pounds on the nose would be a sensible investment.

In the paddock, Jenny Pitman reminded the jockey Phil Tuck of the orders for the day. Tuck was riding because John Francome was claimed by his stable to ride Brown Chamberlain for Fred Winter. Jenny suggested that the best plan would be to allow Burrough Hill Lad to bowl along in fourth or fifth place early on while the others fought for the lead. 'I told him that when the runners reached the top of the hill, I want you right on the heels of the leader and he sat, perfectly placed, behind Brown Chamberlain and John Francome all the way down the hill, ready at any moment to move up a couple of gears. Turning into the finishing straight, Brown Chamberlain ran a fraction wide, Phil pushed Burrough Hill Lad quickly through on the inside, hit the front and it was all over'. Everything had gone according to plan, down to the last little detail. As Burrough Hill Lad passed the winning post, Jenny was delighted and relieved that she had been proved right but she was also so emotionally drained that she felt ill and nearly passed out. Friends helped her down from the stands to the winner's enclosure and there she greeted the hero of the race, Burrough Hill Lad. The previous night she had been out to dinner with some owners and, as everyone was leaving the restaurant, Max Kingsley, a director of the Sportsman's Club in London, had held her arm, wished her luck and reminded her that, when all's said and done, it is only a horserace. Jenny had told him that she did not see it that way – her reputation was at stake. Her reputation was fully vindicated in the most emphatic way. Burrough Hill Lad won by three lengths from Brown Chamberlain with the Irish horse Drumlargan a further eight lengths adrift.

The celebrations that night took place at the stables with a few owners, Jenny's parents, some stable lads and friends. The feast consisted of 23 portions of fish and chips and champagne; Jenny, elated but exhausted, had a cup of tea.

The race had been full of drama and excitement and the huge crowd had been completely engrossed in it as the various incidents unfolded. Jenny's was a hard act to follow but my personal battle with the bookies was not quite over, and I had my nearest brush with success in the Ritz National Hunt Handicap Steeplechase. I had an each-way bet on the favourite, Young Driver, at 4 to 1 and, to my undisguised delight, my support was not actually the kiss of death. Young Driver finished third and, even though I got back slightly less than I had invested, I had the immense satisfaction of standing in the queue at the pay-out window. Of all the horses I had backed that day, this was the only one to finish a race but, despite suffering a severe financial reverse, I thoroughly enjoyed my visit to Cheltenham.

As I was about to leave the course I was introduced to Marten Julian, the much-vaunted racing tipster of *The Sunday Times*, and Mick Lambert, an extremely good trainer from Malton in Yorkshire. Lambert is equally successful on the flat and over the jumps and he has pulled off some clever coups in his relatively short time as a trainer. 'You could do a lot worse,' quoth he, 'than have a tenner on Penscynor in the last at Hexham today.' He was right. I could have done a lot worse, by backing Louviers, Emandar, Marjoram, Boreham Dawn or Tallyrand who finished fourth to eighth. On the other hand, I could have done even better by backing the winner Speed of Light or the second, Raby. Nevertheless, Penscynor, like Young Driver, was placed and it only went to show that I was beginning to run into form just as I was running out of races.

There was a suggestion that I might like to go back to Terry Biddlecombe's house for another game of cards but I declined gracefully, and set off on the long road north to tell my wife how close I had been to winning a fortune at Cheltenham. I now know that fishermen and gamblers have something in common – eternal optimism, a vivid imagination and a romantic view of life.

TWO

ROWING

THE BOAT RACE

The Boat Race, like Guardsmen's bearskins and the Lord Chancellor's Woolsack, is one of those typically British traditions that have survived for years without any debt to sanity. The name 'The Boat Race', like 'The Championships' (Wimbledon) and 'The Open' (British Open Golf Championships), throws out a challenge to the organizers of foreign fixtures to the effect that their crippled contests are mere parodies of the real thing; that they are, in boating terms, up the creek without a paddle.

The first Boat Race, that is to say between the Universities of Oxford and Cambridge upon the Thames, took place in 1829. On account of the many bumping and boring fouls the race was restarted immediately afterwards. Victory eventually went to a jubilant Oxford over the cheesed-off Light Blues on a course from Hambledon Lock to Henley Bridge, and most jubilant of all Oxford undergraduates was Charles Wordsworth whose uncle wrote 'Upon Westminster Bridge', though not while the race was in progress. Young Chas had thought up the idea of a Varsity boat race following on his other 'topping wheeze', the Varsity cricket match. The experiment was a tremendous excess, and didn't take place again for another seven years.

The second race, in 1836, was over a different course: from Uncle William's Westminster to Putney. But Cambridge won, to the absolute chagrin and peevishness of the Dark Blues. Since then the course has been changed again. It now starts at University Stone, 400 feet upriver from Putney Bridge, proceeds in an 'S' for 4 miles and 374 yards and finishes at a point 400 feet upstream from the Ship Inn at Mortlake, allowing enough leeway for imbibers at the Ship Inn to fall in. This has been the course ever since 1845, except for 1846 and 1856 when it went from Mortlake to Putney. And 1863. For the occasion of the race the two opposite banks are renamed the 'Surrey Station' and the 'Middlesex Station', because Middlesex and Surrey faced each other across the Thames in the days before the boundaries were changed.

Although the race takes place during the Easter holiday, preparations are already under way the previous November, when a squad shortlist is whittled down to sixteen, the last 'eight' of whom receive their coveted 'Blues'. Training is serious, and becomes *extremely* serious around January. The final three weeks of practice take place on the sacred course itself, following the racing line, the inside route which picks up vital seconds over the 23m.p.h. average speed of the race. For the first mile the crew on the Middlesex Station has the advantage; for the mid-race the Surrey Station is preferable, and towards the finish the Middlesex Station is again the inside line. A boat is not allowed to impede its rival by crossing abruptly into the opponent's water; crews are always mindful of 1912, when both boats went down with all hands. The race is on the flow tide, 90 minutes before the ferocious tench- and bream-infested waters reach full flood.

Of the 130 races so far run, Cambridge

have won 68, Oxford 61. The longest run of victories is not, as commonly supposed, Oxford's current string of nine, but Cambridge's 13 between 1924 and 1936. The biggest winning margin was also by Cambridge: 20 lengths in 1900. There was a dead heat once, in 1877. 'Honest' John Phelps, the last professional judge ever asked to adjudicate, declared 'a dead heat to Oxford by six feet'. The smallest margin of victory possible is 'a canvas', and this has been the verdict in two excrutiatingly close finishes in 1952 and 1980, both Oxford wins. The 1952 race, despite all the excitement of sub-17-minute runs by both teams in 1984 and Oxford's record victory in 16 minutes 45 seconds, is still considered by many the greatest of them all, when stroke Christopher Davidge hauled Oxford ahead by their bootstraps to snatch the finish in pouring snow.

The Boat Race has brought distinction to many and celebrity to a few. Boris Rankov became, in 1983, the first man to have been in six winning teams. Sue Brown in 1981 was the first female to take part, as cox to victorious Oxford. Equally famous was the 1950 Cambridge cox, Anthony Armstrong-Jones, also victorious. And then there were the Etherington-Smith brothers who frantically rowed against each other in 1900, and Harcourt Gold, the stroke of the Oxford team between 1896 and 1899, the first man to be knighted for 'services to rowing'. But perhaps pride of place, at least in the Cambridge camp, goes to J. H. D. Goldie. Former Cambridge stroke Goldie, whose name is remembered fondly every time the Cambridge reserve boat puts forth, won his last three races and pioneered the sliding seat – a boon to the boating bottom.

The 1984 Boat Race was to earn a special place in history for three very good reasons as we will see later, but in the middle of the week of the race the main point of interest was: can Oxford win for the ninth year in succession, a feat they had not achieved in the twentieth century. I broke the habit of a lifetime and rolled out of bed in my Kensington hotel at six o'clock in the morning on the Wednesday, four days before the race, and drove to Putney to watch both crews training. It was a bright, crisp, sharp morning and shortly after seven o'clock, as the air over Putney Bridge became thick with the commuters' exhaust fumes, heralding the action of the commercial metropolis, a minibus arrived bulging with the heavyweights of the Oxford crew and their cox. In the delightfully fresh and relatively unpolluted atmosphere of the river, the lads prepared to spend an hour and a half covering a few miles of the Boat Race course, well wrapped in sweaters and tracksuits, not for a moment deceived by the bright blue sky and pale sun. For me, sitting on the Oxford launch with their renowned coach, Dan Topolski, it was an invigorating way to spend the early hours of daybreak, but I suppose for the eight men bursting with strength and energy at perhaps the fittest period of their entire lives, it was just a routine part of the daily slog which had begun for most of them six months earlier.

The Oxford President, Graham Jones, the man who is captain of the Oxford boat, explained to me over coffee later that morning that he began training with a squad of 35 in the previous September. He started with the Colleges, rowing in four-man boats for several weeks and winning in the College Fours Races in early October. Any likely candidates for the final selection for the University Boat Race in March should surface at this time, and the squad of 30 or 35 buckle down to a gruelling training schedule from the middle of October. That term the Oxford squad would train every day for between two and four hours, lifting weights and indulging in distance running to increase strength and stamina. At the weekends, the various crews might take to the water in boats but during the week it was generally a physical slog to improve the all-round condition of each and every individual.

In December, when the University goes down for the Christmas holidays and most of the students dream of turkey, Christmas pudding and cream, a liberal sprinkling of festive drink and all the good things of life, the boat crews tighten up their already frugal and spartan lifestyles and increase their physical work-load. The Oxford squad stayed up for a fortnight, during which period they trained for six hours a day. They broke camp over Christmas and New Year but each member of the squad was given a training programme to follow right through the 10 days of the holiday. On 2 January, the squad reassembled at a hotel in London as part of Ladbroke's sponsorship deal, and they embarked on a fortnight's intensive training before the start of the Easter term. They trained morning and afternoon throughout those two weeks and commenced the final elimination process for the first and second crews. They raced regularly on the Thames with fours, rather than full eight-men boats, and the President kept swapping people around until satisfied he had whittled the squad down to the best 16 or 20 oarsmen in Oxford University. He also had a very shrewd idea at the end of this fortnight who would be the first eight and who in the second eight or 'Isis crew', as they are called. The original 30 students, after racing on and off for a fortnight in fours and having been continually juggled around, are finally catalogued and the President takes his eight off for specialized training. The Isis boat goes its own way with the second eight and the rest make their way back to the Colleges, always waiting and hoping for a summons in a case of emergency.

For the last nine weeks up to the Boat Race, the Oxford crew practised four or five hours every day, six days a week. This is a formidable schedule; it has to be remembered that these students are also expected to attend endless lectures, prepare essays, turn up to tutorials and have some sort of vague idea where the University library is hidden. It speaks volumes for the single-minded dedication, discipline, organization and enthusiasm that these young men are able to lead several lives concurrently without suffering any sort of identity crisis.

By the end of the first week of February, Graham Jones had crystallized all his ideas and, following full discussions with the chief coach, Dan Topolski, he was ready to name his crew for the Boat Race. 'The final decision on selection,' stated Jones, 'is actually mine, but when you consider that I was involved in choosing the best crew for the first time, and Dan was doing it for the umpteenth time, it would have been foolhardy not to reach a decision by consensus, and this is what transpired.'

A four- or five-hour training routine is just as demanding and exhausting as it sounds. The crews might begin on the river in two boats of four and, after warming up, they would row separately, working independently on a whole range of drills and exercises. They would work at different rates, alternating some short, sharp bursts with a strong steady pace. Usually the crews would spend an hour on the water and, nearer the race, worked together as an eight most of the time. They would then hightail it back to the gym and spend between two and three hours on the weights, doing circuit training or carrying out special exercises for specific reasons. The weight training would vary between repetitive circuits of medium or light weights to the slower slog of heavy weights. Variety is important to try to sustain the interest.

Graham Jones is an Australian who studied at Sydney University before winning a scholarship to Oxford and, when he finishes at Oxford, he will return to Sydney to complete his studies there. He is reading Clinical Biochemistry which does not sound the sort of subject that can be easily sorted out in half an hour a day. He admitted that rowing had cut pretty deep inroads into his academic pursuits, and being President had inflicted a further drain on his resources. He had to devote a sizeable chunk of the six months up to the Boat Race to training and executing the day-to-day organizational demands of being President, but he explained to me that he had spent virtually the whole of the previous summer, including the whole of the long vacation, at his studies and he would pursue the same spartan policy again in the summer of 1984 to ensure he lost precious little academic ground. There is no doubt that the individual members of the crew all make great sacrifices to fulfil their dreams and ambitions.

Jones claimed he came to Oxford primarily to study at an acknowledged, outstanding seat of learning and academic excellence. Nevertheless, it never crossed

Oxford's chief coach, Dan Topolski – the man who has masterminded Oxford's domination of the Boat Race in recent years

his mind not to row. 'If you have ever sat in a boat,' he explained, 'and held an oar in your hand, you would realize that rowing is a disease, it is like a drug, and it would have been quite impossible for someone like me, with the spirit in my blood, to have come to Oxford and not rowed.'

The Boat Race as a national event of genuine interest survives on bucketfuls of tradition and history, and Jones was aware of the broad canvas of involvement world-wide. 'It is a unique feeling of intense excitement stepping into the boat on big race day,' he asserted, 'in the knowledge that the cream of University oarsmen have been coming down to Putney and doing exactly the same thing for over a hundred and fifty years. It is an awesome thought and one that has gripped the British public.' The two crews both seemed to be pleasantly surprised by the huge press interest in the event in the final month, and there was a full turnout of some unlikely Fleet Street hacks all scrambling around for a different angle in the last week. Television coverage is extensive and recordings of the race are shown all over the world.

Oxford employ 14 coaches and so there is an equitable division of labour when the media arrive *en bloc*, but most people want to hear the prospects from the President himself, and Graham Jones was a very busy man in the middle of March. The total Oxford dominance in recent years, he felt, added to the pressures on him and his crew rather than helping them to relax or pumping confidence into them. Oxford had won the previous eight Boat Races, and Jones did not relish the thought of being the first Dark Blue President to lose since 1975.

He found the burden of responsibility a little onerous to live with but he believed that the 1984 Oxford crew was an exception-ally good one and he was confident and optimistic they would win again. I mentioned it would make a great story for the papers if Cambridge at last broke the Oxford stranglehold and it would be banner headlines splashed all over the back page. 'In that case,' he replied, 'I would happily settle for a line in the Stop Press simply mention-ing that Oxford had won the Boat Race

to notch up their ninth win in succession – a record for the Dark Blues this century.'

I was interested to learn from Graham that winning from Putney to Mortlake evokes much the same emotion as winning a rugby international at Twickenham – about two parts exhaustion to one part elation. In 1983, Graham was surprised Oxford were allowed to poach such a commanding early lead but, no sooner did he appreciate they were a full two lengths up, than he wished the race was all over and he dreaded the thought of another 12 minutes of gruelling rowing to the finishing line. It is both physically and mentally exhausting because it is not just the effort for 18 minutes that day, it is more the culmination and fruition of six months' endeavour, the physical training and mental preparation over a considerable period of time with no competitive match practice, living together 24 hours a day in a house at Putney and working together to a common end several hours every day for half a year of their lives. The end product is just one race over an extended four miles. It is rather like asking Tom Watson or John McEnroe not to play any competitive golf or tennis of any description for six months and then ask them to win the British Open or Wimbledon. To have trained for that length of time and to have had no competitive yardstick by which to judge progress and ability must prove, in the final few minutes, almost soul-destroying; certainly a perverse form of mental torture.

The man mainly responsible for keeping body and soul together is the chief Oxford coach, Dan Topolski. It is his job to motivate, encourage, cajole and inspire the Dark Blues throughout their long, drawn-out preparations from September to March. It is his job to instil confidence and to avoid complacency. It is a job he has been doing with phenomenal success for 11 years but that is hardly surprising with his outstanding track record. He won his Blue at Oxford in the late sixties and he went on to win international honours as an oarsman, coll-ected four medals at Henley and won gold and silver medals in the world lightweight championships.

He was, ideally, far too light and small to

win his Blue at Oxford, but by incredible hard work and determination he made it. He was actually two stone lighter than the next lightest man in the Oxford crew in 1968. He loved rowing but enjoys the challenge of coaching a young, relatively experienced crew almost as much. 'It is exciting every year trying to mould together a crew of eight from raw material which is extremely varied in its quality, shape and size, trying to improve each member of the boat as an individual whilst also trying to develop a cohesive team.'

Dan Topolski is an engagingly forthright man who has packed a lot into his life. He worked for BBC television for four years on 'Late Night Line-Up' and '24 Hours' but, in his own words, he kept taking a couple of months off to travel abroad and the BBC eventually offered him 12 months a year to enjoy his travelling. He travelled through Ethiopia, Uganda and Zaïre down through Tanzania and Zanzibar. Other journeys took him to South America and China. During this time he still rowed and did some coaching; later he published a book about his journeys through Africa and also wrote a series of feature articles. Nowadays, while acting as Oxford's coach, Topolski's first task each September is to whittle down the 50 or 60 aspiring hopefuls into a more manageable 30 or 35 potential Blues. It was interesting to listen to his version of the year's tests and training.

We usually have ten or twelve people back from the previous year's Blues boat and Isis boat, he explained, *and the grapevine spreads news of any promising Freshmen. By the end of October, after an extensive examination in the gymnasium and on the river, the President and myself have usually sorted out the likely first boat, second boat, a junior eight and a lightweight eight.*
From there on in I concentrate on the first two boats and the top four in the junior boat, but by December I know the best sixteen rowers in the University.

As Graham Jones described, the crews then spent most of the Christmas vacation in intensive training. It is during this crucial period that Topolski sorts out the Blues from the rest. They do a running session before breakfast, a physical session in the morning, a rowing session in the afternoon, a land-training session before dinner and a session in the gym in the evening. The coach tests each person individually against everyone else in single-row racing, and he asks the individuals to row against each other over the actual Boat Race course. He puts the whole squad on a rowing machine, one at a time, to measure their strength, the length of their stroke and their basic technique, demonstrating at which point they fall off and where their strengths and weaknesses lie. The test lasts 7 minutes and is fairly illuminating. The coach also tests every one of the final squad of 20 in the gym in circuit training and weight training and out on the track in running. For further selective details, Dan Topolski races them against each other in twos and also in fours, regularly changing one or even two people in a four until he is quite sure he has the best possible balance:

I keep swopping people around, changing one fellow with his opposite number, racing them against each other, race after race after race, to keep the pressure on every single member of the squad and to squeeze the very best out of each of them. I learned the Americans have a very tough selection process in which a man has to prove himself the best all the time, week in and week out, and I tend towards that process because I want each of the men in the Blues boat to know why they are there and why the other seven are there. This open form of meritocracy means that even if somebody is a villain, arrogant, particularly difficult, diffident individual, if he smells or lies or cheats or whatever, the other seven know that he is in the boat because he is one of the top eight rowers in residence at Oxford University. All question marks have been eliminated.

By the last week in January, that situation has been reached, and people who refer to someone being lucky to win a rowing Blue at Oxford are invariably very wide of the mark. From the beginning of February for the last six weeks before the Race, Dan concentrates on channelling all their energy and skill into rowing as an eight, which means everyone doing everything exactly at the same time together and to ensure their pulling pressures through the water are all at exactly the same point and speed. He only tries to correct individual technique at this late stage if it would have a beneficial effect on the eight.

I wondered how important it was to organize the order in which the eight rowers positioned themselves in the boat, and Dan stressed it was critical:

Each person has a slightly different role to play. The stroke sets the rhythm, and he is the pacemaker. He has to read how the race is going and set his boat's rhythm and striking rate accordingly. The number seven man behind him must be a good interpreter of that pace, and he must try to transmit that rhythm to the rest of the crew. The sixth man has to be a big man, capable of anchoring the boat and he has to back up the stroke and ensure the rhythm the stroke wants to adopt can be maintained. The fifth, fourth and third oars are the main engine room, and if I have big, strong but slightly clumsy oarsmen this would be the ideal place to utilize their power. The guys at the bow of the boat will often be a shade lighter to allow the boat to lift a fraction in the water and these men should be technically very sharp, quick, intelligent and efficient.

The Cambridge boat snaps in two shortly before the scheduled start of the Boat Race in March

I was interested to learn from Dan Topolski as we roared down the Thames in pursuit of the Oxford boat in their fourth-last practice before the contest proper, that

he rated his 1984 Oxford crew among the best he had coached. The standard of the Boat Race is still surprisingly high. Rugby, cricket and soccer may be in decline at Oxbridge, but rowing is as good as ever it was. In 1981, the·Oxford crew took on the British National boat at Henley and beat them in the final. Four of the Oxford boat went on to make the National eight and that National eight reached the final of the World Championships. The Oxford crew in recent years have been perched near the top of the pyramid and deservedly so.

They were once again red-hot favourites to win in 1984, not least because they had a considerable weight advantage of around 11 pounds per man. Despite all the predictions of the assorted experts, however, the Cambridge camp was in confident mood when I visited them at their house in Putney during the last week. Their coach, Alan Inns, was an outstanding cox in his day and, in his first year in charge, he firmly believed that Cambridge could spring a real surprise. Around one o'clock on Saturday 17 March everything was set for the hundred-and-thirtieth University Boat Race.

My own plans for covering the event had been severely torpedoed in midweek and had, I thought, sunk without trace. It had been my intention to watch the Boat Race

and, as soon as the second boat crossed the line at about twenty past one, I was going to jump into a car and drive straight to Twickenham to arrive a good hour before the England-Wales rugby International kicked off. But just a few days before the BBC switched me from the Twickenham game to the Grand Slam confrontation at Murrayfield between Scotland and France – who were both unbeaten and chasing the Five Nations Championship in the final match of the season. I assumed this meant I would have to watch the Boat Race on television in Edinburgh but I had not bargained on the exploits of the Cambridge cox, Peter Hobson.

On a cold, grey day with a stiff easterly wind blowing, Hobson took the Cambridge crew on to the Thames to practise a few quick starts prior to the off. However, moments later, there followed a sensational incident, unprecedented in the long history of the event, which led to the Boat Race being postponed for 24 hours. Incomprehensively, the huge crowd lining both banks of the river and standing on Putney Bridge, with a bird's-eye view, watched in stunned silence as Hobson guided the boat flat out straight into a huge, moored barge in the middle of the Thames. Inevitably, there was a sickening thud and the bow of the boat

shattered; Hobson then attempted to steer the crippled boat and his shocked crew towards the safety of the bank of the river. The Oxford crew, roaring towards the start, were greeted with the sight of their opponents paddling furiously towards the bank before their boat sank. They failed. The bow jack-knifed into the air immediately behind A. H. Reynolds, the Cambridge bow oar, and, ignominiously, the stricken boat sank. The crew scrambled to the shore and they realized, even before the salvage operation began, that they they would have to borrow another boat – to which they were not accustomed – for a race that would be delayed or even postponed.

Such a disaster had, seemingly, no logical explanation. The barge in question was exactly where it was always positioned. In the Boat Race programme Hobson had listed among his hobbies, somewhat ironically as it transpired, reshaping barges; but I imagine he normally follows a more conventional path in the pursuit of this pastime. The umpire, Mike Sweeney, was quoted afterwards with the most plausible explanation: 'The barge was huge. The cox was blind because he had so many big men in front of him and is a very little lad.'

Writing in his College magazine two months later, the unfortunate Peter Hobson told the whole sad saga in his own words:

And so the build-up brought us to Saturday. For five of us, this was our first Boat Race and tension was high. The last ten minutes spent in the boathouse were unforgettable, nobody said a word, we just looked at each other, each listening to his own heart-beat and thinking how the finishing line seemed like an eternity away. The crowds and television went unnoticed as we boated, moved off and began the warm-up. Because of bad conditions further up the river, I made the fateful decision to spin and compress the warm-up into the quieter reaches near the start. As we moved off, I took a quick look to check all was clear – noticing a police boat which I did avoid, but was blissfully unaware of what the buttresses of Putney Bridge were hiding from my view. I took the crew off on the first burst, a one-minute piece off the run, not a start as the press said. Once secure in the knowledge that all is clear, a cox will not look

The Oxford boat opens up a gap at halfway as each crew sets new records

again, as to do so unbalances the boat and so it was that I sat still and steered straight into a five-hundred-ton barge. I actually saw it at the same stroke as the collision and there was just time for a stifled cry before the soft crunch of the bow shattering. I think that immediately following the crash, there was a great deal more fuss outside the boat than in it. We were sinking fast and the first priority was to make the shore. The boat finally sank in less than three feet of water and so there was no danger of being swept away or any further catastrophe. Shock had well and truly set in by now and the enormous crowds of disbelieving people went unnoticed. For my own part, my mind seemed unable to accept that this could happen twice, so I suppose disbelief was my main feeling, although shock was doing its best to finish me off.

By the time we had cleaned ourselves up and calmed down – about two hours later – things did not really seem all that bad. The fact that every Sunday paper was making us front-page news and that the BBC was having rescheduling crises never reached us. Our main thought soon became the race on Sunday and by about five o'clock we had simply put the clock back twenty-four hours. As the person who had caused it all, I suppose I was in a fairly delicate position, but the crew and coaches were marvellous. They understood the circumstances and to them, it was as simple as that. In fact, one or two felt relieved as a 'dress rehearsal' was just what we needed!

And so, with a borrowed boat we set out again on Sunday. The rest you probably all

know. We lost, but we did have the race of our lives and came off the water knowing that we had given the best we could. Next to this, the result almost comes second, but not quite.

Over the next few days, the size of the whole affair gradually dawned on us. It certainly seems that the first Sunday Boat Race has given the sport and the Varsity Match a great boost in terms of public interest. Whatever the long-term implications, one thing is for sure, I'll never be able to live it down. So I may as well learn to laugh about it!

Cambridge, as Peter Hobson wrote, did lose but they did so only narrowly and in a time so fast it would have won any of the previous 129 Boat Races. They broke all previous course records and I noticed in *The Times* report it said the cox 'steered the finest course seen on the sideway for many a long year'. Congratulations to Peter Hobson and the Cambridge crew for a magnificent effort and also to the winners, Oxford, on setting the new course record of 16 minutes and 45 seconds. This beat the old record by 13 seconds – Cambridge beat the old record by 1 second.

I am indebted to Hobson for allowing me the opportunity to watch the race live on the Sunday and I was immensely impressed by the dedicated approach of the young men of Oxford and Cambridge to this great traditional event. They earned my respect and admiration. A large part of the continuing attraction of the Boat Race lies in the fact that it is one of the last great amateur sports in a professional, generally over-commercialized sporting world. The two crews take part for no material ends, simply for the love of rowing. They race on an unusual course – no one else rows over four and a quarter miles on a winding river even vaguely similar to the Thames from Putney to Mortlake – and capture the imagination of the whole British public for one afternoon a year. Or in the case of 1984 – two afternoons. As Dan Topolski says, it is an eccentric, oddball, British, madcap thing but it is a great spectacle with a wonderful tradition; the public have always loved it and will no doubt continue to do so long into the future. I can only echo these words.

THE CALCUTTA CUP

There is only one real, tangible trophy to be won in the International Championship, and that is the Calcutta Cup, awarded annually to the winners of the Scotland-England match. The 'triple crown' may have existed in King Lear's day, but sadly there's no such rugby coronet.

The Calcutta Cup was presented by one G. A. J. Rothney and the officials of the Calcutta Rugby Club in India after their own little club, formed in 1873, was disbanded, after four years, for want of decent opposition. The idea of international rugby competition had been a dream of these Old Rugbeians, inspired by the first established 'international' between England and Scotland, who had been playing each other since 1871. The Calcutta Club drew all their funds out of the Indian bank and commissioned local craftsmen to fashion a suitable commemorative pot. The result was a rather unusual object with three snake handles and an elephant on the lid; the stand bears the inscription: 'The Calcutta Cup. Presented to the Rugby Union by the Calcutta Football Club as an International Challenge Trophy to be played for annually by England and Scotland – 1878'.

The trophy is the property of the Rugby Football Union and spends most of its time in a vault, except for the week prior to the annual match when it goes on display to surprised onlookers. The first match for the Cup took place in 1879 at Raeburn Place in Edinburgh but, perhaps out of deference to the Cup's unusual appearance, both sides contented themselves with a draw. The Calcutta Club was actually reformed in 1884 just seven years after it disbanded but, strangely, didn't ask for the trophy back.

The International Championships were first held in 1883 when the four home countries took part. France joined in later to make it a Five Nations tournament in 1910. It is interesting to see how the honours have been divided in the various competitions. The Calcutta Cup has been contested 92 times, with England winning 44, Scotland 35, and 13 drawn. In the International Championship, though, England have achieved 18 outright wins, Scotland 12, Ireland 9 and France 7, but they have all been surpassed by Wales with 21. The Triple Crown honours have followed a similar pattern, with 15 to England, 9 to Scotland, 5 to Ireland and 16 to Wales. Grand Slam wins have gone as follows: 8 to England and Wales, 3 to France, 2 to Scotland and 1 to Ireland.

Among the most memorable of Cup matches was the Murrayfield showdown of March, 1925. Scotland had gone into the game undefeated all season but England scored first, leading 8-5 at the interval and pressing home their advantage with Wavell Wakefield's score from a Len Corbett cross-kick to make it 11-5. But suddenly Scotland staged a rearguard action with a corner-flag try by A. C. Wallace, a touchline conversion from A. C. Gillies and a late, heart-stopping goal by H. Waddell to pull victory out of defeat. Apart from the Championship itself, Scotland won both the honours that year: the imaginary Triple Crown and the all-too-real Cup with its elephant and snakes.

The 1984 Calcutta Cup match gained historical significance being the hundredth meeting of the two countries. In 1871, before the actual Cup came into existence, about 4000 curious onlookers turned up for the inaugural battle between Scotland and England at Raeburn Place to watch a match played in wind and rain. Scotland won by a goal and a try to England's try. Sadly, from my point of view, not much has changed 113 years and 100 matches later – the 1984 game between these two intense rivals was played in persistent rain, and Scotland again emerged victorious.

The build-up to the match was interesting because both countries had played the All Blacks in November during their short tour in Britain. Scotland drew 25-25 to salvage some pride after two particularly inept and disappointing performances, one by the South of Scotland, who lost 30-9, conceding 5 tries to the New Zealanders, and one by Edinburgh, who lost 22-6 and conceded 3 tries in the process. Meanwhile, hopes of a great revival for English rugby were given enormous encouragement by the North of England, losing narrowly to New Zealand by 6 points in a high-scoring game, and the two notable victories of the Midlands at Leicester and England at Twickenham.

This was England's first win over New Zealand at Twickenham since the famous 1936 match which was highlighted by the try-scoring exploits of Prince Obolensky. There is no doubt in my mind that England's display against the All Blacks in November was more decisive than Scotland's and, if the two teams had met a week later, I'm sure England would have beaten Scotland. In fact the Calcutta Cup match took place three

months later, and by then the balance had tilted perceptibly in Scotland's favour.

Not, I hasten to add, that the two countries' respective final trials in early January gave the French anything but hope. The Irish team, who had done so well in the previous two seasons, were beginning to fall apart and Wales, in the middle of a rare trough, had only just scraped home against Japan. England struggled, in a most ungainly fashion, to beat their junior side in the trial, a last-minute drop goal saving their pride and honour; while Scotland were actually convincingly beaten by their junior side. As one of their established players told me at the time, I think tongue in cheek, the Scottish team knew that the trial would be their only really difficult game all season, and it proved that Scotland had two great sides – one good enough to share 50 points with the mighty All Blacks, and another good enough to thump that team.

For England the warning lights should have been flashing in every direction after the trial. They had stubbornly, though understandably, stayed loyal to the team that beat New Zealand, and to exactly the same dull, but effective, tactics that had been employed in achieving that victory. That both the team and the tactics failed against a very scratchy and fragile Rest of England side in the trial should have forced the selectors to progress from the firm base established against the All Blacks at Twickenham. Instead, they decided to stick to the same team and, despite a flood of warnings in the media, committed themselves to the same tactics.

In fairness to the England squad, the time from the disastrous trial in the first week of January to the Murrayfield encounter four weeks later was a chapter of accidents, carried out against a backcloth of disruption caused initially by the weather and eventually by fate. The worst of the winter hit their weekend squad session with a vengeance, to force them off the playing fields indoors, where little of use was accomplished. At their only opportunity to consolidate the outstanding work of their pack from the November International, Peter Wheeler recalled it was virtually a waste of time and energy:

I was nursing a broken bone in my hand which meant we did no worthwhile line-out practice, apart from the fact that Maurice Colclough was also unfit. Both props had injury problems and, in effect, we did no scrummaging in the entire build-up to the Scotland game. We arrived in Edinburgh to train at the Hibs soccer ground on the Thursday afternoon, only to be told that they would not allow any scrummaging on the pitch itself or any of the surrounding area. On the Friday we were promised a full pack to scrummage against but, for reasons which I never did fully comprehend, the guaranteed opposition failed to materialize. Our game plan against New Zealand and our ultimate success had been based on our formidable set-piece platform, especially our scrummaging, but this decisive advantage in our favour had been allowed to evaporate through force of circumstances. Just as the intensive, concentrated preparation for the All Blacks game had been well-nigh perfect, the build-up to the Calcutta Cup contest had been a catalogue of disasters.

In stark contrast, Scotland had advanced apace. Setting aside the temporary hiccup in the Scottish trial, the team had developed understanding and genuine confidence from their All Blacks result, which was reinforced by the seeming plight of the Welsh players and the slightly eccentric behaviour of the Welsh selectors. Scotland, supported by its tartan army of faithful fans, marched on Cardiff in far more exultant mood than at any time in recent memory. After all, Scotland had laid to rest one hoodoo in 1982 by trouncing Wales in Cardiff, a feat last achieved 20 years previously. Playing much the better rugby, they repeated the medicine in 1984 to begin their Championship campaign in the best possible style – with an away win. The squad sessions prior to this match and the game itself meant, inevitably, that Scotland went into the Calcutta Cup match tuned to their peak by their shrewd coach, Jim Telfer, and firm favourites to beat an England side ill-equipped for the task ahead – a side, through no real fault of their own, lacking in organization, physical fitness and match sharpness.

Peter Wheeler, a good friend of mine and a player I shared some wonderful matches with through the years, did express

misgivings to me going into the match, and he admitted afterwards that with hindsight the pitfalls were there for all to see. Of course, deprived of the advantage of hindsight, the selectors adhered too rigidly to their conservative policy and they suffered the consequences. Once the team had been selected, Peter defended the tactics, although afterwards he admitted the English team were unable to execute them with anything like the forthright aggression and control that they had displayed against New Zealand. Scotland on the other hand, had intended to be very much more ambitious than England.

John Rutherford, one of the few outstanding successes on the British Lions tour to New Zealand in 1983, and one of the most gifted footballers in British rugby, had fully intended, encouraged by coach Jim Telfer, to run the ball wide from the set-pieces generally and the loose invariably, to stretch the big, ponderous English pack. However, torrential rain during Friday night and heavy

The look of anguish on Peter Wheeler's face says it all

rain all Saturday morning persuaded the Scots to adapt and adopt a more realistic but similar approach. Instead of running the ball wide, the new plan was for John Rutherford to kick the ball wide and for John and Roy Laidlaw to keep turning the English back in defence by lobbing the ball over their forwards.

The master strategy worked admirably and it was largely responsible for Scotland finishing the game two-thirds of the way towards their first Triple Crown success since 1938, and for England finishing the game on the scrapheap and playing the role of also-rans almost before the season had started. It says a great deal for Jim Telfer that, having wound up his exhaustive preparation for the game in ideal weather on the Thursday and fully intent on moving the ball about, he was able to change the tactics radically on the Saturday when the playing conditions had deteriorated so markedly. He went down on the morning of the game to examine the pitch and he ordered the whole squad to go out for a walk in his absence, just to get used to the driving rain and wind.

John Rutherford recalled:

We had a pretty good idea that they would play exactly the way they did against the All Blacks and, knowing that, we had worked conscientiously to organize our defence to contain their attacks. We were well organized to cope with their powerful scrum-half Nick Youngs trying to break on his own or link with his back row. By destroying their scrummage we really eliminated that threat, although to our surprise it did not stop England trying to outmanoeuvre us in this way. Fortunately our loose forwards, Jim Calder, Iain Paxton and David Leslie, were well organized and fully competent to sniff out any offensive close to the forwards. We also anticipated that Youngs and Cusworth would kick a lot, and we felt by hounding them and pressurizing them as much as possible we could force them into making mistakes, which is what happened. But the fact that this was what transpired was not due to their shortcomings so much as to the rousing performance of the Scottish pack and, in particular, the back row. They laid the foundations of our victory in Cardiff and did exactly the same against England.

The heavy rain, the wet pitch and the greasy ball ensured it was never going to be an entertaining, running extravaganza, but I felt beforehand that if England could reproduce their early-season form the conditions would not affect them adversely. This was the first Calcutta Cup game to be played in the shadow of the new East stand, and, because of the reduced space on the terraces, the ground capacity of 60,201 turned up to brave the weather and endure a tedious opening quarter of an hour, in which the packs were fiercely engaged in a war of attrition. England's scrummage, as I had feared, was poor and early on they were disrupted, shoved back and wheeled round to make life extremely difficult for the half-backs, Nick Youngs and Les Cusworth. Youngs, doubtless on instructions, spent most of the match kicking the ball over his forwards or breaking close to the scrum, and he certainly did this more than he actually passed to his backs. It proved pretty futile as the Scots defence was rock solid and more than equal to the occasion. Sitting alongside the redoubtable Bill McLaren in the BBC television commentary box, I was becoming increasingly frustrated at England's rigid approach; their lack of flexibility contributed to their downfall. Plan A was patently not breaking down the Scots resistance and, at the end of 80 minutes, it was apparent that there was no Plan B to use instead.

On the assumption that the Scots, with much more match practice to sustain them in the inevitable slog which the weather had ordained, would prove fitter and more durable, it was very important for England to pinch a healthy lead by half-time. They had their chances. On the day that Dusty Hare became the most capped full-back in England's history, his normally ruthlessly accurate goal-kicking deserted him. In the first half he missed four kicks at goal and he failed with two more after the interval. As if these were not bad enough, Clive Woodward and Les Cusworth both missed, by a whisker, attempts at drop goals. At the end of the day those eight kicks were worth 24 points and could well have killed off the Scottish challenge. As it was, the tide of the match changed in a short burst of activity during

Scotland fly-half John Rutherford, architect of Scotland's victory over England, drives the visitors back with a brilliant display of kicking

the 10-minute period on either side of half-time, and thereafter England were always swimming hopelessly upstream.

After Hare had missed with his first three kicks at goal, Scotland won a scrum half-way on the right-hand touchline. John Rutherford, one of the rare breed of ambidextrous fly-halves, floated a glorious 50-yard, left-footed diagonal deep inside the English 25-yard line on the far touch-line. Hare gathered the ball but was promptly and abruptly tackled into touch by Roger Baird. At the line-out, Colin Deans threw the dripping wet ball with deadly accuracy to Leslie at the tail. He won the ball and Scotland launched an attack with the ball on the ground. Clive Woodward and Huw Davies hesitated for a fatal split second, waiting for the other to kill the ball, and Iain Paxton hacked it forward. David Johnston exploded through onto the loose ball 15 yards from the English line and, summoning up the array of skills he acquired as a professional footballer in two years with Heart of Midlothian in the Scottish first division, he flicked the ball neatly past the onrushing defence and then outsprinted

Ewan Kennedy scores the crucial try to set Scotland on their way to victory over England at Murrayfield

Woodward to score the crucial first try of the match. Dodds converted. Right on half-time, Hare at last kicked a penalty goal but the Scots' star was in the ascendancy.

During the interval Bill Cuthbertson left the field with a strained groin to be replaced by John Beattie, but this change did little to affect the Scottish momentum. From quick, mauled possession 35 yards from the English line in the opening minute of the half, Calder and Tomes set up a driving ruck which spreadeagled the English defence. Laidlaw chucked out a poor pass along the ground to Rutherford but the fly-half scooped it off his toes superbly and flicked up a perfect, short pass to the strapping 6-foot, 5-inch and 14-stone centre, Ewan Kennedy, who stormed through the hesitant and flat-footed defence to score a try near the posts. Dodds again converted to give Scotland the luxurious cushion of a 12-3 lead. In the very next minute Hare kicked his fiftieth penalty goal for England after Beattie had tackled Scott without the ball. 12-6. Within four minutes of the restart, Scotland had restored their 9-point lead. Hare failed to find touch from a penalty, which was an elementary but costly error because Keith Robertson fielded the ball and hoisted it high into the English half in the middle of the pitch. Woodward caught the ball but was simultaneously tackled by Johnston. Kennedy kicked the ball forward but he was immediately, blatantly, obstructed by John Scott, and Dodds landed the penalty.

England by this time had lost Peter Winterbottom with a bruised hip – he was replaced by John Hall – but, with the Scots controlling the loose and Rutherford and Laidlaw kicking magnificently, the match as a two-sided contest was over. Before the end Ewan Kennedy, who had made such an impact on the game, left the field with an injured knee but England could receive no comfort from this because he was replaced by Scotland's number one talisman, Jim Pollock. He has an amazing record for Scotland, having played three times previously and never been on the losing side. That tells only part of the story. The first of those matches was against Wales in Cardiff in 1982, where Scotland had not won since 1962. The next was against England at Twickenham in 1983, where Scotland won for only the second time in 45 years, and the other was against the All Blacks, a team Scotland have never beaten in 79 years of competition. When the invincible Pollock appeared, England had every cause to raise the white flag and take to the lifeboats.

There were those statisticians up on the BBC gantry who said all Scotland needed to do to guarantee the Triple Crown and the Grand Slam was to pick Jim Pollock for the last two Internationals. The selectors did, with dramatic effect. Dodds managed a second penalty in the last quarter of the match to make the final score 18-6 and few, if any, Englishmen would deny the better equipped and organized side had won. As I set sail from a depressingly wet and windy Edinburgh that night I realized the euphoria over England's victory in November was a false dawn yet again. Admittedly, we had won the Grand Slam at Murrayfield in 1980 but, that season apart, England had not topped the Five Nations Championship table on any other occasion since 1963. They were destined to win only one of their next five Internationals and the immediate outlook remains as bleak and distressing as ever.

To compound the suffering of the loyal English follower, the picture is the same over a fairly wide canvas. Our cricketers have not only been destroyed by the West Indies this summer but they managed to lose a Test series against New Zealand and Pakistan in the first three months. The English soccer team flopped in the European Championship, the rugby league side were wiped off the face of the earth in Australasia, and no Englishman came too close to winning Wimbledon or the British Open Golf. But enough of England's problems.

At Murrayfield at four o'clock on the 4 February, Scotland were huddled, dripping wet, in their changing room, their grip on the Calcutta Cup still secure.

Before we had even begun to change out of our kit, recalls the hero of the hour, John Rutherford, *we were chatting excitedly about the prospects of the Triple Crown showdown in Dublin against the Irish. We heard that the Irish, already beaten convincingly by France, had lost that afternoon to Wales in Dublin. We had waited forty-six years since Scotland's last Triple Crown success and everyone in the dressing room knew, players, reserves, the coach, the selectors, we had never had a better chance of realizing the seemingly impossible dream.*

What John did not know was that 1984 was in the most emphatic possible style going to go down in history as Scotland's year. Not only were they two-thirds of their way towards a first Triple Crown since 1938, they were also half-way to their first Grand Slam since 1925.

FOUR

EQUESTRIANISM

BADMINTON HORSE TRIALS

Of all the trials our four-legged friends undergo in the name of sport, three-day eventing is perhaps the most exacting. Spectacular spills are par for Badminton's tough cross-country course with its 35 frightening and wearying obstacles including Bechers, Giants' Table, Faggot Pile, Luckington Lane and Pheasant Feeder. A fierce test, but then the Badminton Trials were designed to put British equestrianism through its paces in preparation for the Olympics.

Launched in 1949 by the late Duke of Beaufort, of fox-hunting fame, in the heavily wooded park of his Badminton House in Gloucestershire, the Trials were initially called 'The Badminton Olympic Three Days' Event'. The first winner was Captain J. Shedden on Golden Willow, and army riders dominated the early years. The Event became so prestigious, firing as it did Britain's Olympic successes, that it was soon emulated not only by other British Three Day Events, such as Burghley and Harewood, but by competitions across the world.

'Badminton' became international in 1951 and, after riding out the storm of a Swiss team taking most of the initial honours, Britain's equestrians have mounted a successful challenge against stiff oppositions, particularly from Ireland and Australia, with such successful home-team partner-ships as Frank Weldon on Kilbarry and Lawrence Rook on Starlight.

Three-day eventing, which incidentally can last five days, is one sport in which women can compete on an equal footing with men and, even on the rigorous cross-country phase, they have achieved spectacular successes. Sheila Willcox (Waddington) scored a hat-trick of victories in 1957, 1958 and 1959 and two wins on the same grand horse, High and Mighty. Anneli Drummond-Hay rode Merely-a-Monarch to a clean sweep of all three phases in 1962. But the most successful Badminton rider of all time, not excluding Captain Mark Phillips with his distinguished record of four wins, is Lucinda Green (*née* Prior Palmer).

Lucinda, born in London on 7 November 1953, made her début at Badminton in 1972 when she finished fifth; since then she has won six times. Married to Australian rider David Green since 1981, she was the first eventer to attract sponsorship, signing a deal with OCL in 1977. She was awarded the MBE in 1978.

The Horse Trials were a whole new world for me and I headed towards Badminton on Friday, 13 April intrigued at the prospect of learning about the trials and tribulations confronting the competitors who participate in the Three Day Event. I was fortunate, however, to have been able to enlist Lucinda's help; she was going to guide me very gently through the intricacies of a highly complicated art, and it was thanks to her great patience and friendly cooperation that I now have a fair idea of what goes on.

The Three Day Event seemed to me to be a thorough test of the athletic versatility of a horse, in much the same way as the Decathlon in the Olympic Games gives an athlete like Daley Thompson the perfect vehicle and opportunity to parade *his* extraordinary versatility. Of course it is also an exhaustive test of the skills of the rider and the person who has trained the horse, and the Badminton Horse Trials each year are the highlight of the Three Day Event calendar in which the very best horses and riders are united in a supreme test of their skill and courage.

At the outset Lucinda had to explain to me that the Trials are divided into three separate categories which are carried over three separate days. On the first day the Dressage takes place, followed by the Speed and Endurance tests on the second day – including the cross-country – and, finally, on the third day the Showjumping rounds off the examination.

I began by watching the Dressage on the first day and, after an hour, Lucinda was not best pleased when I said I thought it looked about as exciting as watching the grass grow. However, once she pointed out exactly what each horse was trying to do, I began to appreciate the infinite skill and expertise which had gone into the background preparation to produce the finished effect. In a way, it was like going into the circus and trying to remain unimpressed when the trainer puts his head into the lion's mouth or the lovely lady allows the African elephant to place one foot on her tummy or head as she lies on the ground. The act looks very easy but, after giving it some thought, it becomes apparent that the demands of the show are extreme. Just as the chimpanzees on the well-know television adverts have been carefully, indeed meticulously, trained to perform unnatural feats and tricks, so it is with the horses who take part in eventing.

The Dressage is the most unnatural part

Lucinda Green checks her watch before the start of the cross-country course during the Badminton Trials

of all, and it came as no surprise to me to learn that it takes several years to train a horse up to the very high, very demanding standard required to participate, let alone win, at Badminton. Lucinda estimated that, starting with a three- or four-year-old horse, she would take five or six years to overcome and master all the challenges which the Three Day Event brings. The length of training required helps to explain the remarkable patience, dedication and determination of the people involved in the sport. It should be remembered, too, that it costs about £5000 a year to train each horse, with no possibility of recouping that outlay from prize money. Sponsorship is essential.

At Badminton the Dressage consists of each horse attempting 20 separately defined movements for which they will be awarded marks by the judges between 0 and 10, giving a maximum of 200 points. Over and above this they will be awarded further collective marks in four different categories up to a maximum of 10 each, making a possible 40 points. The grand total for Dressage comes to 240 points.

In 1984 there were 107 horses entered

for the Trials of which 75 actually participated; Lucinda Green had two of these, Beagle Bay and Village Gossip. I watched her ride the striking grey Beagle Bay into the arena for the Dressage and looked as carefully and critically as I could at her performance, granted my limited knowledge and experience of the event. The arena is a rectangle measuring 20 metres by 60 metres, and the horse and rider must execute the 20 different movements from memory. Lucinda, on the 14-year-old Beagle Bay entered, as prescribed, at a canter and covered 30 metres down the centre of the rectangle before halting abruptly. The horse stayed still, the rider then saluted before moving off at a trot.

The second movement had the horse tracking off to the left, breaking into a medium trot in which the horse's stride was lengthened, and then completing a circle 20 metres in diameter to its left. The next movement was called a half-pass to the left; the horse executed an awkward-looking sideways movement that appeared to the uninitiated as if it was crabbing as it shuffled across the rectangle. This was followed by the horse halting and taking five steps backwards before moving off forwards, without any pause, at a trot. The sixth, seventh and eighth disciplines were the same as the second, third and fourth, except they were to the right instead of the left. The next few movements had the horse trotting and then walking at various different but precise speeds whilst maintaining the overall rhythm. The animal then had to produce a circle to the right 10 metres in diameter at a canter, which is about twice the speed of a trot, and this was followed by the same discipline done to the left.

I had never appreciated that a horse leads with one leg when it canters. Lucinda had Beagle Bay zigzagging down the full length of the rectangle, leading first with the right leg and later repeating the exercise leading with the left. The remaining four movements involved the horse changing direction at set points as it went round the perimeter of the rectangle first at a trot and, finally, at a canter.

To fulfil the stringent standards laid down, the Dressage demands enormous discipline and concentration on the part of both the horse and the rider. For every mistake made during the 20 movements, marks are deducted from the maximum of 10 per section and, as yet, no one has ever scored the maximum 200 marks out of 200. Lucinda and Beagle Bay incurred 51.4 penalty points to lead the field at the end of the Dressage tests from Richard Walker on Accumulator with 53.2 penalty points; Mike Tucker on General Bugle was third with 53.6 penalty points. Right behind, on the heels of the three leaders, came the New Zealander Mark Todd on Charisma (57.4) and the Scotsman Ian Stark on Oxford Blue (58.2).

According to the three judges, Tony Buhler of Switzerland, François Lucas of France and Jack Burton of America, there were no really outstanding performances and there was little to choose between the extremely competent displays from the leading dozen competitors. Half of the 75 entrants came within 20 penalty points of Lucinda, which meant there was plenty of interest in the Speed and Endurance section on the Saturday.

I gathered the general impression from Lucinda that the Dressage is not her favourite part of three-day eventing but comes at the bottom end of her list. She explained:

It used to be very much the prerogative of the continentals to dominate the Dressage, but in recent years the British have made enormous progress. In the past it was psychologically disappointing to be invariably trailing at the end of the first day of three days of competition, and a great deal of effort was concentrated to improve the performance of our horses in Dressage. The benefits have been dramatic and well worthwhile, and now our leading riders and horses are just as good as the best of the cross-channel Europeans even if we do not relish the task quite as much as they do.

Once again, the sun shone brightly on the Saturday and in ideal conditions the Speed and Endurance began in front of a crowd of over 200,000. Lucinda went second of the 68 horses which had survived the opening day, on her second horse Village Gossip who had 61.8 penalty points after the Dressage and was in about twelfth place. The skill in the second stage of the Three Day Event is to show the speed, stamina and ability to jump well in the cross-country as well as to judge pace accurately. There are four separate challenges, which run consecutively and last one and a half hours with only a 10-minute rest during which the horse is examined by a vet to ensure it is sound enough to continue. It is a ferocious test of horse and rider and is the most spectacular highlight of the three days. First, the horse has to cover 3¼ miles on roads and tracks around the Badminton estate in no more than 20 minutes. This is not an impossible time limit but, if the rider goes too fast and the course is completed in 16 minutes, the horse will be shattered and unable to fulfil the rest of the really

demanding examination. If the horse takes more than 20 minutes the rider incurs one penalty point for each second in excess of the 20 and faces automatic disqualification and elimination if the finishing time exceeds 24 minutes. The problem and art in this section is to restrain a fresh, keen horse and to judge the pace in order to finish *just* inside the 20 minutes by covering the trip at a steady, sensible pace.

The horse then proceeds to jump the steeplechase course which is not especially demanding, and only one of the 49 eventual finishers collected any penalty points for poor jumping. The fences are similar to those at a typical point-to-point course and are easily negotiable by horses and riders proficient enough to be at the Horse Trials in the first place. There is a time limit of 4 minutes and again the skill is to utilize all 240 seconds but not to go over the time to incur penalty points. To rush a horse through in about three minutes would inevitably tire it and reduce its capability in the later stages. Only two horses were eliminated at the steeplechase section, but seven of the eventual finishers picked up penalty points for exceeding the 4 minutes.

From the steeplechase the horse continues straightaway with the second journey on the roads and tracks – 6 miles, on this occasion, with a horse considerably less frisky and fresh than it was 24 minutes previously, and a time limit of 45 minutes. None of the final 49 horses collected any penalty points for this part of the Speed and Endurance test and, after being examined by the vet, they proceeded to tackle the cross-country course.

This, in my view, is the best part of the Trials, as the horse, in a race against the clock, has to negotiate 27 fences or obstacles. There is a time limit of 11 minutes, 38 seconds, and a competitor is penalized 0.4 of a penalty point for every second over that time. If a rider takes more than 29 minutes, 28 seconds, he or she is eliminated. It was a magnificently designed and picturesque course which took six months to construct and featured a whole range of ingenious and imaginative obstacles. Out of the 27, the ones that stick in my

Lucinda Green and Beagle Bay safely negotiate the cross-country course

memory are the high stack of Whitbread beer barrels, a huge tree trunk suspended off the ground at nearly four feet, zigzag rails over a big ditch, the Whitbread beer lorry about four feet high and a spread of 5 feet 6 inches, a huge bridge over a stream, a couple of large banks which have to be cleared with nasty looking drops on the far side, and a catherine wheel which the horse has to spin round, jumping all the rails. It is easy to understand why 200,000 turn up every year to watch the cross-country; the course is fascinating enough almost without the horses, and to see the riders eating up the ground to clear the 27 obstacles in double-quick time was my abiding memory of three great days at Badminton. Lucinda Green on both Village Gossip and Beagle Bay had clear rounds to leave her with Beagle Bay lying in first place and Village Gossip in seventh. The 16 gruelling miles had been covered in the one and a half hours allotted and Lucinda, tired but delighted, had worked hard and earned a good night's rest.

At the end of the second day, nine of the horses had succeeded in completing the Speed and Endurance without incurring any penalty points, and the leaderboard had, as a consequence, changed noticeably. Mark Todd on Charisma had moved into second place with Ian Stark on Oxford Blue third. They were 6 points and 6.8 points behind Lucinda which meant that, going into the final event on the Sunday, the Showjumping, Lucinda had the luxury of knowing she could afford to knock over one fence to incur the statutory five penalty points and still emerge triumphant.

The Showjumping course is not particularly arduous or difficult in its own right, but it has to be remembered that the horses and riders have already had two rigorous days of competition on the Friday and Saturday; the Showjumping is the survival of the fittest. A lot of the stuffing has been knocked out of the horses; this usually results in slower reactions for which the rider must be mentally prepared. The emphasis is placed on the strength, boldness and courage of the horse and rider and Lucinda Green, equal to every challenge, enjoyed clear rounds on both her chargers.

She did have an anxious moment one jump from the finish when Beagle Bay rapped the first part of the double fence with an almighty thump. The pole bounced up in the air before miraculously landing straight back into the cup with a fair old rattle, much to the relief of Lucinda and her army of supporters. Watched by Her Majesty the Queen, she glided over the last to capture her record-breaking sixth victory in the

Lucinda Green and Beagle Bay in perfect harmony during the Show-jumping at Badminton

Badminton Horse Trials.

This marvellous achievement may never be equalled let alone beaten, and certainly not the way Lucinda has done it, on six different horses. When you consider that she has taken approximately five years to train each horse up to the highest possible standards, it puts into perspective the brilliant achievement of one of the world's greatest equestrian personalities. She won Badminton first as a teenager in 1973 on Be Fair, and continued her remarkable run with Wide Awake in 1976, George in 1977, Killaire in 1979, Regal Realm in 1983 and Beagle Bay in 1984. To win Badminton once is a great pinnacle for any competitor; to triumph six times borders on the dream world of the fairy tale come true. I was delighted that I was there to see Lucinda Green rewrite the record books.

THE WORLD CHAMPIONSHIP

The game of snooker began in 1875 on the mess tables of Jubbolpore, India. A young subaltern, Sir Neville Chamberlain, was enjoying a variation of billiards called Black Pool (using extra coloured balls) when his opponent suddenly got him in a tight corner with the help of a lucky 'fluke'. Chamberlain felt bound to say a rude word, and the rudest one he could think of was the nickname for a greenhorn at the Woolwich Military Academy – 'snooker'. The name, and the game, stuck.

Billiards, the grandfather of snooker, is a grindingly slow non-spectator sport. The highest score, achieved in 1907, was 499,315 (unfinished!), compiled by Tom Reece, and snooker itself began as a protracted affair of 73-frame epic struggles that went on for weeks. The matches were of interest chiefly to the dinner-jacketed clientele of Thurston's – the pre-War Leicester Square Hall where you could be ejected for trying to light a pipe in the back row.

The World Championship began in 1927 with one main attraction – Joe Davis. 'Old Potato Face' beat T.A. Dennis without breakin sweat – picking up £6 10s along with the original silver trophy – and went on to virtually own the title for the next 19 years, until 1946. Having beaten everybody in sight Joe retired, and snooker retired just as gracefully from the public interest. The first television coverage had featured Alec Brown Junior, Horace Lindrum and Willie Smith, in 1936 (– it's true! Alec Brown told me). It didn't seize anybody's imagination. Later on, viewers were given endless permutations of Joe Davis *v.* A.N. Other and, for many years, snooker was slotted edgeways between other more pressing sporting events on BBC's 'Grandstand'. ITN staged 'pro-am' matches in 1961, but these degenerated into prearranged 'grapple-fan' bouts and snooker was taken off the air.

The advent of colour TV, BBC2 and cult personality players like Irishman Alex Higgins, inspired the BBC to adopt an idea suggested by Ted Lowe, a veteran of the game. The long snake of snooker was chopped up into single-frame, 'sudden-death' matches and 'Pot Black' was born in 1969 with commentary from 'whispering' Ted Lowe himself. It was an immediate hit. BBC 1 continued to feature a snooker filling in 'Grandstand' sandwiches. Park Drive (Gallahers) followed John Player in sponsoring the World Championship and the tournament was slimmed down from its former girth to two weeks of intensive competition. TV coverage of the climax became possible and snooker as a spectator sport hotted up, literally: the terrific TV lights curled up the cushion rails on the table and players burned their bridge fingers going after the new improved prize-money. Ray Reardon squinted his way to victory over Australian Eddie Charlton amid the glare and dazzle of the 1973 final, clearly annoyed by the new limelight. Sponsors were *not* bedazzled. The 1975 World Championship had no sponsor at all, save Eddie Charlton in his native Australia, where the tournament was staged amid considerable acrimony about the draw and the venues.

In 1976, Embassy (W.D. and H.O. Wills) bravely sponsored a Championship which was in many ways the worst fiasco of all, disorganized by a firm called Q Promotions, now defunct. There were arguments over everything from the tables to the two tournament venues (Middlesbrough Town Hall and Wythenshawe Forum, Manchester). The mercurial Higgins reached the final by the seat of his pants, there to backfire 16-27 against Reardon, still worried about the lighting. Play was overshadowed by a table shade and blazing TV illuminations which made each ball look like a pile of eggs. The £15,300 in prize-money was divided by 27 players (compared with £200,000, £44,000 to the winner, in 1984) and the game was still a sight for sore eyes.

Snooker needed an organizer and in 1977 in Mike Watterson, player and businessman, it found one. The Championship moved to a plush little 900-seat venue in Sheffield – the Crucible Theatre; it has been there ever since. The new era broke Reardon's stranglehold. John Spencer beat Canadian Cliff Thorburn in 1977, using a 'revolutionary' two-piece cue. In 1978, with seven million now watching on television, South African Perrie Mans defeated veteran Fred Davis in a semifinal so gripping that his great brother Joe collapsed in his chair. He was fatally ill.

1979 was memorable chiefly for the choirboy features of Welshman Terry Griffiths who won the final at his first attempt (like Joe Davis, Spencer and Higgins before him). His semifinal against Charlton went on until 1.40 a.m. In 1980 Cliff Thorburn broke the hearts of Higgins' frenzied followers to snatch the world title away from Britain, but in 1981 Steve Davis emerged from Plumstead to dominate the game. A cool, technical craftsman capable of potting balls like shelling peas, Davis fought off Welshman Doug Mountjoy to take the 1981 title and £20,000. Oddly enough, Davis was beaten 10-1 in the first round the following year by 'unknown' Tony Knowles, and eventual victory went to Alex Higgins – the self-styled people's champion'. But Davis restored order in 1983 with an awesome victory over Thorburn, despite the Canadian's early 147 maximum break.

Daily BBC coverage of the Championship, which began in 1978, has turned the nation into late-night snooker gogglers, intimately familiar with the game's leading players. In 1984, over 100 hours of television coverage of the tournament were shown, with prime audience figures ranging from three or four million to nine million or more. The pros are models of sartorial elegance and self-control under pressure. Only Higgins has occasionally broken the mould, licking cue balls and taking his tie off – a hanging offence.

On my first visit to the Embassy World Championships this year I was fortunate enough to meet Ted Lowe – a walking snooker encyclopedia and the man who has done so much to popularize the game. During our conversation he remembered that it was in 1946 – the year Joe Davis retired – that he had been appointed general manager of the Leicester Square Hall in the centre of London, and that it was from then on that professional snooker began to evolve into the Championship as we now know it. Ted was responsible for two innovations. He initiated, firstly, the interval and, even more significantly, the concept of playing in a dinner jacket or, at least, a stiff white shirt and black bow tie.

The reason for this innovation was beguilingly simple. Billiards and snooker tournaments were played in the evenings over several hours and it was the custom in the forties for gentlemen to dress for dinner. These gentlemen, who comprised the bulk of the crowd at a championship or challenge match, would watch the snooker and then go out for dinner, or would go out for dinner and then round off the evening at the snooker match. Either way, they would be dressed in dinner jackets and Ted Lowe believed it would be appropriate for his players to be similarly attired.

The Hall, which seated 200 people, earned total gate receipts for one day of around £65. The old-timers did not make a fortune; the leading players would receive a large slice of their money playing exhibitions for which, in the old days, £10 would be an acceptable fee. (Nowadays the top players demand between £2000 and £5000 for special exhibition matches.) However, they could certainly play to a consistently high level.

Ted Lowe went on to tell me that he has played, followed and been involved in snooker for 50 years and, through the years, has always rated Joe Davis as the greatest player. In an impressive list of his top five he adds John Pulman, Fred Davis, Ray Reardon and Steve Davis. The last three all took part in the 1984 Championship and it is fascinating to see the differences in ages between the competitors. At 70, Fred Davis is 51 years older than John Parrott and there are few, if any, world championships in which there is such a great disparity.

I watched Dennis Taylor playing John Parrott and Cliff Thorburn playing Willie Thorne on my first venture to the Crucible Theatre during the 17-day Championship. The first thing to strike me about the venue was that I could watch both matches at the same time. Watching on television I had not appreciated that the two tables are in the base of the amphitheatre only a few feet apart, separated by a thin, mobile, dividing wall. This partition prevented a third of the crowd of 1000 from seeing more than one game at a time, and it cannot have made life easy for the players. Just as one player behind the partition was concentrating, about to play a crucial shot, he was more than likely to be interrupted and put off by a burst of rapturous applause for the player on the other table who had pocketed a particularly difficult shot. Admittedly, at the final stages of the tournament the partition was removed and only one table was used, but it must have been extremely distracting for the less experienced players in the early stages.

The outside courts at Wimbledon or parts of a championship golf course must have similar distractions, but to me it seemed like an unfair pressure on the competitors and, to some extent, the spectators.

The ninth seed, Terry Griffiths, whom I appeared with on one of the 'Question of Sport' television programmes, fully endorsed this view:

It is definitely not an ideal situation and it can often be very distracting and frustrating. People are unlucky from time to time and miss shots when the crowd instinctively react to an incident on the other table, but the conditions are the same for everyone. To enable the BBC to cover the event fully they must prefer the two tables in operation simultaneously, and we players have to acknowledge that without the television coverage we would lose some of the sponsorship and the fact that we are playing for £200,000 is entirely due to sponsorship and television.

I found it all abnormal and I asked Terry if the presence of the two mobile TV cameras and their cameramen prowling round the table right behind the players as they lined up their shots was not equally disturbing. He agreed:

It definitely has a disruptive effect being hemmed in by two moving cameras, a partition and half a crowd and it is quite incredible the difference when it comes to the single table for the semifinals. Up to that point it is cramped and claustrophobic and it feels small and tight and when you miss a few shots it soon feels a lot bloody smaller, I can assure you. I have more space round my practice table in my snooker room at home and that's a very compact little room.

One thing I was surprised to learn was that different tables and snooker balls play differently. Terry spent an hour practising in the dungeon of the Crucible Theatre the night before his quarterfinal clash with Steve Davis and as I chatted to him he explained that although the two practice tables were made by the same manufacturers as the two competition tables from exactly the same materials, every table has its own individual idiosyncrasies. It is up to the players to react to the particular table and set of balls.

As he practised he explained how each

every shot in the Championship; with more frames in each round than most other tournaments, the pressures are so outrageously enormous that it becomes highly probable the best player will win in the end. Terry pointed out that the duration of the individual matches is longer in the World Championships and even though, like other tournaments, 32 top players assemble on the starting line, the intense mental stress ensures that only the fittest and best survive. 'I think all players come to Sheffield at the peak of their form but we all know we need to be on a "high" for a lot longer than a normal tournament. The winner will be the one who stays the course best mentally over seventeen days when it is difficult to relax, to sleep, to eat and generally to escape from the immense pressure. That is why the less experienced players have a lot of difficulty.'

The first round of the Championship proper is the best of 19 frames, the second round and quarterfinals are the best of 25 frames, the semifinals are over 31 frames and the final is the best of 35 frames. That is a lot of snooker concentrated into a short period and, when I enquired how Terry Griffiths had spent his two free days following his win over the eighth seed Bill Werbeniuk and before his quarterfinal confrontation against Steve Davis, he astonished me by saying he had spent betwen 10 and 15 hours on the practice table both days. It would not be my ideal way of spending a day and it suggests that a snooker player's life is a lonely one. The players move from one tournament to the next or to a special challenge or exhibition match, living out of a suitcase in an assortment of hotels, and there is an air of the old Wild West about it. Instead of two gunslingers riding into the town (dressed to the nines) for the inevitable shoot-out, the centre stage is held by two immaculately attired snooker players, cult figures now in their own right, ready for sudden death. Terry does not regard it as either a hard or unpleasant method of earning a very good living. He won the World Championship in 1979, simply adores playing snooker and doesn't really mind slotting in all those endless hours on the practice table.

In the hope of a long career at the top,

time he attacked a difficult red he would weigh up the various options before deciding whether to play a safety shot or not. Against Steve Davis, he admitted he would resort to safety tactics more often than against a lesser player:

Steve and I will both use a lot of safety shots trying to leave nothing freely available on the table, with the one ball nestling against the cushion preferably behind a couple of colours. If there is a simple red for the taking, I would also work out which colour I was going for next and then play for the next shot.

Every single shot demands great concentration because you don't ever get another chance at that shot. Miss it and you'll never have it again in a million years – it's gone.

The stark truth is that there is pressure on

Intense concentration etched on the face of the world snooker champion, Steve Davis

Terry believes it is important to be not only mentally alert but physically fit too. Although he is very grateful to tobacco sponsorship in snooker he gave up cigarette smoking once and for all because he firmly believes that will add 10 years to his playing career. In the summer he runs regularly and indulges in light exercises every day. He looks fit and relaxed and clearly enjoys every moment he spends bent over his cue under the spotlight, literally and metaphorically, in the big tournament matches.

The margin for error is so small I felt that there might not be much difference in performing well and performing badly, and Terry agreed. 'There's hardly any difference at the top level. Even in the same night, even in the same frame, there's very little difference in it, two balls making contact in a certain position. You can play brilliantly one moment and badly the next and the difference can be just the thickness of a coat of paint.'

It was a marvellous experience to watch Terry Griffiths rattling the balls round the table with such amazing accuracy, and I enjoyed watching it so much that I hoped he would win the title again in 1984 – especially when I discovered, chatting to his father, that he had played rugby with a fair degree of success as a youngster. In fact, he was in the same Coleshill School 1st XV at full-back as both a promising fly-half Phil Bennett and a useful forward called Derek Quinnell. His father, Martin Griffiths, now a septuagenarian, travels to watch the major championships and he recalled that Terry, now 36, began playing snooker at the age of 12 in the family house on a 50-year-old table, 4 feet by 2 feet, with just 10 snooker balls which were smaller than full-size. From little acorns grow big oak trees. After playing with his father for four years, he began to play in the highly competitive local leagues round Llanelli and he went on to play as an amateur in local competitions. Eventually, in 1979, in his first tournament as a professional, he lost to Rex Williams in the qualifying round of the UK Professional Championships. In his second tournament, he won the world title.

Fred Davis, a sprightly 70-year-old, won the last of his 8 world titles in the fifties but it was still a pleasure to see him win through the qualifying stages to face, and lose to, Bill Werbeniuk in the opening round. In going down by 10 frames to 4, Fred Davis earned £2200 to add to his old-age pension.

At the other end of the scale, 19-year-old John Parrott, the youngest player in the Championships, earned £4350 when he lost to Dennis Taylor in an exciting second-round match. He is widely tipped as a future champion and he was pleasantly unassuming and open when we talked briefly later that

night. He came into the sport by chance just before his thirteenth birthday. He was going to play bowls with his father one night but it was raining so heavily that they switched plans and popped in to the local snooker club instead. He became a snooker junkie in no time at all and has never looked back.

Unlike most of the older professionals, John Parrott has never had a job and judging by his meteoric rise this year he should be capable of earning an extremely good living on the snooker circuit. He is an intelligent, witty individual with a batch of 'O' levels and would have sat his 'A' levels two years ago if his current manager had not spotted him playing snooker for his local team, the Dudley Institute in Liverpool. With his side 3–0 down he stepped up and cleared the board, and in 1983 he turned professional. He made a remarkable first appearance on television in the Lada Classic when he reached the semifinal before losing to Steve Davis by 5 frames to 4, but the disappointment of defeat was cushioned by a cheque for £7000. He acknowledges that he is likely to earn very large sums of money for such a young sportsman but he is confident he can handle it. 'Obviously there is a danger of going off the rails but I intend to keep my head screwed on and my feet firmly on the ground. I live at home with my father in Liverpool and my manager is only two miles away. We work everything out between us and I don't intend to jeopardize a promising career.'

He was naturally disappointed losing to Dennis Taylor but he had the satisfaction of playing well in defeat. 'I tried everything except breathing on Dennis's spectacles between shots and the fact that I was in good form took the sting out of the defeat.' He did not appear to me to suffer unduly from nerves or lack big match temperament but he felt, curiously enough, that he was more likely to suffer from the importance of the occasion when he was an established player. After beating Tony Knowles in the first round he chose to watch Liverpool at Anfield, to relax as he waited for his next match. He played soccer at school. 'I was a dashing outside-left, you know, but in my spare time now I play a bit of golf and listen to music – everything from classical to jazz funk.' I have a feeling he will not have a lot of spare time in the future as he rockets up the ladder of success.

Dennis Taylor proceeded to win his quarterfinal against Doug Mountjoy, but lost to Steve Davis in the semifinal. In the other semifinal Jimmy White, the eleventh seed, beat the Canadian professional champion Kirk Stevens by 16 frames to 14.

The stage was set for what turned out to be the best final – the experts agreed – in recent memory. I had a long chat with Steve Davis a few days after the epic contest and it was interesting to hear him say that winning the Championship again was far more important to him than the prize-money involved. He wanted the prestige and the title and he admitted that it was far harder defending the title and the top-seed billing than it was winning the Championship in the first place. Steve Davis won the title in 1981 but made a hasty exit the following year when he lost in the opening round to Tony Knowles. He took the title again in 1983 and he was determined to hang on to it in 1984. He said his hardest match up to the final was a thrilling quarterfinal victory over Terry Griffiths which was desperately close and exciting. The rest of his matches he won relatively comfortably, whereas Jimmy White had had a far tougher path to the final culminating in a gruelling confrontation with Kirk Stevens which went on until late on the Saturday night, leaving White undoubtedly a little jaded for the first session of the final on the Sunday. Steve Davis relaxed during the two and a half weeks of the tournament by trying to lead a normal life as if he was at home and not in an hotel, and to that end he had 3 or 4 of his close friends in the hotel with him. He spent a lot of time in his room, engaged in a long, drawn-out battle with an electronic chess game, and when he wanted to spend time on the practice table he steered a wide berth around the Crucible Theatre and went to a health club in Sheffield where he was left to himself and not disturbed by the club members.

For all these reasons, when the final began Steve was probably. in the better frame of mind though he admits he has to endure greater pressure because, from the first ball to be pocketed on 21 April until the last ball dropped on 7 May, he is the target for all snooker's head-hunters. Just as Liverpool have found in soccer, John McEnroe and Martina Navratilova have found in tennis, Tom Watson in golf or the All Blacks in rugby, there are no easy matches because everybody makes an extra special effort to beat the best in the world. Steve Davis won all his matches only because he was able to keep producing his very best form whenever it mattered, and when he hits top form it is breathtaking to watch.

By the end of the first day he led by 12 frames to 4, needing just six more to clinch the crown. Jimmy White is a very quiet, bold player and, when he had a hot streak from time to time, he looked unbeatable but those moments of magic did not last long enough to trouble the champion initially.

However, on the second day, it was quite different. White began brilliantly and with the adrenaline coursing through his veins he began to dominate the final. The crowd became excitable as the underdog asserted himself and, in oddly typical British fashion, they gave him their support. Davis was philosophical:

One of the wives of my friends said that if I had been playing against Adolf Hitler the entire crowd would have been behind Hitler because they just love to see the favourite beaten. The decisive point in my favour as Jimmy stormed back into the game with a whole succession of big breaks, was my ability to score steady breaks of fifty, sixty and seventy consistently. That won me the Championship in the end. I never emulated Jimmy's fantastic purple patches but I never cracked either, and I kept getting decent breaks of around 60 even from difficult positions. I kept waiting, sitting powerless on my chair, for Jimmy's bubble to burst as I knew it was impossible to maintain his scintillating, blistering form for ever and I knew when he did weaken for a moment, I had to be mentally prepared to cash in. That is precisely what happened.

White took seven of the first 8 frames on Holiday Monday with some stunning snooker which included a break of 119 in the

Right on cue, Jimmy White helped to make the final a fantastic match

opening frame. He clawed his way back into contention 14–11, then recovered from 16–12 to 17–15 before staging his most fearless exhibition of aggressive play. In the thirty-third frame, needing only one more frame to win, Davis opened up a 60–0 lead and was attempting to pocket the blue rather than an easier colour because going for the blue would have made it easy to come back on to a red prior to going for the black and putting himself well out of reach. The blue went straight for the pocket, tantalizingly spun slowly round the rim and remained on the table hovering over the pocket. White immediately seized the initiative and cleared the table to win the frame 65–60. Steve thought he had lost the Championship at that moment. 'I had made a mistake and allowed Jimmy to continue the phenomenal momentum he had enjoyed throughout the final day. I thought the gods had decided to have a new champion.' But, as Terry Griffiths had stressed to me, every game is completely different and White looked set to clear the table in the next frame to tie the match with just one frame left when he missed a relatively easy green to the top left-hand pocket while leading 40–32, and Davis stepped in smartly to win the frame 77–40 and a truly classic final by 18 frames to 16.

They say good snooker play in an average

Joe Soap is the sign of a misspent youth, but for the millions glued compulsively to the television coverage of the World Championships, they must all be guilty of a misspent adulthood. Happily, I was one of those riveted by the events of those 17 intriguing days of play. When I was not actually at the Crucible Theatre, the most ideal amphitheatre, I was in front of the goggle-box.

The great strength of the sport is that it makes excellent television. The table fits perfectly onto a television screen and the viewer can follow every move in close-up. It fits the screen much better than a football, rugby or cricket pitch, a golf course, a race track – be it for horses, motor cars, or athletes – and better even than a tennis court. This partly explains the massive popularity of snooker as a spectator sport. Nevertheless much of the interest is in the personalities who play at the highest level and the incredible degree of skill which they share. British snooker players are the best in the world and I was delighted to be reminded of that undeniable fact this spring at the Crucible Theatre in Sheffield. It was indeed a pleasure to watch all the stars in action, but especially the single-minded excellence of Steve Davis, world champion for the third time in four years.

THE CUP FINAL

There have been a lot of things broken in the history of the Rugby League Challenge Cup – apart from stand-off Peter Ramsden's nose in Huddersfield's 1953 victory over St Helens when Ramsden scored two tries on his nineteenth birthday. The first breakage was the sundering of the northern clubs from the English Rugby Union. The principle at issue was 'broken time' – expenses paid to working players who missed their Saturday shifts in order to turn out for their clubs. The clubs wanted to pay: the English Rugby Union refused. A meeting at the George Hotel, Huddersfield on 29 August 1895, broke up with the decision to form the Northern Rugby Football Union. The first Challenge Cup final of the breakaway League, with its own championship and 22 teams, was held in 1897 under the name of the Northern Union Cup. The Cup in question was slightly taller than the 3 feet it is now: a bit broke off the top. It cost 60 guineas and was made by Fattorini's of Bradford who later made the FA Challenge Cup original – half the size of the rugby one. In that first final Batley drubbed St Helens 10–3. A crowd of 13,492 paid a total of £624 for the privilege of witnessing the inaugural 'do' at Headingley, compared with 84,745 who coughed up £666,000 to see the 1983 affair.

There were new rules for the new League, mainly designed to sell the game as a spectator sport. By the 1898–9 season the players were full professionals. In 1906 sides were reduced from 15 to 13, and ready for anything. There are some 34 teams in the League now, though many have come and gone over the years and about 70 squads have seen membership. The first Northern Rugby Football League winners were Manningham, the Bradford side.

Although the record gate for any Challenge Cup final (or indeed Rugby League match) was the 102,569 who jammed in to see Warrington beat Halifax in a 1954 replay at Bradford, Wembley has now become the showdown venue. The man behind the shift was a Welshman by the appropriate name of John Leake, who piloted the idea through the 1928 conference in Llandudno. So the 1929 final was staged at Wembley, where attendances have varied from 98,536 in 1966 (St Helens *v.* Wigan) to 36,544 in 1930 (Widnes *v.* St Helens). There have been 'full houses' on only four occasions, in 1966, 1969, 1978 and 1980, but then the authorities don't put a 100,000 limit on the gate as they do for the FA Cup final. They reckon your average league supporter is bigger than your soccer supporter and takes up more room. 41,500 heavyweights paid £5,614 to see the first Wembley final in 1929, when Widnes beat Dewsbury 13-2. One spectator who must have added a few tons to the calculations in 1938 was Don Bradman, peerless Aussie cricketer, who presented the trophy.

The Challenge Cup broke new ground with a man-of-the-match trophy before either cricket or soccer had one. The coveted Lance Todd Award, named after the player and manager, has been a feature of the final since 1946. The first winner was

Wakefield's Billy Stott. The great day has produced many larger-than-life characters: men like 'Ahr Albert' Goldthorpe who captained the fantastic Hunslet side of 1908, winners of the Cup, championship, Yorkshire League and Yorkshire Cup. Their pack was called The Terrible Six. Another giant of the game was Jim Sullivan of Wigan, who amassed a century of goals in 18 consecutive seasons and kicked the very first goal at Wembley.

Records have been broken in 1984: both Wigan and Widnes made their twelfth Wembley appearance, and both had already won the trophy six times at Wembley. The Widnes trio of Keith Elwell, Mick Adams and Eric Hughes made their seventh appearance in a Wembley final – another record. But the biggest breakages have not been the records or the bones, but the hearts. Half-back Dai Davies finished on the losing side twice with Warrington, again with Huddersfield and yet again with Keighley. And in a 1968 final played in Wagnerian thunder and lightning, Wakefield Trinity's Neil Fox sliced the decisive last kick wide to make it 11-10 to Leeds in a stunning finish. Fox did his crying in the rain.

I was brought up in a small village called Adlington which is only six miles from Wigan so, from a very young age, my heart was with Wigan. Naturally, I was delighted that they reached the final of the Challenge Cup in 1984, for the first time in 14 years and I was looking forward to their reappearance at Wembley. I have always enjoyed watching rugby league and am still a fair-weather supporter of Wigan; I have been along to Central Park several times in the last three seasons and I was particularly impressed with their match against the fabulous touring Australians in 1982. The Australian team was one of the finest collections of rugby players I have ever seen in either code of the game, and there were important lessons to be learned by any youngster, irrespective of whether he preferred union to league or vice-versa. Their breathtaking speed and accuracy of passing, their direct, hard, straight running, brilliant support play and superb, aggressive tackling made them invincible; their game was an object lesson for league and union player alike.

It was very much in the hope that some of the glamour and skills with which they had captivated the British public on their tour had been absorbed by the top British clubs and would be reproduced at Wembley on 5 May, that I set off on the journey from Preston to London in optimistic spirits. The Cup final is an annual pilgrimage for all the diehard supporters of the game in the north and they plan well in advance to make a weekend out of it. The atmosphere pervading the entire trip is one of warmth and friendliness inspired by a deep-rooted, genuine love and affection for the game. This was brought home to me most emphatically on the motorway when I overtook a coach filled with 30 or so Wigan supporters, decked out in cherry and white hooped scarves, hats and rosettes, and 30 or so Widnes supporters, suitably covered in their club's white and black colours. I could hardly imagine any other big Cup final in which the rival supporters would happily agree to share a coach on a 200-mile journey to the match, presumably share a hotel and the return journey.

There is no better way that I can sum up the wonderful atmosphere than to say that the coach typified the shared intensity of interest with which the Challenge Cup final is riddled every year. It is a great occasion, a great day or weekend out and a special, once-a-year event which whole families often enjoy together.

I booked into a small London hotel to discover that over 20 York supporters were also staying there. They told me they had booked well in advance and come every year, even though they accepted that their team, currently languishing in the Second Division, was never likely to make it all the way to Wembley. They come every year simply to watch the biggest rugby league club match in the world, for its own sake.

Curiously enough, York came close to making it to Wembley in 1984 but lost in the semifinals to Wigan by 14 points to 8. En route to Wembley, Wigan beat Bramley, Oldham, St Helens and York whilst Widnes defeated Dewsbury, Fulham, Hull Kingston

Rovers and Leeds. The increasing interest as the competition develops is best illustrated by the fact that the average gate attracted by Wigan and Widnes for the first three rounds was under 8000 for the seven matches, whereas 31000 watched the two semifinals on neutral grounds and three times that number turned up for the final at Wembley.

I learned early that Saturday exactly why the event is so popular. Of all the great sporting occasions that I attended in 1984, none was more friendly and more fun than the Challenge Cup final. Everybody was in good spirits on their way to the stadium and there was a total lack of animosity and aggression amongst the rival groups of supporters. They were courteous, witty, amiable and obviously out to have a really good time, which is the way all groups of supporters should behave at a sporting occasion. The police said that year in, year out they never have any trouble at the rugby league final and it is a pleasure to deal with such civilized fans. To me, it shows up in a true light the disgraceful behaviour of some British soccer fans, who give football such a bad name. In this context, I am referring to the growing minority of hooligans and 'yobbos' who are exactly what they purport to be – hooligans and 'yobbos'.

The atmosphere inside the stadium was akin to that of a rugby union international at Twickenham and it was a pleasure to see how orderly and helpful everyone was. I bumped into the Chairman of Castleford and he asked me if, now I was a professional, I would fancy joining and playing for his club. I told him that there was no way I would like to play rugby league for Castleford or any other club to which he replied, I hope tongue in cheek, that on second thoughts he realized that I would not be good enough for Castleford, anyway. Much as I had anticipated, my appearance at the rugby league Cup final meant I came in for a fair bit of stick, but it was light-hearted banter of the most genial kind and I had a marvellous day out.

I tucked into a slap-up lunch in one of the hospitality boxes and shortly after one o'clock the crowd were entertained by the 100-strong combined bands of the Coldstream, Irish and Welsh Guards. They provided a stirring spectacle and so did the Hull and Oldham Under 11s who took over at two o'clock in their Bertie Bassett mini-challenge match. At half past two the massed bands returned and this time they were accompanied by the well-known disc jockey, Ed Stewart, who led the community singing of such popular songs as 'She's a Lassie from Lancashire', 'Sailing', You'll Never Walk Alone', Land of Hope and Glory' and 'Abide With Me'.

This rousing sing-song was a fitting prelude to the arrival of the two teams who were greeted with a full-throated roar – this would do a mischief even to the most unreceptive eardrum and tickle the emotional strings of the hardest heart. The teams were presented to The Right Honourable the Earl of Derby, the President of the Rugby League. The National Anthem was played and at three o'clock the eighty-third Challenge Cup final kicked off.

Unfortunately for the clubs in England, all future rugby league players and big matches will be compared to the great Australian squad about whom I have already elaborated and, judged by their amazingly high standards, the 1984 Challenge Cup final was not a great game. The tackling was typically ferocious and decisive but the two teams lacked the ingenuity, imagination and inspiration which the Australians had shown and even the passing and handling were substandard.

None the less the crowd was engrossed in the war of attrition being enacted on the famous Wembley pitch, and the fact that both sides were guilty of so many elementary mistakes did not seem to detract unduly from the overall entertainment. In fairness to Wigan, who failed to capitalize on their pressure and slight dominance in the first 20 minutes, their players in their first visit to Wembley since 1970 were likely to suffer more from nerves than Widnes players. They should have been a couple of scores in front by then, but they made too many unforced handling errors and their chance of upsetting the favourites slipped away.

Widnes were much the more experienced side and, as it is with every sport the world over, you cannot buy experience and

you cannot survive so easily without it. Widnes and Wigan were each making a record twelfth appearance at Wembley and each had won the Cup six times. The winners were destined to take the trophy for a record seventh time and Widnes were hot favourites because their recent history has been vastly superior to that of Wigan. Widnes were appearing in their seventh Wembley final in the previous 10 years and they had won the Cup in 1975, 1979 and 1981. They had won the Premiership Trophy in 1983 and, in 1984, they had been runners-up in the John Player Trophy and the Lancashire Cup.

Their current squad was steeped in experience of big-time matches and that counts for a lot in a one-off confrontation in a knock-out competition. It was essential for Wigan, if they were to win, to grab a good early lead and not just the one penalty goal they managed and, though they certainly built up the platform for such an advantage, they hesitated and were hustled out of their

rhythm by a Widnes team confident of its own ability and quite capable of absorbing and soaking up the anticipated early onslaught. Wigan has, historically, been the stronghold of rugby league in the north and they had three times as many supporters in the capacity crowd as Widnes, but their loyal and devoted fans, who have supported them right through their recent famine, knew their fate when they failed to add to Whitfield's penalty.

The turning point in the match came in a three-minute flurry of activity which produced two great tries late in the first half. Wigan were on the attack and Colin Whitfield hacked the ball forward, but he was beaten in the race to retrieve possession by the Widnes full-back, Mick Burke. In a trice, Burke exploded through five tackles and made a rampaging run up to half-way before linking with Andy Gregory the scrum-half who set the 34-year-old veteran campaigner Stuart Wright free on the wing. When he was tackled, Widnes launched two

Widnes scrum-half Andy Gregory initiates a sniping counter-attack during the Rugby League Cup final

The Widnes defence is as strong as their attack; Kerry Hemsley, the Wigan forward, is the meat in the sandwich

more bullocking offensives by courtesy of Mick Adams and then Joe Lydon. From this position, about 30 yards from the Wigan line slightly to the right of the posts, Keith Elwell spun the ball left along the line and Mike O'Neill, showing tremendous pace and power for a big, strapping second-row forward, burst through the first lines of defence and created space for John Bassnett on the left wing. Bassnett jinked off his left foot to slice inside and, as he was engulfed by the covering defenders, he popped the ball up to his fly-half Kieran O'Loughlin a couple of yards from the line. 25,000 Widnes supporters held their breath as O'Loughlin failed to take the pass first time, knocking the ball forward and up into the air. He sprinted over the line in hot pursuit and regathered the ball in mid-air in outstretched hands just like a circus juggler and crashed to the ground to score the first try of the match. Mick Burke, the man who started the move, added the conversion to give Widnes a lead of 6 points to 2.

Three minutes later, Wigan were on the

attack again near the Widnes line when Mark Cannon had a delicate chip ahead charged down by Mick Adams; Les Gorley collected the ball and timed a quick, accurate pass to Kevin Tamati on his left shoulder. Tamati fed Joe Lydon as he himself was tackled and Wigan, one moment sweeping forward to follow up the kick from Cannon, were suddenly caught flat-footed on the retreat. Lydon was clear to sprint 75 yards to score a spectacular and, as it transpired, match-winning try. Burke converted and Widnes had a commanding lead of 10 points.

In a sense, I felt sorry for Wigan because I thought they had played the better rugby in the first quarter of the game, and they certainly showed tremendous character to hit back in the last minutes of the half, attacking non-stop in a prolonged assault on the Widnes line. But it was to no avail against a magnificent, solid defence. What pleased me most about the two dramatic tries was that both were made to some extent by the footballing skills of the two second-row forwards. As a member of the second-row union myself, I noted with respect the efforts of Mike O'Neill in setting up the first try and the legerdemain of Les Gorley in sparking off the second try a few moments later. And, while on the subject of forwards introducing some of the subtleties of the game to telling advantage, I wonder what my former colleagues, Frannie Cotton and Mike Burton, two redoubtable rugby union props, would have done if they had attempted to drop a goal from 20 yards in the middle of a Twickenham international. That was precisely what the Widnes prop forward, Steve O'Neill, succeeded in doing 10 minutes into the second half.

He landed his fifth drop goal of the season, which is an enviable record for a prop and, furthermore, it was a crunching tackle by his fellow prop, Kevin Tamati, on Gary Stevens near the Widnes line which propelled the ball out of Stevens' grasp and led to the third try of the match. Joe Lydon swooped onto the loose ball, scooped it up and streaked down the left wing at breakneck speed to score his second try with another unforgettable 75-yard dash. That ended the match as a contest – Wigan were well and truly dead and buried. In a final flourish Wigan did manage to score when Kerry Hemsley surged over the line for a try carrying three defenders with him, but by then their names had been earmarked for the losers' medals.

When the final whistle was blown by Billy Thomson, refereeing his last rugby league game before retiring at the age of 50 after a long and distinguished career, not only were Widnes deserved victors but Joe Lydon was guaranteed the man-of-the-match award for his two electrifying tries. The Widnes captain Eric Hughes led his triumphant team up the famous steps and he received the State Express Challenge Cup from Lord Derby. He also received congratulations from the leader of the Labour party, Neil Kinnock, and from the former leader of the National Union of Mineworkers, Joe Gormley.

Widnes then set off on the customary lap of honour with the cup held high and I was glad that they were given a great ovation by the Wigan fans as well as by their own. The winners, as always, were awarded a fantastic ovation and the players and the Widnes hierarchy were submerged in a spontaneous wave of hysteria and adulation. It makes a wonderful, emotional sight and a suitable end to a great sporting occasion, but I was equally intrigued to examine life from the other end of the tunnel and share the disappointment of the Wigan team and their legion of supporters.

I was able to do this through the eyes of their centre-threequarter David Stephenson. David was a member of the England Schoolboys international rugby union team which included Mick Burke, the current Widnes full-back, and also players like Huw Davies, Marcus Rose, Tony Swift and Nick Youngs who all went on to play rugby union for England at senior level. David was a member of my own rugby union club at Fylde for two seasons before he signed professional forms for rugby league. Understandably, he was very dejected at the end of the match at Wembley because he and the rest of the Wigan team knew that they had not produced their best form.

The forwards had not won enough possession,' he felt, *'and the whole team made too many errors in attack to justify our belief and hopes that we would spring a surprise. At half-time the coach Alex Murphy, not a man noted for sitting on the fence, gave us a right rollicking and most of what he said is unprintable but he pointed out, quite correctly, that the two tries which Widnes scored both arose from our errors when we were actually on the attack.*

The inference is that Wigan lost the game rather than Widnes won it, but this is not a completely fair assessment as it ignores the thoroughly professional and totally organized approach of the winners. They were good enough to take their chances as they arose, no matter how they were created.

Stephenson also believed that the whole glamour and razzle-dazzle of Wembley affected them more than it did Widnes. The Wigan team were not accustomed to eight motor-cyclists giving them a high-powered police escort to the ground from the hotel. He, himself, was shocked and disturbed by a BBC TV camera crew and interviewer bursting into the dressing-room while the team were changing, and mingling with the players for about a quarter of an hour. I agree that this may be welcomed by the large, armchair audience at home, but it would never happen in rugby union or cricket or at Wimbledon and it strikes me as an outrageous invasion into a player's liberty and privacy.

These are not valid reasons for denying Widnes victory and the Wigan players admit the better side won on the day. All the more reason then, when it was all over, for David and the lads to feel disappointed, disgruntled and depressed. David recalled:

I was emotionally and physically drained at the end. I remember congratulating Mick Burke and wandering slowly off the pitch. I was trying to hide my feelings but I did start to cry as the reality sank in when Widnes climbed up the steps to collect the trophy and the medals for the winners. Our boys felt like lepers with the plague at that moment because we were left on the edge of the pitch isolated and unwanted. The photographers and the press were swarming round Widnes and nobody wanted to know or even seemed aware of our existence.

I saw Alex Murphy, the substitutes and the

Scorer of two brilliant tries, Joe Lydon had every right to think it was his Rugby League Cup

assistant coach come on the field to console the Wigan team but they accepted the old adage that you do not get any bouquets for coming second in a two-horse race. Of course, the cognoscenti were aware that it was not initially a two-horse race at all but a 34-horse race with every team in the first and second divisions participating. That meant little at quarter to five in the afternoon on 5 May. David elaborated:

I can honestly say that the walk from the pitch up to the box to receive my loser's medal felt like the longest walk of my life. The mammoth contingent of our supporters were still chanting 'Wigan', 'Wigan' and I felt dreadful because the team had let them down. As I descended the steps, head bowed, I thought we had let down ourselves, let down our families, let down our friends, let down our fans and let down the town of Wigan. But then our skipper, Graeme West, came round each player individually and ordered us to hold our heads high and run round the pitch to acknowledge our fans before going back to the dressing-room.

The players did just that, waving to a sea of cherry and white colours in every imaginable combination, the supporters reassuring the players each with glazed eyes. It was a moving scene and so was the one in the dressing-room which followed. 'Alex Murphy came in and shut the door and told us that he was proud of us. Even though we had lost we had made it to Wembley for the first time in a long time and we could hold our heads high because we had nothing to be ashamed of. Several of us were in tears and others were trying to choke back the disappointment but Alex and the captain persuaded us that there was life after defeat.'

The team returned to their hotel outside London and tucked in to a five-course banquet followed by a few short speeches. Surprisingly, the team claimed they had a smashing night with their wives or girlfriends at a disco until the early hours of the morning and they recovered from the setback of the afternoon more readily than they had expected.

The Sunday was going to be another challenge. They set off on the return journey to Wigan in mid-morning and the plan was

to arrive at the centre of Wigan at four o'clock. If they had won they knew they would be given a magnificent reception with every man, woman, child, dog and cat turning out swathed in cherry and white to greet them. But, in defeat, they wondered if a single soul would bother to turn up in the town or at their ground at Central Park. They decided that, in case anyone did bother to turn out, they should have their jackets, shirts and ties to hand. But David remembers with obvious pride:

When we hit town just after four o'clock we could hardly believe our eyes. We were given a hero's welcome with the whole town covered in cherry and white and we drove straight to the ground. We went to our dressing-room and, on schedule, emerged from the tunnel onto the pitch at half past four to the most phenomenal reception I have ever experienced. The ground erupted with rapturous applause and we knew we had the best supporters in the world. There was hardly a dry eye in the house and it was hard to believe that we were the losing team the day before. We walked round the ground mixing with the crowd, having our pictures taken with young babies and old-age pensioners and every age-group in between. We signed hundreds of autographs, smiled and chatted to as many people as we could, but it was impossible to speak to a tenth of the gathering. As the treasurer and the Chairman said ruefully, it was the biggest gate of the season. People kept wringing us by the hand and telling us how proud they were that we had got to Wembley. There was a lump in every throat and when we returned to the dressing-room ages later there were an awful lot of wet hankies. It was the most moving, unforgettable day I can ever recall at Central Park. Next year we will simply have to win the Cup because our fans deserve it.

For Widnes, I dare say, the celebrations were even greater but it is nice to know that the old American football coach's maxim – 'Winning is not the most important thing; it is the only thing' – is not always the case. Like Wigan and Widnes, I also had a memorable weekend and I shall be back at Wembley again in 1985. I hope Wigan might be there again too and that when the final whistle goes, they will be first up the Wembley steps.

SEVEN

RUNNING

THE LONDON MARATHON

In 490 BC a Greek courier, Pheidippides, was dispatched from the small town of Marathon to Athens 24 miles away with an important message: the Greeks had thrashed the Persian garrison. The poor man ran all the way and, having conveyed his message, collapsed and died.

When the first modern Olympics were held in Athens in 1896 there was a commemorative Marathon–Athens run in Pheidippides' honour, and the first 'marathon' race was won by Greek shepherd Spyridon Louis, whose training had consisted largely of forced marches in the army. His time for the 40 kilometres was 2 hours, 58 minutes, 50 seconds. There was also an unofficial entrant: a Greek woman, Melopene, finished the distance in about four and a half hours. It was, however, several decades before women were officially allowed in the race; married women found at the Olympics were tossed off a cliff.

An important London marathon took place in 1908, as part of the Olympics. The distance from Windsor Castle to the White City Stadium – 26 miles, 385 yards – was to become standard for the marathon course, and this was reflected in the 1924 Olympics. The first runner to reach the White City Stadium in that London race was Italian Dorando Pietri. Poor Pietri failed to drag his body round the last lap and; having been helped over the finish line, was disqualified.

In the 1954 Empire Games in Vancouver, Britain's heroic Jim Peters looked set to carry all before him, having broken 2 hours, 20 minutes in 1953 – the first man so to do over an undisputed marathon distance. The crowd roared loudly as Peters entered the stadium 15 minutes ahead of the field, but his speed nearly killed him. Peters staggered and crawled round the track for 11 minutes and had to be helped away, heartbroken, with just 200 yards to go.

The marathon is the litmus test of a runner's character and veteran Finn Hannes Kolehmainen showed his in the 1920 Olympics, winning the longest-ever marathon (26 miles, 990 yards) in 2 hours, 32 minutes, 35.8 seconds. Emil Zatopek forced his wiry frame through the marathon in 1952, having already completed a track 'double'. Grete Waitz, who in 1983 ran the distance in 2 hours, 25 minutes, 29 seconds, produced the first women's run in less than two and a half hours – the Norwegian had cracked the barrier just eight years after the first female time under three hours.

The London Marathon may not be the oldest such race in the country (that was the Windsor Polytechnic Marathon), but it certainly gripped the interest of the British public. Most of them were in it! The inaugural race, held on 29 March 1981 from

Greenwich Park to Constitution Hill, boasted 7000 starters, 6255 finishers inside five hours, 144 inside two and a half hours. It ended, incredibly, in a dead heat, with Dick Beardsley (USA) running hand in hand over the line with Inge Simonsen of Norway. Their time was 2 hours, 11 minutes, 48 seconds. Joyce Smith was the fastest woman and the first girl in Britain with a time under two and a half hours (2 hours, 29 minutes, 57 seconds).

The second London Marathon was even bigger, with 80,000 entries. There were 16,350 starters, 15,758 of whom made it. Hugh Jones was first in 2 hours, 9 minutes, 24 seconds, and Joyce Smith became the oldest British record-holder in any event at 44 years, 195 days with her time of 2 hours, 29 minutes, 43 seconds. Roger Bourbon ran the entire race dressed as a waiter; the Californian crossed the line and poured himself a glass of wine from the bottle he'd carried all the way on a tray. Shamefaced onlookers thought it had been stuck down. Marathon madness knows no bounds. In the 1982 Honolulu race Don Davis covered the distance in 4 hours, 20 minutes, 36 seconds – running backwards. And the Athens Marathon of 1976 saw Dimitrion Yordanidis complete the course in 7 hours, 33 minutes. He was 98.

My great regret about the 1984 London Marathon was the fact that I could not run in it. It had always been my intention to participate and I began training for it in December with regular runs of three or four miles. Gradually, I increased the distance of each training spin until, by the beginning of March, I was covering the best part of 15 miles two or three times a week. I set the alarm for six o'clock in the morning and completed two hours round the streets and fields on the outskirts of Preston before setting off to the office for a day's work. On the days when I did not do a strong early-morning run, I tried to do a few miles at lunchtime and, with eight weeks to go to the Marathon, I was in excellent shape and looking forward immensely to the challenge. Sadly and infuriatingly, the persistent pounding on the roads and on the pavements during that four-month period caused a recurrence of the neck injury which ended my rugby career and I was grudgingly forced to accept some sound medical advice: it would be foolhardy in such circumstances to flog my 17 stones round the streets of London for 26 miles.

I was very upset when the specialist broke the news to me because I had thoroughly enjoyed and become accustomed to the routine and discipline of training and felt very much fitter and better for it. I believed that I would be able to complete the course under 4 hours and that not many people of my size and weight would be any faster than that. Not only was I very disappointed at having to drop out, but I was also a little embarrassed because the fact that I would be participating had received publicity in the papers and on the radio.

Nevertheless, I decided that the London Marathon was undoubtedly one of the great sporting occasions of the year and, even though I would not be able to give my own description of the event as a competitor, I would still be able to see the agony and ecstasy through the eyes of a handful of runners. I travelled down to London on the Saturday afternoon in readiness for a marathon runner's typical gourmet meal the night before the actual race. I had been invited to the home of John and Kari Hegarty in Highgate to guzzle the sort of specialized, carefully balanced bill of fare which gives the right sustenance for someone about to run 26 miles.

During my own training I had cut down on cigarettes and alcohol and the regular marathon runners explained that they would have an extremely low alcohol intake, if any, during the week of the race. I am delighted to report that we drank some excellent wine with the magnificent meal Kari cooked that evening, as it was generally agreed that watching a marathon was less demanding than participating. I had heard so much conflicting advice in the four months I had been training that I had consulted an excellent paperback by Neil Wilson and Andy Etchells called *The Marathon Book*; it confirmed that a lot of nonsense is talked about the importance and significance of diet and how it affects the performance of a long-distance athlete. They point out that all foods are broken down into a fairly small number of simple 'building-blocks' – sugars, fatty acids, glycerol, amino-acids, vitamins, minerals, and water. These raw materials are absorbed into the bloodstream and are either stored or broken down as part of the process which produces energy. Wilson and Etchells point out that as long as the weekly diet is well balanced, it does not seem to matter hugely what marathon runners eat during their long training period. They cite that in Japan the natives train on rice and fish, in Mexico on a maize, eggs and beans diet, the American top runner Bill Rodgers survives on 'junk' food while other Westerners stick to a vegetarian diet; yet all these different parts of the world produce first-class marathon performances.

The balance is the vital ingredient and any diet which includes meat, fish, salads, fresh fruit, green vegetables, milk, eggs and wholemeal bread will give the individual what he requires. It certainly suited me in training! It should go without saying that it is essential to drink considerable amounts of fluid to replace liquid lost on long training runs. This general diet is really a matter of common sense. What needs to be borne in mind is that anyone running long distances is burning up far more calories than someone just sitting in an office and, in consequence, requires more food. I reckoned that when I was running 40 or 50 miles a week, I was burning 4000 or 5000 calories per day and I did not feel any sense of guilt sipping a pint of beer at the end of a ten-mile journey.

However, there is general agreement nowadays that, in the final build-up to the actual race, a special diet packed with carbohydrates can be extremely beneficial. As Kari Hegarty was to prove, it can also be exceedingly tasty. The theory is that the body runs on muscle glycogen – the principal source of energy for the long-distance athlete – and a carbohydrate-packed diet increases glycogen in the body.

In normal circumstances, a fit runner on a normal diet would begin to run out of glycogen soon after halfway; people experience 'the Wall' when fatigue sets in and the athlete's strength starts to drain away. The carbohydrate-packed diet is designed to counteract this sensation. The runner should, after his final long-distance run of

Horseplay during this year's London Marathon

about 18 miles and intending to run on a Sunday, stop eating carbohydrates altogether on the Monday, Tuesday and Wednesday before. The body tries to compensate for the sudden loss of glycogen by producing its own. Then the runner should pack carbohydrates into the body again on Thursday, Friday and Saturday. By so doing, the runner should have enough glycogen to last through the entire 26 miles.

Whatever the theory, a great many of the runners in the London Marathon would have tucked into a high-carbohydrate meal on the Saturday evening, similar to the one I enjoyed in Highgate, in the hope and expectation that extra glycogen would help them avoid 'the Wall' the following day. For the record, I joined the two men and one woman who had run marathons previously, John Hegarty, Robin Dow and Sophie Hansson in tabouleh (cracked wheat salad) followed by fettuccine al gorgonzola, then cannelloni with spinach and finally spaghetti bolognese. We all ate until our eyes were popping out of our heads and I must confess the last thing on my mind that night was the thought of pounding the streets of London for four hours the next morning.

During dinner, I asked John Hegarty what had made him, the Creative Director of the highly successful advertising company Bartle, Boyle and Hegarty, in his late thirties choose to run in his first marathon. He recalled that:

The whole idea of accepting the challenge to run 26 miles inspired me. I saw one of my friends run in the New York Marathon and I just thought the event was so fantastic and emotional that I wanted to take part. I play tennis regularly and golf occasionally but I know that I'll never play in the same tournament as John McEnroe or Jimmy Connors, or Tom Watson or Jack Nicklaus. In the London, New York or Tokyo Marathons, I would be able to run in the same race as the best marathon runners in the world in the same conditions and I felt it would be a great experience. I always remember in the 1982 London Marathon there was a huge sign which said 'You are all winners', and I believe that summed up the general feeling of the competitors in the best possible way.

John reflected on the marvellous cama-raderie amongst the runners before, during and after the race and it is hard to think of many other sporting events which attract participants from such a wide, cosmopolitan cross-section of society and, especially, from all areas of the British social structure. The runners include members of the nobility, Members of Parliament, high-powered tycoons, top-class business executives, cloth-capped workers, unemployed people, sportsmen from every conceivable sport and a fair sprinkling of entertainers from the world of show business.

John continued:

As I was saying, I have never experienced before my first marathon, or since it, quite the same tremendous warmth and friendship at such a sporting occasion. Nearly twenty thousand runners will line up aware that they are all about to embark on a rare adventure in which they will all share the same emotions, the same inevitable suffering, the same disappointments and almost ninety per cent will share the same experience and satisfaction of completing the course. Each and every individual who crosses Westminster Bridge at the end of the twenty-six point two miles is a hero and a winner in his own right.

John reckons that part of its attraction, fascination and popularity is the actual availability of it; there is plenty of evidence to show that increasing numbers are becoming involved every year in marathons round the world.

John began training in October – six months before he ran his first marathon – and his first run was about a mile in an old pair of tennis shoes. The decision the following morning, after waking up with sore knees and aching calves, was to buy the proper equipment. He bought proper running shoes and could scarcely believe the difference they made. He was able to run three miles right away without any detrimental side effects and gradually he increased the punishment until, by the end of the month, he was up to three runs of five miles every week. During the next couple of months he ran five miles twice a week but slowly increased his Sunday distance from five miles to eight, then 10 in December and finally 15 miles in the middle of January.

Because of severe business pressures he was never able to undertake more than three training runs a week and he accepted that he was trying to survive on a bare minimum.

To become fitter and stronger he increased his speed at training, rather than the distance, and he worked to a set pattern. From Southwood Avenue in Highgate, he would run to Regent's Park and circumnavigate the Park once, twice or three times before running back to Highgate. The journey there and back was 8 miles and each lap was 2.7 miles; so three laps of the Park plus the journey there and back was approximately 16 miles and the ideal trip for the 12 Sundays before the race itself.

What pleased John most about his preparation was his simple-minded determination to fulfil his limited training schedule in sincerity and not cheat himself. 1982 was a bad winter with plenty of snow and frost on the ground and there was a big temptation on a really cold and wicked night to miss the agony of pounding through the snow for a five-mile spin, but he knew that he was already only doing the bare minimum of training miles and he could not afford to opt out when the weather was not too inviting.

On race day, John made the mistake of accepting the advice in the books and magazines on marathon running and decided not to put forward too ambitious a time. He hoped to finish in well under four hours but put himself down in the 4 hours-15 minutes bracket. The huge numbers at the start, however, meant that the people out of the front ranks crawled the first two or three miles and he found that very frustrating. 'In fact, I found the first five minutes extremely torturous,' claimed John, 'because I was trying to duck, weave, and side-step past people and tying to avoid tripping up anyone or being tripped up myself.'

As the field stretched out he struck a rhythm and was feeling very good and confident by the time they cruised past the *Cutty Sark*. He felt fine crossing London Bridge and trekking along Cable Street, but then the course turns away from itself so that the runners double back and head in the opposite direction. John, along with several other runners I spoke to, found this psychologically disheartening; his suffering was further increased at that point because, having completed half the course, he heard on a radio blaring out in the crowd that Hugh Jones had just crossed the finishing line to win the 1982 Marathon. 'People were finishing the race and I had thirteen miles to go'. He gritted his teeth and ploughed on until he passed the 19-mile mark; then he began to move into the world of the unknown having never been this distance before in his whole life. He did not experience 'the Wall' but at 22 miles he desperately wanted to confront the man who determined the marathon distance of 26 miles, 385 yards and ask him just what his objections were to a race of precisely 22 miles.

At that moment, with thoughts of Ancient Greece flooding through his mind, he reached the Tower of London and had to run across the cobblestones. Apart from the additional pain to every blister, he was terrified he was going to go over on an ankle and fail to finish the race. He negotiated the cobblestones with extreme caution and suspicion and headed off in the glorious knowledge that with just three miles to go he was definitely going to finish.

The Mall looked amazingly foreboding, stretching out into the hazy horizon, but I knew at that point if I could accelerate slightly, I could cover the whole course in three and a half hours.

If someone had leapt out of the crowd and offered me a million pounds to beat three and a half hours, I realized that there was nothing I could have done. I was running along at a steady pace and could not possibly have put one blistered foot in front of the other blistered, aching foot any faster.

He drifted off into a sort of hypnotic trance over the last stretch, recognizing certain people in the crowd and hearing some of the comments people were shouting which, earlier in the race had simply melted, unintelligibly, into the general barrage of noise bombarding the eardrums. It was a strange sensation but quite a pleasant one. There followed a moment of sheer undiluted elation and ecstasy as John Hegarty crossed Westminster Bridge and the finishing line.

Television personality Jimmy Savile raising money for charity on one of his many marathons

John briefly relived the moment:

As I clocked in, the guy behind me lurched forward and collapsed completely on top of me. He was out for the count as he clung on to me and I can honestly say that I have never felt anyone so frighteningly cold. He was a sickly grey colour and icy cold. The officials quickly wrapped him in aluminium foil and helped him through the barrier to make sure he was registered before he was taken off for treatment and first aid. I was met at that stage by Kari and the family and, swathed in aluminium foil, went home to the best bath of my life. To me, the achievement and deep, glowing satisfaction is a long-term experience which I still recall with pride and pleasure rather than an immediate feeling of I've done it, great, that's it.

He finished in a highly commendable time of 3 hours, 35 minutes and, though he has no inclination to run another marathon, is openly delighted he ran it once.

One of John's friends, Robin Dow, the General Manager of Northern Europe for Levi Strauss & Company, has had his way of life changed since he first ran a marathon. He also first competed in the 1982 London Marathon and, also in his late thirties, recorded a staggeringly good time of 3 hours, 6 minutes after only six weeks of training. He had been a keen athlete at school 20 years previously but he had done no serious running in the intervening period. His interest in the Marathon was aroused the previous year when he went to watch it and was intrigued by the large entry, the huge crowds and the excitement it generated. He felt then it would be nice to run in 1982 but actually did nothing about it until somebody at Levi's entered a team for a cross-country race in Sweden. As the boss, he had a moral obligation to turn out and he began light training. He enjoyed the training and the discipline of the routine and, in his own words, 'became excited at the prospect of running 26 miles'. He is by nature a competitive animal and wanted to run a fast time but, with the limited training imposed by the absurdly tight schedule, he was pleased to do just over three hours in the Marathon.

In training, he had run mostly five or six miles a day and never more than 10 miles but, on the Sunday of the race, he was swept along by the general euphoria of the occasion to produce a much better time than he could reasonably have expected. He completed the second half faster than the first, which is unusual, and enjoyed overtaking hundreds of runners as they tired in the latter stages. The last three miles were a nightmare though, as he suffered cramp and intense fatigue, but he shuffled down the Mall and over the bridge to finish. He felt totally wrecked but decided there and then that he could and would do better.

He ran his second marathon – the Inverclyde – five months later at Strathclyde in Scotland and he finished it in 2 hours, 40 minutes. For this race he trained right through the summer and he continued, and even increased his rigorous schedule, in the autumn to improve his time yet again in the Heart of England Marathon near Birmingham three months later. The importance of that race centred round his desire to finish in under 2 hours, 35 minutes because that was the qualifying time for automatic entry into the London Marathon. Robin completed the course in 2 hours, 31 minutes.

With entry to the London race guaranteed, he had the incentive to slog on with the training right through the winter and into the spring.

I averaged about seventy or eighty miles a week without fail, including a twenty-mile run every Sunday, often done with the Highgate Harriers. During the week, I would alternate a hard day and an easy day. On an easy day I would do about seven miles at a steady six and a half minutes a mile. On a hard day, I would do ten miles but mixing up five very fast miles with five much slower miles. This interval running is soul-destroying but is of enormous benefit. In the four months before the race, I trained every single day and it is essential, like a camel with water, to store up a huge reservoir of miles. There is no question that the miles and miles covered in training make the difference when it comes to the big race. The training has to be a rigid discipline and I enjoyed the regime and way of life. I ran every night after work and found it therapeutic after a hard day at the office – a perfect way to unwind.

The reward came in the 1983 London Marathon. Robin Dow finished on the heels of the leading runners and his best time of 2 hours, 29 minutes, 54 seconds. It was a marvellous achievement. In 12 months he had improved by 24 per cent. Another 10 per cent and he will smash the world record. A significant proportion of the field in the Marathon at the Olympics in Los Angeles took longer than 40-year-old Robin Dow.

Apart from feeling fitter and the pleasure of actually completing, Robin has also been sponsored in both the Heart of England and Inverclyde Marathons. He raised enough money on these two occasions to buy a guide dog for the blind. It is a pleasant side-effect of so many marathons that staggering sums of money are raised each year for charity.

Nowhere is this more evident than in the show-business participation in marathons. In 1982, the well-known and highly successful comedian Lennie Bennett decided, with plenty of encouragement from his friends, to raise a team of show-business personalities to run the London Marathon for charity. Lennie explained to me that he is heavily involved in supporting and raising money for Leukemia Research; he told his team that he thought if they all completed the extended 26 miles, a target of £100,000 would not be impossible. None of his team, which included, amongst other celebrities, Kenny Lynch, Suzanne Dando and Alan Minter, had ever run a marathon before and there was a certain apprehension about entering unchartered territory.

However, it was all for an excellent cause and the team attacked the training with varying degrees of commitment. Lennie believed that if he was going to do it, he would do it properly and he trained conscientiously throughout the eight months up to the race. He kept a diary of his runs and the total came to 1587 miles. This is roughly the distance from London to Moscow and follows the guidelines of good marathon training that you must have the miles under your belt. He ran about 50 miles each week, although latterly he sometimes did 100 miles in a week and he did not smoke and drank in moderation. Once he had established a pattern, he stuck to it and actually enjoyed it.

The basic groundwork was done in the middle of winter, said Lennie, *and it was invigorating, if semi-lunatic, pounding along Blackpool promenade in howling blizzards, snow and ice and rain with the temperatures below freezing and high winds knifing straight through the various tracksuits, sweaters and jerseys. Sometimes, I left home and ran six miles along the promenade at the crack of dawn and I would be the only human being there.*

From left to right, Kenny Lynch, Suzanne Dando and Lennie Bennett, enjoying training for the London Marathon

The week of the Marathon, Lennie adopted the high-protein, high-carbohydrate diet. He had no carbohydrates at the beginning of the week and packed them in during the last three days. On the morning of the race, he had a bowl of cereal and three cups of black coffee. He reckons that the one thing guaranteed to destroy people in a marathon is setting off too quickly. He ran 8½-minute miles for the first 10 miles and felt terrific because he had gone faster than that in training. He covered the next 10 miles at even 7½ minutes which put him bang on course for completing in three and a half hours. He never experienced 'the Wall' and, with the crowd yelling encouragement as they recognized him, he stretched out down the Mall and the haunting, nagging doubt which had lingered in his sub-conscious for eight months that he might not finish, suddenly evaporated. 'With only two miles to go, I knew that I would finish and I just felt utter elation and immense, unbelievable satisfaction. I think running over Westminster Bridge was the happiest moment of my life.'

He went back to his London flat, had a shower, lay down for an hour's rest and then drove off to take part in a Charity Dinner in Wolverhampton that night. Not only did that charity benefit, but his TV Times team, with the help of a Telethon on London Weekend Television on the Friday night before the race, raised a staggering £250,000 for Leukemia Research. Lennie Bennett finished in a time of 3 hours, 22 minutes. Kenny Lynch who had been less committed to the idea of hard training – according to Lennie his idea of training was simply to drink one glass of champagne less each day – suffered badly at the 18-mile distance when he hit 'the Wall' as he ran through the Isle of Dogs. He was on the point of stopping and giving up and just wanting to lie down and die when he came across a large group of his friends and relatives who screamed en-couragement and almost shamed him into carrying on. He completed the course in 4 hours, 20 minutes.

Suzanne Dando, Britain's best-known and most glamorous gymnast, was an outstanding sportswoman and, as British champion, did well in the Moscow Olympics. But running 26 miles is an entirely different proposition and not one she particularly enjoyed. Her television engagements and long list of personal appearances severely restricted her opportunities to train in the same selfless way she had as a gymnast and running 30 or 40 miles a week for three months was not the ideal preparation. She recalled the drawn-out suffering of the day:

I felt bad after six miles and it got gradually worse. It was a warm day and it seemed to me I hit this mythical 'Wall' at about eight miles! I kept going, got my second wind and though tired and aching, I was absolutely determined to finish even if it took until Tuesday. I hit a slow, steady pace and was surviving adequately until Tower Bridge and those horrific cobblestones. I thought I was going to break an ankle but I carefully negotiated this unnecessary obstacle course and walked, staggered, shuffled along, trotted and ran intermittently the last six miles to finish in just over five hours. I had a real sense of achievement but was disappointed to discover the rest of the TV Times had all gone. I was the last of the team to finish and the rendezvous point was deserted. Wrapped in my aluminium foil, a kind soul gave me money for my bus fare home and I set off alone. It was not quite the perfect end to a memorable day but it gave me a chance to think of a good argument to defend my slow time. The first woman to finish, Joyce Smith, only ran for two hours, twenty-five minutes, and forty-three seconds. I had been able to keep running for well over double that time!

The following year, Lennie again entered his team to raise money for charity, even though he had only just recovered from a knee injury. He did a good time in the circumstances of 3 hours, 40 minutes but was ashamed to admit that the lady member of his team, the lovely British pentathlete, Kathy Tayler, beat him by one minute. Without an inordinate amount of training, only two months' at about 30 miles a week, this exceptionally gifted all-round athlete did, according to Lennie, an amazingly good time. Kathy averaged 8½-minute miles and believes that she could, with a full training programme, chip into that sort of time with some effect. Since then she has proved the point with two half-marathons in fast times.

In 1984, several well-known personalities ran. I went along with John Hegarty and Robin Dow early in the morning of the race. We wanted to soak up the atmosphere so we boarded the 7.50 a.m. from Charing Cross to Greenwich. Packed in like sardines with hundreds of competitors we listened to their nervous apprehensive chatter as the train crawled the six miles to the start of the race. The platform at Greenwich could scarcely cope with the heaving mass of humanity and the overpowering smell of wintergreen and other magical potions brought back memories of afternoons spent in rugby changing rooms round Britain. The runners were laughing, joking and generally good-humoured, but clearly a little on edge.

Greenwich Park was covered with 'Joe Joggers' as they are affectionately known and the start, from two separate points, was a magnificent sight. 20,000 people of every size, shape, colour, religion, section and class of society intermingled as they headed off at 9.30 a.m. towards the Woolwich Road on the first of the 26 miles. The runners were preceded at 9.25 a.m. by the wheelchair competitors who were given a great reception by the massive crowd lining the whole route. We then ran about a mile across the Park to the *Cutty Sark*, to pick up the leaders completing their sixth mile. The field was just beginning to stretch out at that stage and, by the time we crossed the Thames to the Isle of Dogs, there were plenty of gaps between runners. Later, with eight miles still to go, the Norwegian runner Ingrid Kristiansen was out on her own, leading by a fair distance in the Women's

race while Charlie Spedding overtook the pace-setting Tanzanian athletes Juma Ikangaa and Zakaria Barie to hit the front in their Men's race.

Just over half an hour later, Kristiansen and Spedding won their respective events and well did they deserve the enthusiastic response and cheering of the Londoners lining the route several deep along the Embankment, down the Mall and on Westminster Bridge. For the next six hours, runners continued to stream over the Bridge, odd ones dressed like Superman, Spiderman, Tarzan, clowns, film-star look-a-likes; there was even a pair representing the front and back ends of a donkey. All were exhausted; all were elated.

I was astounded at the phenomenal speed the leading runners maintained throughout and impressed by the stamina and sheer determination of the slower finishers. A remarkably high number of competitors usually finish marathons – about 95 per cent – and I take my hat off to every one of them. Lennie Bennett summed it up best:

I've topped the bill at the London Palladium, I've played all the great theatres in England, I've done my own show on television, but I can put my hand on my heart and say that finishing the Marathon in 1982 was the greatest single achievement of my life and the one moment of which I felt proudest. The combination of pain, fatigue, blisters and suffering just melted away as I ran down the Mall on the final mile and a half. The crowd lifted me and with immense pride I relished every moment in the finishing straight because I was about to conquer the toughest race in the world, and me comfortably on the wrong side of forty years of age. It was a marvellous, magical moment and gave me the most enormous high I have ever experienced in my life. Anyone who has never run a Marathon won't really understand; anyone who has, will know precisely what I mean.

Having trained for it, listened to the reflections of those who have run in it and having watched the 1984 London Marathon for seven hours, I think I do know what Lennie Bennett means. The message on that bill-board of congratulation to all runners is true: 'You are all winners'.

Former champion pentathlete Kathy Tayler, who ran a fast marathon for charity

HEAVYWEIGHT CONTEST

The noble art of rearranging a man's features was invented, according to the Ancient Greeks, by an Ancient Greek; Theseus of Athens even tried to popularize spiked gloves for the purpose but they never caught on. Greek boxers, like the ones who fought in the 688 BC Olympics, usually wore oxhide knuckle thongs. The Romans were more drastic, introducing the *caestus*, a leather glove loaded with lead and later studded with brass or iron spikes.

When Rome fell, so did the sport of fisticuffs. It was revived in the early eighteenth century in the fairground booths of England, when pugilist and promoter James Figg brought bare-knuckle bouts to Southwark, Moorfield and Smithfield. Fighters stood toe to toe on a chalk-line 'scratch' and eye-gouging, wrestling holds and 'purring' – booting a felled opponent – were par for the course. Giants emerged, like Jack Broughton who divided his time between poleaxing pugs and coaching delicate young gents at his Haymarket Amphitheatre using 'mufflers' – rudimentary gloves. In 1743 Broughton devised a crude set of rules, such as: 'No person is to hit his adversary when he is down, or seize him by the ham, the breeches, or any part below the waist'. They still left a lot of scope.

In a championship bout of 1750, Broughton was blinded in the ring by a blow from butcher Jack Slack. 'I am blind, not beat,' Broughton told his patron the Duke of Cumberland, requesting to be pointed in the direction of his assailant. Slack won; the Duke lost £10,000, and his temper, and rushed a bill through Parliament making prizefighting illegal. Legal or not, boxing soon regained all its former glory. In 1786 the Prince of Wales, later George IV, and assorted nobles turned out to watch Richard Humphries fight Martin the Bath Butcher at Newmarket. From then until the Regency boximania of the 1820s, knuckle fighting vied with hanging as England's most popular sport. The public flocked to see bouts lasting six or seven hours and 80 or 90 rounds, and aristocratic young swells and the poet Lord Byron knocked each other about.

Fists were pickled in brine and turpentine to harden them up; faces were pulped into anonymity. After 43 rounds with Henry Pearce in 1805, John Gully's apparently eyeless head swelled up like a pumpkin. Often damage was so bad that spectators could not tell the front of a fighter's cranium from the back. A prizefight in 1821 between Neat of Bristol and Tom Hickman was not atypical. After one particularly savage blow in the eighth, Hickman 'hung suspended,' writes essayist William Hazlitt. 'His face was like a human skull, a death's head, spouting blood. The eyes were filled with blood, the nose streamed with blood, the mouth gaped blood.' There was no time limit; pugs fought till they were finished, and were pushed back into the fray if necessary by interested cornermen. In one bout between Deaf Burke and Simon Byrne, Byrne was literally carried back into a fight that lasted 98 rounds. When it ended Byrne was dead.

Champions who could do something more than stand and slog often earned the soubriquet 'Gentlemen' in front of their names, and men like Richard Humphries and Daniel Mendoza brought a little footwork and bobbing-and-weaving to what was essentially artless thuggery. In 1810 the first 'world championship' was held, between English champ Tom Cribb and former Virginian slave Tom Molineux. Molineux began promisingly but after 39 rounds sank to the canvas wheezing, 'Me can fight no more.'

The fight game in general was getting out of hand. Fixing or 'crossing' was commonplace and riots were regular. In 1814 the Pugilistic Club was formed in an effort at control. After a spate of fixings, fatalities and manslaughter charges, boxing ran foul of the law again. New rules were drawn up in 1838, followed in the 1860s by the famous Marquess of Queensberry rules introducing fixed rounds and the ten count. The gloves went on and knuckle fighting went out.

Boxing – gloved – became respectable again. The London Prize Ring Rules, substantially those of today, were adopted and the National Sporting Club took championship bouts out of the hands of riffraff and watched them themselves, in dinner jackets. World title fights became orthodox affairs. In 1892 San Francisco bank clerk Jim Corbett knocked out John L. Sullivan of Boston to take the world title in gloves. Corbett was called 'Gentleman Jim'. Since 1929 in the UK, the sport has been under the eagle eye of the British Boxing Board of Control.

The twentieth century has seen a golden age of 'hungry' fighters from poor backgrounds. The first negro to win the world championship was Jack Johnson in 1908, followed by a succession of great black boxers at all weights, like Jersey Joe Walcott, Floyd Patterson, Sonny Liston, Sugar Ray Robinson and the great Joe Louis. The golden age also produced a string of 'white hopes', starting with cowboy Jess Willard. Willard was dethroned in 1919 by Jack Dempsey, the Manassa Mauler, who broke the cowpoke's jaw. Dempsey fought Gene Tunney in 1926 in Philadelphia before 130,000 spectators, and again in 1927 in Chicago before 145,000. Many could hardly see the ring, let alone who won. During the 13-second count, which the referee delayed until Dempsey was in a neutral corner, five radio listeners suffered fatal heart attacks. Similar tension gripped London's Highbury in 1966 when the young American Cassius Clay, alias Muhammad Ali, performed surgery on British Henry Cooper's left eye to dash his title hopes. Ali brought the fight game into the technological age, spurning hay-maker punches in favour of the jab, lightning speed and verbal intimidation. Absorbing American George Foreman's thunderous bodyblows in Zaïre, Ali delivered the *coup de grâce* with two pistol cracks in Foreman's chops. He had rope-a-doped the old bludgeonry of boxing into a very sweet science indeed.

Since Britain's last world heavyweight champion, the Cornish blacksmith Bob Fitzsimmons, in 1899, only a handful of truly outstanding fighters have surfaced to give genuine hope that the richest and arguably the greatest prize in sport might return to Britain. Gunner Moir in 1907, Jack Palmer and Dewey Smith in 1908, all fought for the world title. Tommy Farr put up a magnificent display before losing on points to Joe Louis in 1937 and, since the last war, Don Cockell, Brian London, Henry Cooper, Richard Dunn and Joe Bugner have all fought for the world title. (Cockell and London lost to Rocky Marciano, Cooper, Bugner, London and Dunn were victims of the incomparable Muhammad Ali.) Now, in the eighties, another British heavyweight has emerged as an exciting world title contender in the remarkably impressive shape of Frank Bruno.

Born on 16 November 1961, he took part in his first weigh-in that day and scaled a not particularly noteworthy 6 pounds and 3 ounces. He was soon to become relatively big for his age, and he first took up boxing when he was about nine. His initial flirtation with the sport which was later to become his way of life ended when he went to a special boarding school two years later.

The interest in boxing was rekindled on leaving school at the age of 16, and he boxed as an amateur for the next two years before becoming the youngest boxer to win the ABA heavyweight title at the age of 18, narrowly beating Rudi Pika on points. His enormous potential was fully exposed by this time and he was approached by Terry Lawless, the renowned East End manager, who had skilfully guided flyweight Charlie Magri, lightweight Jim Watt, light middle-weight Maurice Hope and welterweight John H. Stacey to world title triumphs in the past decade.

The following year he needed a special-ized eye operation in Colombia before he was able to join the Terry Lawless stable of boxers, and he signed as a professional in March 1982. His first opponent was one Lupe Guerra who was knocked out in the first round to confirm the impression that Bruno could punch with venomous power. With the magnificent physique of a Mr Universe and weighing in at around 16 stone, he is an awesome sight in the ring, and his next nine victims bore witness to his brutally destructive powers by surviving less than 16 rounds between them. Of his first 10 opponents in 1982, nine lost in less than two rounds.

1983 proved equally successful with 10 more wins inside the distance. However, his nineteenth adversary, Floyd 'Jumbo' Cummings had the temerity to poleaxe Bruno in the first round of their contest with a cracking right hand which would have inflicted a first defeat on Bruno if it had not come nearer the end of the round. The bell saved him. He recovered to stop Cummings in the seventh, but for many critical ringside observers the inevitable seeds of doubt had been sown – could Bruno take a punch?

Lawless, a benevolent father figure devoted to his fighters, to their welfare and their future, had selected the first 20 opponents for Bruno with extreme care and, perhaps, almost undue caution. Not one was a noted explosive puncher and not one was famed for being unduly durable. Neverthe-less it would certainly by hypercritical to describe them all as being, in pugilistic parlance, 'bums of the month', and it is generally accepted that Lawless was right to hand-pick these 20 fighters to give Bruno as much experience as possible before moving into the more rarified atmosphere of the world's top 50 heavyweights. After three or four victories at that level Bruno would be catapulted into the top 10 and Lawless had to be sure his man would be ready.

In a curiously negative way, the events of the 13 May 1984 were to justify the over-protective policy indulged in by the Lawless camp. The 671 seconds that Juan Antonio Figueroa of Argentina lasted in Bruno's twenty-first fight in February 1984 added precious little to the impression held by boxing's cognoscenti, but the announce-ment of James 'Bonecrusher' Smith as opponent number 22 caused not so much a ripple as great tidal waves of interest on both sides of the Atlantic. Here, at last, was someone who would be a worthy yardstick by which to judge the world-title dreams and aspirations of Frank Bruno.

Smith had no family background in box-ing and began his amateur career at the remarkably advanced age of 23 while serving with the US Army in Germany. He won 35 of his 39 fights as an amateur including 25 knock-outs, before turning pro in 1981 at the age of 26. He was nicknamed 'Bonecrusher' because he injured not only his opponents but also his sparring partners. 'I crushed a few bones, broke a few noses, fractured a few ribs.'

He lost his first contest as a professional when he was knocked out in the fourth round by James Broad, but he claimed afterwards he was hustled into that fight at very short notice. After that defeat he built up an impressive sequence of 13 wins including 11 inside the distance. In his fifth fight in September 1982, screened live on national television, he caused a major shock when he outpointed the hitherto unbeaten Chris MacDonald. It was at this point that two New York entrepreneurs, real-estate dealer Alan Kornberg and mortgage banker

Steve Nelson, put him under contract, and they have jointly managed him ever since. Kornberg and Nelson made their mark at once by persuading former world middle-weight champion and one of boxing's great legends, Emile Griffiths, to take over as Smith's trainer. Under the shrewd tutelage of Griffiths, Smith made dramatic progress and in 1983 he was described by Randy Gordon, editor of *Ring*, as the most improved heavyweight in America. It was generally acknowledged that at last Bruno had a worthy opponent.

The build-up to the fight was much the same as Bruno had undergone in his previous 21 contests, only a little more intense. Once again top-class sparring partners were engaged to help during the preparation in March and April. The first-floor gymnasium in the Thomas A'Beckett pub in the East End of London is home for Terry Lawless's stable of boxers, and the daily routine does not alter all that much for the boxers as they prepare for a big night.

It was fascinating for me to learn how the boxers spend a typical day. The gym is about two-thirds of the size of a tennis court with a ring at one end and some heavy exercise equipment at the other, including a few enormous punch bags and an exercise bicycle. In the middle of the room on the wall is a full length mirror where former world flyweight champion Charlie Magri spent much of his afternoons training shadow boxing. After some lighthearted banter from Terry Lawless the lads buckle down to a serious work-out. A handful of boxers work out at any one time and in the fortnight building up to the 'Bonecrusher' Smith clash, Frank Bruno trained in the gym each day at lunchtime. In the week before the fight he went for a run early in the morning to increase his stamina and he spent between two and three hours in the gym every afternoon. The strain was beginning to creep in 10 days before D-day but the sheer professionalism of the approach by every-one involved was most impressive.

The various smells and sounds of a boxing gym are peculiar to that sport, and I can understand how they become an intoxicating drug. The senses are soon aware

The impressive figure of Frank Bruno in training

of the various liniments being smoothed over the combatants, and the sounds of a gym have a beguiling hypnotic effect on the ears. The heavy atmosphere is alternatively pierced and punctuated by the repetitive thumping and thudding of the punch bags, the smacking of a skipping rope as it hits the wooden floor once every second, the continual whirring, humming buzz of the exercise bike, the shuffling of boots on the canvas and the snorts and grunts from the shadow boxers and those sparring in the ring.

Bruno loosened off and warmed up before sparring with four different partners over 2 or 3 rounds each in quick succession. His opponents included an American heavyweight, Mark Lee, who was due to fight on the same Wembley bill, and two other promising heavyweights from each side of the Atlantic – Ronnie Turner and Adrian Elliott.

There was a cool, clinical precision surrounding everything Bruno did during his sparring, and he had the aura of a future champion as he went to work in the ring with an air of invincibility and seemingly limitless enthusiasm. Terry Lawless explained that Bruno always drove himself very hard in the gym and it was psychologically important to him to put maximum effort into his sparring. The gruelling session completed, the big 16-stone athlete goes off to relax at home with his attractive girlfriend Laura and two-year-old baby.

The lifestyle could be thought tedious but the rewards are phenomenal for the few who make it to the top. The inclination to criticize a boxer's way of life recedes rapidly when one ponders the thought that Frank Bruno with skilful handling and guidance, and a little bit of luck, could be a millionaire within two years. Bruno, Lawless and the 10,000 fans packed into Wembley knew what was at stake at ten o'clock in the evening on the second Sunday in May. The lights went out in the arena, and a single spotlight picked up James 'Bonecrusher' Smith as he made his way to the ring against a background of muffled, almost muted, applause. He entered the ring and instantly became the focus of attention as he smiled

Frank Bruno on the retreat against James 'Bonecrusher' Smith at Wembley

and stared into the darkness, his big brown eyes nearly popping out of his head. Clearly he was relishing his first encounter with the big time.

Moments later the spotlight settled on Bruno and his entourage as they pushed their way through a heaving, screaming throng of loyal supporters, accompanied by a musical fanfare, to reach the ringside where I was sitting in the best possible seat. After all the usual preliminaries on a big fight night, during which time several former British world champions were introduced in the ring, Smith and Bruno were ready for the showdown.

Watching the two gladiators sizing up for the first round I was acutely aware of the description of the ring as the loneliest place on earth. The early exchanges went firmly in Bruno's favour and the crowd went nearly hysterical when he looked to be on the verge of finishing Smith in the opening three rounds. But the fight continued. I'm no expert on the scoring system but I could appreciate that Bruno was well on top throughout the first seven rounds and was cruising to his first points victory in reasonably, if not spectacularly, convincing style. Unlike so many of Bruno's earlier victims, however, Smith was extremely durable and, as befits a college graduate, more intelligent than any fighter Bruno had met previously.

The first evidence of this was in fact in the first round. Lawless had suggested to Bruno that Smith kept his left hand rather low and he would probably be susceptible to a good right-hand punch. Video film of his previous fights strongly supported this theory but Smith, sensing the potential danger from Bruno's right hook, kept his left hand and arm surprisingly high throughout the contest. A week after the fight Bruno told me how confusing and frustrating this tactic was, but he admitted it was a part of the education of a young 22-year-old boxer on his way to the top.

The stance adopted by Smith may have drastically reduced Bruno's opportunity to finish the contest with his right, but it became a shade easier for Bruno to land his left jab. This he did with telling effect in the early rounds, and it seemed to those of us at ringside that it would be only a matter of time before Smith would be worn down and defeated. Neither Bruno nor his armada of supporters had expected the outstanding fitness and resilience of Smith to soak up the punishment for seven rounds and yet still dredge up the energy to hit back with a ferocious onslaught at the end of the fight.

It must have been disheartening for Bruno to dominate the evening with such authority and discover that, despite liberally spraying most of his best shots in the general direction of the American's head and even occasionally his body, Smith was still able to smile through his more uncomfortable moments and bounce back. Furthermore, the pressure of the occasion had reached Bruno. He was not the first British sportsman to feel psychologically drained by the realization that he was carrying on his massive shoulders the fervent hopes of 10,000 British supporters inside Wembley and another 10 million outside the arena. As so many of our best individual sporting stars have learned to their cost, be it playing tennis at Wimbledon, playing golf in the Open Championship or running the 100 metres at the Olympics, carrying the hopes and dreams of a whole nation imposes a terrific strain. Many have found it insurmountable.

Certainly Bruno in the tenth round appeared to be overcome as much by the significance of the event as by the skills of James Smith. He had built up such a commanding lead by the tenth that he was guaranteed a handsome points victory and the lure of some very rich pickings if he could just survive the final three minutes in a vertical position. This he would have comfortably done if he had not sensed the crowd, accustomed to his happy knack of separating his previous 21 opponents from their senses with great alacrity, demanded of Bruno another win inside the distance. Instead of consolidating his impregnable points advantage, he made the fatal mistake of chasing a knock-out victory.

Tired and a little bewildered by Smith's stuffy resistence, Bruno lurched into the attack, prepared to take the odd risk in his

search for the big pay-off. Such a bold, but foolhardy, plan backfired on him painfully. He was caught on the ropes by a long, lunging left hook which left him rooted to the spot, paralysed into a state of hopeless, helpless inactivity as he tried to unscramble his instantly scattered thoughts. His apparent hapless confusion was mercifully short-lived. A furious flurry of punches from Smith rained on his head from all angles and, in a trice, he was dispatched into that dark and forbidding world of the semi-conscious, hovering somewhere between painful reality and complete oblivion. A final, wicked right to the side of the head was ultimately responsible for, in boxing parlance, switch-

ing out the lights and leaving Bruno to drift into never-never land. He landed with a sickening thud right beside me in a neutral corner of the ring, his head about two feet from mine, staring blankly at his corner.

Wembley was almost silent as their hero lay motionless on his side. There was surprise that he had been unable to defend himself after the first two destructive blows landed. There was shock that he didn't move off the ropes the moment he was stunned by the initial blows. There was disbelief that he lacked the worldly-wise ring craft to hold on to Smith, to clinch and lean and smother Smith's secondary offensive or even take a count of eight to clear his befuddled mind.

Frank Bruno, eyes closed, knocked over and out by James Smith

There was incredulity to see their hero, the East-End-man-in-the-street's alter ego, lying crumpled in a corner of the ring, poleaxed.

The sad truth was unpalatable but unavoidable. Frank Bruno was no better equipped to take a good punch than most other twentieth-century British heavyweights and, in consequence, he was no more likely to win the world title than any of his predecessors.

The newspapers made little of the referee's scorecard which had Bruno coasting home by 7 rounds to 2 going in to the tenth. Instead they analysed the ability of James Smith to see if he was about to take over the world as some latter-day Muhammad Ali. It was generally concluded that he was no great world beater; he would probably make the top 20 on the strength of this one notable victory and then enjoy two or three decent paydays before fading from the limelight as quickly as he entered.

I left Wembley feeling desperately sorry for Frank Bruno, realizing his world had collapsed. It was a cold, miserable night, and on the four-hour drive back to Preston I thought how I had suffered similar setbacks on the rugby field before England eventually won the Grand Slam in 1980. To be written off by the media is not the end of the road, although I knew for the next few days it would seem like that for Frank Bruno.

Perhaps my lasting memory would not be the sad denouement but the great dignity with which Bruno accepted the situation. When he recovered his wits he crossed the ring to congratulate the winner. He stood in the centre of the ring, bowing to all four corners of the amphitheatre as if apologizing for letting down his fans and friends, and then he insisted on posing with Smith in front of a posse of photographers at a time when most defeated boxers would have preferred the refuge of the loser's dressing-room. In these actions Bruno had shown courage and character, and in the lonely world of professional boxing I dare say they will be valuable attributes in the years ahead.

It came as no surprise to me that Bruno showed the same dignity the following morning at the press conference. The drama behind that appearance in a West End hotel in London gradually unfolded as lunchtime approached. Terry Lawless informed Bruno after the fight that he had had enough disappointments in his career as a manager and he had decided to quit boxing. Frank replied that if Lawless was going to retire then he would too. The next morning Frank phoned Terry to arrange to travel to the press conference together. Terry said he just wanted to pull the sheet over his head and stay in bed all morning and felt this was one press conference it might be better to miss. Frank argued it was their duty to attend, and he persuaded Terry to join him and also to continue their partnership.

Much was made at the press conference of Bruno's youth and the assembled Fleet Street hacks could think of only three heavyweights who had reached the top by the tender age of 22 – Joe Louis, Floyd Patterson and Muhammad Ali. Without doubt, Bruno has time on his side, and a defeat at this stage of his career is far less damaging than at a later, more critical, stage. Other evidence produced to confront the home camp came from a most unexpected source: the record of Joe Bugner. It was pointed out that Bugner lost to Jack Bodell and Larry Middleton in a short space of time, but recovered to beat Jurgen Blin for the European title, and six months later he fought Ali in Las Vegas for the world title.

No doubt this was succour to the Bruno camp, but in the last analysis it had to be admitted that he was beaten, however unfortunately, by a mere journeyman who had about as much chance as me of winning the world championship. It was amazing to hear Kornberg and Nelson claiming that they were on target for a title shot for Smith and, with the Bruno fight having been screened live on national television throughout the United States, their man was now one of the hottest properties in the fight game. The truth is that they were guilty of huge self-delusion if they actually believed that sort of razzmatazz, and they had to acknowledge that if the fight had been scheduled for 9 rounds and not 10, their man would have been on the wrong end of a comprehensive defeat.

To talk of Larry Holmes in the same

breath as James Smith was simply an eccentric example of American bravado. Smith, 30 next birthday, was a man with his future behind him although he could reasonably anticipate two decent paydays against top-10 contenders before leaving the boxing scene. Bruno, on the other hand, still has plenty of time to make his mark, and the theory that only the rarest exceptions could be good heavyweights at the age of 22 was part of his philosophical approach when I met him, along with Terry Lawless, for dinner on the Friday night five days after the fight.

Frank and Terry, accompanied by their respective better halves, Laura and Sylvia, chose the Trattoria Parmigiana in Leytonstone for our rendezvous, and we had an excellent meal and a very enjoyable evening. I was delighted to find that Frank Bruno was as charming and dignified as I had imagined. It could not have been easy to indulge in social intercourse with the memory of James Smith so near the surface but he was relaxed and friendly, and talked openly about the night his career was shunted temporarily into reverse gear.

He confirmed that the pre-fight instructions from Terry Lawless had been simple and emphatic – he was to keep moving in the centre of the ring and try to land the right hand early on, and on no account was he to get caught on the ropes or in a corner. It was failure to fulfil this last instruction that proved to be his undoing. In the last three or four rounds he was caught flat-footed on the ropes on more than one occasion, and he soaked up several hard punches. He admitted that night at dinner that he knew it was tactically dangerous and he confessed that Terry had been screaming at him between rounds to keep off the ropes. Those were his orders immediately prior to the fateful tenth round, but he was powerless to act.

Both Terry and he pointed out that, though he was physically as strong as any boxer in the world and at a peak of fitness on the night, he was in fact mentally tired before the first punches were thrown. The psychological pressures had affected him to a far greater extent than he had expected, and he had begun the most important contest of his life suffering from mental fatigue. He was drained of his usual energy, and even his concentration had suffered. He told me he would be in a much better frame of mind next time, but he stressed the Frank Bruno who lost to James Smith was a mere shadow of the real Frank Bruno. Terry Lawless concurred fully with these thoughts; Frank had apparently repeated between rounds that he was feeling tired although he had hardly done anything.

This helps to explain the performance of Bruno; I've seen tension adversely affect all sorts of sportsmen at the highest level of competition, and it is not easy to overcome. Terry reflected that Frank, in winning his first 21 bouts so easily, had been like a fourth-division footballer scoring 60 goals in a season. He had learned the hard way that life in the first division is a great deal tougher and, it should be remembered, James 'Bonecrusher' Smith was far nearer the bottom of that first division than the top.

Terry was every bit as disappointed about the defeat as Frank, but by the Friday night both had recovered sufficiently to look back critically, analyse where they went wrong and, much more significantly, plan for the future. Everyone is entitled to one off-night no matter which sport they pursue and now, instead of chasing the world title and millions of dollars in the immediate future, such a prize will be part of a long-term plan.

All I know is that I enjoyed the occasion despite the smoky atmosphere at Wembley and, in retrospect, I had a memorable night out with two of the very best ambassadors that boxing can lay claim to in Britain. I wish them both well in the future and, though I do not really believe Frank Bruno will be the first British world heavyweight champion this century, I know that far stranger things have happened in the topsy-turvy world of sport. I, for one, would be absolutely delighted if he did make it. He, like Terry Lawless, is a credit to a sport that has thrown up more than its fair share of rascals over the years, and he deserves every success. I am confident of one thing: in the next three or four years he will make an extremely lucrative living out of boxing and will give thousands of people a great deal of pleasure through his pugilistic exploits.

NINE

FOOTBALL

THE FA CUP FINAL

It cost a shilling to see the first FA Cup Final in 1872. M.P. Betts, the winning goal-scorer in Wanderers' 1-0 victory over Royal Engineers, did his stuff in front of a crowd of 2000 at Kennington Oval (compare this with 1984, when 100,000 paid nearly £1,000,000). Right-back for the Wanderers was C.W. Alcock. Charles Alcock dreamt up the whole affair, was winning captain, Secretary of the Football Association, and the first man to collect the FA Cup. Betts, the goal scorer, kept a lower profile, playing under a pseudonym – A.H. Chequer.

The silver trophy of those days stood 18 inches tall and cost £20. It was eventually stolen while on display, the pride of Aston Villa, in a shop window in Newton Road, Birmingham. The replacement was given to Lord Kinnaird in recognition of his 21 years as FA President, and the third trophy, 175 ounces and 19 inches high, is the one played for now. It cost 50 guineas and was made by Fattorini's of Bradford in 1911. The first year it didn't travel far: Bradford City won it.

The FA Cup is an unpredictable showdown and there have been enough upsets and giant-killings to arouse suspicions of a jinx. When Wanderers retained the original Cup in 1873, they did so with the help of a challenge system, going straight into the final and picking the venue. Since then this system has been abolished, and some strongly fancied teams have not been so lucky.

Preston North End in 1888, for example. The team had been hand-picked to challenge the might of triple-Cup-winners Blackburn Rovers, and the 'Invincibles' were practically being photographed with the trophy before the match against poor little West Bromwich Albion. Shocked by West Brom's 2-1 victory, Preston were fired to do the 'double' the following season. Winning the League without a defeat and the Cup without conceding a goal, the Invincibles this time left nothing to chance.

Even more upset than Preston in 1888 were Newcastle United. Between 1905 and 1911 they reached five finals and were bridesmaids at four of them. The Cup's history is littered with underdog victories, jinxes and superstitions. Walsall's 1933 win over Arsenal; Yeovil's victory over Sunderland in 1949; non-League Worcester's defeat of Liverpool in 1959; fourth-division Colchester's win over Leeds in 1971 – the list is almost endless. No surprise that pre-war Portsmouth manager Jack Tinn wore 'lucky' spats; that Major Buckley gave his Wolverhampton Wanderers monkey-gland treatment in 1939; that Don Revie wore a 'lucky' suit for the 1973 Final between Leeds United and Sunderland (the suit didn't do any good – Sunderland won).

There's even an injury jinx, blamed on the hallowed Wembley turf, resulting in a good many broken legs and even a broken neck for goalie Bert Trautmann in 1956. With so much uncertainty prevailing, conservatism is often the better part of valour. Extra time has been played in the last three FA Cups and the last three Finals have gone to replays. Unlucky for some. Of course, fortunes can change. Newcastle United may have had four out of five disappointments between 1905 and 1911, but these losses were all at Crystal Palace. What they needed was a change of venue. Wembley Stadium saw them victorious in 1951, 1952 and 1955.

The first Final at Wembley in 1923 was unlucky for somebody else – the spectators. It was not an all-ticket affair and 200,000 reportedly squeezed into the grounds to witness the proceedings. There wouldn't even have been a kick-off had it not been for the heroism of one mounted policeman, PC Scorey and his horse Billy, driving the overspill off the pitch to make room for Bolton to beat West Ham.

The hundred-and-third Cup Final – the fifty-sixth to be played at Wembley – was Watford's first appearance and Everton's eighth (including three previous wins). Arsenal and Newcastle United have been in it 11 times, and Aston Villa and Tottenham Hotspur have won the trophy seven times each.

A fortnight after watching the Rugby League Cup final at Wembley, and a week after watching the Frank Bruno fight at the Wembley Conference Centre, I was back again in north London for my first visit to the FA Cup Final. If I had been allowed to choose the two finalists back in January, I doubt very much if Everton and Watford would have been the first two names on my list but when the dust had settled on the semifinals, I saw a lot to commend the impending battle.

Many of the ingredients necessary for a classic match were there, although neither side was overendowed with great individual personalities. On the other hand, the match was an ideal contest between the north of England and the south; there was the romantic image of Everton, who had spent so many years languishing in the vast shadow cast by their Merseyside neighbours Liverpool, trying to escape and re-establish their own identity; and, of course, there was the fairy-tale story of little Watford rocketing from the bowels of the fourth division in the late seventies to their first-ever appearance at Wembley. All the Walter Mitty people of Merseyside and Watford had seen their dreams realized in the semifinals on 1 April; now they were ready to play out their final fantasy in the last great showpiece of the season.

The Final was another episode in the long-running saga of David against Goliath. Everton had been winners of the FA Cup on three previous occasions; the nearest Watford had come to Wembley before was in 1970 when they reached the semifinals. But, that year apart, Watford's Cup record has a distinctly fragile look about it. They had been known to beat a retreat with their Cup hopes dashed from such unlikely places as Northwich Victoria and Workington and, just as certain unfashionable clubs regularly succeed in exciting the interest of the soccer world with their heroic deeds in Cup ties, Watford had been careful never to fall into that category.

The team had obviously worked hard to reach the Final. They began their campaign with a 2-2 draw at Luton and squeezed through in the replay by 4 goals to 3. They followed up with wins over Charlton, Brighton and Birmingham, each by 2 goals, and then edged past third-division Plymouth in the semifinals when Reilly scored the only goal of the game. To reach the Final in only their second season in the first division was a wonderful achievement, and it did much to vindicate their style of play – described by some ungenerous critics as kick-and-rush tactics. None the less, they emerged from the tunnel into the bright sunlight and, with the famous Wembley roar wrapping itself round them, they trotted on to the most famous arena in England. At best they were underdogs; at worst, rank outsiders.

In the belief that Everton would win, I arranged to meet Howard Kendall, the Everton manager, two weeks before

Wembley. I thought Everton would be more relaxed and more confident than Watford because of their history, and also because of their current strength. However, Howard Kendall pointed out that there was a dreadful fatality rate which afflicted favourites in the FA Cup Final and, in a sense, it would be easier for Watford to reproduce their best form because no one expected them to win. With nothing to lose, they could play their normal uninhibited game and hope a couple of chances came their way to clinch the match.

Howard had had the benefit of previous experience of Cup Finals at Wembley. He first appeared there as a player for Preston North End against West Ham in 1964 and he made history in that day by becoming, at 17 years and 345 days, the youngest player ever to play in a Cup Final. Preston lost 3-2 and Kendall fared no better when he returned to Wembley four years later as a member of the Everton team which lost to West Bromwich Albion in extra time. In the middle of that four-year period, in 1966, Everton enjoyed their last major Cup success when they won the FA Cup with a 3-2 win over Sheffield Wednesday. Everton won the First Division Championship in 1970, but there followed a famine which lasted for 14 years.

Howard Kendall explained that such a time would be long for any club to live with failure, but he reckoned it was 10 times worse on Merseyside when near-neighbours and arch-rivals Liverpool can boast a trophy cupboard over at Anfield genuinely creaking under the weight of silver they accumulated during the all-conquering reigns of Bill Shankly, Bob Paisley and now Joe Fagan. In purely economic terms, the recession and depression have generally hit Merseyside extremely badly; down Goodison Park way, the fans have had a soccer depression to add to the socio-economic one.

In his three years as manager of Everton, Howard Kendall has had to live with the contrasting fortunes of the two Merseyside football clubs. There was promise of great riches in 1984 as Everton gradually advanced towards the Final of the Milk Cup as well as the FA Cup. Looking back at the whole season, he avowed that:

The main turning points came in the Milk Cup. We were a goal down to Coventry and recovered to win with two goals in the last ten minutes. Then we trailed against Oxford and showed tremendous character and resilience to fight back and eventually eliminate Oxford in the replay. It was after these two games that I knew we had a side good enough in every respect to win a major prize, and my fears for the future of the club after our poor start to the season in the League were all part of history.

Nevertheless, the unpalatable truth is that Everton, having reached the Final of the Milk Cup, found Liverpool on the other side of the halfway-line at Wembley. The Everton manager admitted he would desperately have liked to win that match because it would have been as good as winning two trophies; to win the Milk Cup for the first time would have been a special achievement in its own right, but to do so by beating Liverpool would have doubled the glory and the satisfaction. In retrospect, I thought Everton were unlucky not to win the Milk Cup Final at Wembley outright. The game ended in a goalless draw and Liverpool won the replay at Maine Road, Manchester. Everton played outstandingly well on both occasions and they were two excellent, tight matches, but all the Everton supporters understood and gleaned from the two encounters was the fact that the trophy would sit for the next year at Anfield rather than Goodison Park.

Howard was fed up sharing the feelings of old Mother Hubbard and he was quick to take encouragement from a couple of recent historical statistics. In 1982 Tottenham Hotspur lost the Milk Cup Final and went on a few weeks later to win the FA Cup and, in 1983, Manchester United did exactly the same. Could Everton make it a hat trick? Kendall admitted:

The problem for us all season has been scoring goals. We have created plenty of opportunities but our finishing, though thankfully it has improved dramatically during the last eight months, still lets us down far too often. Our defence is just about the best in the Football League and I can guarantee Watford will find it damnably hard to score against us at

Wembley. To win the Cup we will have to capitalize on our chances.

Clutching at encouraging statistics – for example, only one club had ever won the FA Cup at Wembley on its first appearance there, as Watford were trying to do – Howard Kendall was well aware of another interesting and salient fact. Liverpool had won most things more often than Everton but they had only won the FA Cup twice and Everton were now attempting to capture it for the fourth time. Howard mentioned over and over again the peculiar problems at Goodison Park of trying to repay and satisfy the loyal fans when, on the other side of an imaginary 'Berlin Wall', over at Anfield the Liverpool supporters enjoy endless success, winning cups, trophies and medals, not to mention European victories, every year. The overall scenario at Wembley on 19 May has to be seen against this particular background.

Most of the advantages lay with Everton and their experience of playing the Milk Cup Final at Wembley had to be of enormous benefit to them. They were far less likely to be overawed than Watford and although I felt Watford played rather well early on – their fans were in excellent spirits on their way to the ground and they, like the rugby league supporters a fortnight earlier, were especially well behaved. In chatting to some of the police on duty it was disappointing to hear that outbreaks of violence and crowd disturbances are all too common nowadays, but I'm delighted to report that the 1984 Cup Final had no such unsavoury incidents to report before, during or after the match. Having said that, it was still easy to see the presence of the mob element, as they tend to hunt in a pack and act as a pack. While I was struggling through the vast army of Everton fans to find my spot in the stand, they joined together in some light-hearted verbal ribbing that mostly referrred back to a 'Question of Sport' on BBC TV and the fact that I occasionally lost to Emlyn Hughes, a refugee from that great unwashed area of hell known as Anfield.

They feed off each other and tend to gravitate towards their leader or chief spokesman and, as demonstrated by all their chanting, there are a large number of sheep who merely follow. In a friendly atmosphere on Cup Final day, the mood was reasonably harmonious and kept well under control, but not too vivid an imagination is needed to appreciate how easily and how quickly it could, and does, get hopelessly out of control. Merely investigating another branch of the same tree, when Ian Robertson and I were trapped in a slow-moving crowd, Ian found it a shade disconcerting to put his hand in his back pocket and find there was already someone else's hand in his pocket. Obviously the someone else soon discovered he was a Scotsman with no money at all! The basic attitude of the Everton fans appeared to be more aggressive than the smaller, more amiable army of Watford supporters, and less socially acceptable than the respective followers of Wigan and Widnes in the first week of May. These were my views at the time; but it is only fair to repeat that the match and the aftermath passed off without incident, and both sets of supporters behaved admirably.

Once seated in the stadium with a perfect view, high up, overlooking the centre line, the 90,000 plus spectators were treated, as is the custom, to two hours of entertainment before the kick-off, beginning with the massed bands of the Guards Division playing a musical medley, followed by a display of aeronautical aerobatics, a motor-car cavalcade and a youngsters' soccer skills competition, before the singing of the traditional Cup Final hymn 'Abide With Me'. The teams were then presented to His Royal Highness the Duke of Kent, the President of the Football Association, before the game kicked off.

Contrary to the general expectations of the professional critics and pundits, Watford did not suffer from nerves and allow Everton to dominate the early proceedings. In fact, Watford almost made the best conceivable start, to confound those who indulged in verbose pre-match analysis of how the game would develop. In the opening seconds of the game, their teenage centre-half Lee Linnott took one of the long throw-ins in which he specializes. The tall, rangy George Reilly headed it deeper into the Everton goalmouth and John Barnes nodded it

Graeme Sharp gives Everton the lead against Watford at Wembley in the Cup Final

Sharp's goal seems to have the stamp of approval, judging by the reaction of his teammates

goalkeeper Neville Southall dive on the ball just as it was about to cross the line.

In the first half an hour, Watford seemed to me to be playing just as well as Everton although neither side struck the sort of fluent rhythm which might have produced a soccer classic. It was all frenetic endeavour and fierce industry, but the match lacked aestheticism and ingenuity. In the middle of this hustle and bustle with no clear pattern of play emerging, I thought it was just as likely that Watford might win. However, they had the wretched misfortune to be playing without their captain, and also without left-back Wilf Rostron, who was suspended after being sent off, and his absence made a crucial difference to the final outcome. He was replaced by 20-year-old Neil Price, who had only a handful of first-team games behind him and who turned out to be the weak link in the Watford defence. He was cruelly exposed by Trevor Steven in particular and others in general, and his lack of experience

and awareness permitted Everton the freedom to mount a stream of profitable attacks down his flank during the match, until he was substituted by Paul Atkinson midway through the second half.

Having made such invasions down the wing, Everton tended to follow up with a series of high crosses, which may have been planned as a shrewd tactic against a supposedly suspect goalkeeper but which produced little reward. On the other hand, the Merseyside men could argue that the goalkeeper Steve Sherwood inspired precious little confidence in his judgement, positioning and handling, and a cross was in fact directly responsible for the second goal. That is as may be, but it did not make for an attractive game. Everton never seemed to take full advantage either of the susceptibility of Sherwood or of the hesitancy and immaturity of the very young and inexperienced Watford back four.

Gradually, as half-time approached, Watford became frustrated, less confident and less composed; their attacks became more sporadic and Everton looked the more likely to score. Just seven minutes before half-time, they struck. Richardson and Reid combined to launch the ball into the Watford penalty area. Linnott headed the ball away to relieve the immediate danger but it was an ineffective and indecisive clearance which Gary Stevens quickly fastened on to, and he shot for goal. He mistimed his kick but the ball broke to his team-mate Graeme Sharp who had time to steady himself, turn and hit the ball past Sherwood into the goal, off the inside of the left-hand post.

The goal deflated Watford and, though they tried to fight back before the interval, I think from that point on Everton were always going to win and the Watford team and their fans sensed the inevitability of it. That was certainly the consensus of opinion around me during the half-time break. I was reminded at this time of just how glamorous an occasion the Cup Final can be. Sitting just behind me was Rod Stewart with a very attractive blonde girl and I waved and chatted to Sharron Davies who was a few seats away. I spoke to Dickie Jeeps, the

former England Rugby Union captain and now Chairman of the Sports Council and I spotted quite a few celebrities from various sports, also Members of Parliament and people from the world of show business.

Nobody I spoke to believed Watford would recover, and a second goal five minutes into the second half realistically ended their challenge. This goal provided the major controversy in the match and was the main talking point after the match; but as far as I was concerned, it looked a good goal. Trevor Steven neatly eluded Price and floated a high, hovering ball across the goalmouth. Sherwood, in my opinion, misjudged the flight of the ball and he had to rapidly back-pedal to try to retrieve his position. In doing so, he was definitely off-balance as, still leaning back and with his whole momentum and body weight going away from the direction of the cross, he got his hands above his head as Andy Gray came in to attack the ball. Gray went in to head the ball and made contact as Sherwood struggled, and failed, to get both hands on the ball at the same time. Gray headed the ball out of the goalkeeper's tentative and inconclusive grasp and into the net for the decisive match-winning goal. Sherwood, who bumped into one of his own defenders as he leapt backwards initially, fell to the ground but he was not fouled by Gray and the referee, who was in a perfect spot to see the whole drama unfold in front of him, was absolutely correct in awarding the goal.

Watford might have been one or even two goals up in the first 30 minutes but luck was not on their side and, for the last 30 minutes of the match, they had no option but to play out the role of gallant losers. It was commendable to see the Watford players and their legion of loyal fans accept the second goal in the most sportsmanlike manner, and they ended a thoroughly sporting contest with their bold reputation enhanced. There were only 20 fouls in the whole game which was enjoyable and exciting, though falling well short of being a spectacular or epic Final. It was good, wholesome stuff and Everton, with their greater experience and composure, gave an efficient, disciplined, controlled and utterly

professional performance of solid quality.

Afterwards, the Watford manager, Graham Taylor, refused to blame his goalkeeper in any way for the defeat and he believed he was fouled when Andy Gray scored the second goal. But, whatever the rights and wrongs of that particular saga, it is worth mentioning that Neville Southall had a superb game in the Everton goal and, if the two goalkeepers had been swopped round, the result may well have been different.

As it was, Kevin Ratcliffe led his team up to the Royal Box to receive the Cup and, holding it high over his head, he turned to the crowd to allow the Everton supporters their cherished opportunity to raise the roof and unleash the resounding cheers they had been nurturing during the past 14 years. For them, it was a golden moment, worthy of the

long wait. The team set off on their lap of honour and were given a warm reception by the generous Watford fans, magnanimous in defeat, and a delirious reception from the thousands who had travelled from Liverpool. Immediately behind me, a little boy with a Watford cap, red and yellow scarf and rosette was nearly drowning me in a flood of tears while his Dad tried to console him and, in the end, he accepted that really he should be proud of his team for reaching Wembley and putting on such a brave display.

Shortly before the match started a message was flashed up on the big screen at the end of the ground. It announced that a new record by the Chairman of Watford, Elton John, entitled 'Sad Songs', was about to be released, and I wondered if the ensuing 90 minutes were going to be too much for Elton. Obviously, he must have been sad at the end, but also immensely proud of this, the culmination of a series of heroic achievements since he took over as Chairman. Dressed typically in his own individual hat, spectacles and an amazing shining, glittering suit, he waved to the crowd and consoled his players and, despite his disappointment at the result, clearly enjoyed his day at Wembley.

On reflection, 1984 was a pretty good year for Merseyside. Liverpool won the First Division League Title, the Milk Cup and the European Cup. Everton won the FA Youth Cup to safeguard their interests for the next 14 years, and their most treasured prize, the FA Cup. I went for tea in the banqueting suite after the match and heard some of soccer's more knowledgeable men – Bobby

Andy Gray, extreme left, heads the second goal to clinch the Cup

Charlton, Laurie McMenemy and Bobby Robson – all agree that it had not been a very good game of football, just as many other Cup Finals had previously failed to rise to the occasion, but it still had enough entertainment to sustain it.

I began the long drive back to Preston at six o'clock and, as I had anticipated, I spent nearly four hours surrounded in every lane of the motorway by cars, vans, dormobiles, lorries and coaches, all decked out in Everton's blue and white colours, with flags and scarves draped out of the windows, fluttering in the wind. At the many hold-ups along the way, there was plenty of drinking being done by the passengers, a chaotic amount of noise from the mass tooting of countless different car horns, and a lot of laughing, joking and high-spirited celebrating being undertaken with relish. It was quite an experience travelling back that night and if a foreigner had been driving along the motorway in the opposite direction, I hate to think what sort of reaction the scenes would have provoked. People would have been excused for thinking that an alien army was about to invade the north of England.

The town of Liverpool was alive and buzzing on the Sunday when the conquering heroes returned to an emotional reception. They toured the streets in an open-top bus and hundreds of thousands of Liverpudlians lined the route to give them a truly unforgettable welcome. After this I spoke again to Howard Kendall to find out if he was satisfied with the manner in which Everton had procured their victory. He said that he was disappointed with the early play; his players were much more nervous than he had expected and the team's normal fluency was missing. He had felt that their Wembley appearance in the Milk Cup would have ensured a relaxed approach to the Cup Final, but he admitted that the players had still allowed the importance of the occasion to affect them adversely and they had not produced their best form.

He knew in the dressing-room before the game that the players were suffering from tension and apprehension and he was concerned in the first quarter of the match that Watford, who appeared happy just to be at Wembley in the final, might sneak a lead and hang on to it as his team struggled to string their game together. It was impossible for Howard to enjoy the game before Andy Gray's goal gave Everton a comfortable cushion, because so much was dependent on the result. 'A win meant we would be in Europe in 1984–5,' Kendall said, 'and we would also be back at Wembley in August for the FA Charity Shield clash between the winners of the Cup and the first-division champions. It was a fantastic bonus to think that a win in the Cup would lead directly to another crack at Liverpool at Wembley.'

Even after Andy Gray's goal, Howard found the second half a nerve-racking experience which seemed to last forever and a day. When the final whistle did go his overwhelming feeling was one of huge relief and, of course, delight that the Cup would be going to Goodison Park. It was interesting that, while the players embarked on their lap of honour, the crowd started to chant his name; although he did not want to take anything away from the players as they acknowledged the plaudits of the fans, he was persuaded to walk round in their wake and, in the nicest possible way, join in the waving, cheering and general adulation, and became part of the newly-formed Merseyside mutual admiration society.

I saw the manager being interviewed on BBC television on the Saturday evening and was surprised to learn that he was celebrating with the club directors and wives while the players had decided beforehand to have a players-only dinner and party. He told me that he was, naturally, disappointed but he respected the wishes of his players to celebrate alone and he was grateful to them for the pleasure and joy they had given him in the afternoon. He was speaking sincerely from his heart when he said the Cup Final had been a great day for him, for his family, for the club, for the players, for the fans and for the town of Liverpool. It laid to rest Bill Shankly's old line; he claimed there were two great sides on Merseyside without any doubt – Liverpool and Liverpool reserves. On 19 May, Everton restored a large chunk of honour and pride to the other side of the city.

TEN

FLAT RACING

ROYAL ASCOT

In the summer of 1711, Queen Anne, driving from Windsor over Ascot Heath, looked out of her carriage window and decided that here was a very suitable place for racing. The day before the subsequently arranged meeting she personally inspected the course, being saluted by a number of onlookers, among them Jonathan Swift, the great satirist. 'We saw', wrote Swift to Stella, 'a place they have made for a famous horse-race tomorrow, where the Queen will come.' A notice appeared in the *London Gazette* announcing 'Her Majesty's Plate of 100 Guineas' to be run on the Heath, and on 7 August the first Royal Ascot was under way. It was such a huge success that a second meeting was promptly arranged for the following month.

The meeting was on and off after that for the next 150 years, as a succession of monarchs showed their interest in or satiety of the Sport of Kings, but Ascot has been a regular event since the late eighteenth century. The Royal Meeting starts every year with the Queen Anne Stakes (now held in June) and is the most colourful spectacle in the British racing calendar. It occupies four days – Tuesday until Friday – although racing is also held on the Saturday without the 'royal' status. The meeting is a haven for both punters and gossip columnists, rubbing shoulders with the gents in their morning coats and ladies in high fashion and extraordinary millinery. The focus of attention, apart from the races themselves, the society and the pageantry, is the royal procession, first introduced in 1828 by George IV and little changed since. Princess Victoria first appeared at Ascot in 1834 and attended the meeting many times until the death of Prince Albert, and there have been royal guests a-plenty, including a couple of Czars (Alexander I and Nicholas I).

Her Majesty Queen Elizabeth II's first public visit to any race meeting was on Whit Monday, 21 May 1945, two weeks after the war was over. The young Princess and her father George VI moved inconspicuously in uniform (ATS subaltern and Field Marshal) among other khaki-clad racegoers in the paddock, and the Princess watched excitedly as Finchampstead Handicap-winner Historic, his saddle removed, rolled on the grass and kicked his legs triumphantly.

Ascot meetings go on throughout the year with steeplechase, mixed and flat races, but the royal event is the highlight. Top-class horses, trained to the peak of their fitness, contend at Royal Ascot, with the meeting's principle race being the Gold Cup, for stayers of three years and upwards. The Gold Cup was first run in 1807, and West Australian (the 1854 winner), Gladiateur (1866) and the famous sire St Simon (1884) distinguished themselves among nineteenth-century stayers. The filly Quashed in 1936 fought off American champion Omaha in a stirring finish, and the name of Alycidon, who won the Cup in 1949, is remembered also for Cup wins at Goodwood and Doncaster. The most valuable Ascot race is the King George VI and Queen Elizabeth Diamond Stakes, instituted in 1951; its first winner was the three-year-old Supreme

Court. Perhaps the greatest winner of the era, though, was the Italian Ribot, who thundered to victory over the Queen's own High Veldt and an international field. The leading jockey in both the Cup and the King George Stakes is Lester Piggott.

In 1983, the mare Stanerra showed unusual strength and courage in winning the Prince of Wales Stakes and then, at the same meeting, the Hardwicke Stakes, breaking the course record on the second run. Whether or not she did a victory roll in the grass goes unrecorded. It is on record, however, that champion jockey Terry Biddlecombe, having won on Penharbour in the Territorial Handicap Hurdle at Ascot in March 1967, tossed his silver trophy in the air out of sheer exuberance, having strolled up and introduced himself to the Queen during the presentation ceremony. The innocent Biddlecombe was drawn aside by the old Duke of Norfolk afterwards and told that Ascot jockeys, however triumphant, must never speak to Her Majesty unless first spoken to.

Preparations for my visit to Royal Ascot on Wednesday, 20 June began early, when I set about hiring a morning suit for the occasion. I ordered it well in advance but my unusually efficient organization was to no avail: when I went to collect it on the Tuesday, my attempt to squeeze into the trousers was a miserable failure. Hiring clothes for someone of 17 stones and 6 feet 4 inches can always present problems and I was lucky that someone of similar build to myself had ordered a suit to be collected from the same shop for the Friday. I tried his trousers on and they fitted perfectly. I promised to return them on the Thursday and, on this condition, the shop packed them up for me.

I drove to London from Preston early on the Wednesday morning in my ordinary suit and I called in en route for the races to discuss some business with a friend. I embarked on the last leg of the journey at noon and stopped at a garage to fill up with petrol and, at the same time, slip into the toilets to change into my morning suit. The petrol-pump attendant assured me I was not the only person executing that particular manoeuvre during Ascot week.

I arrived on the course before one o'clock and linked up right away with Ian Balding. He trains a dozen horses for the Queen but, before becoming one of the best trainers in Europe, was an outstanding rugby player, winning a Blue in a very good Cambridge side and playing for donkeys years for Bath and Somerset at full-back. He was able to spend a couple of hours taking me round to see the most significant parts of the course and introducing me to some fascinating personalities.

We went first to the top of the grandstand which presented us with a magnificent view of the course and Ian showed me where the starting stalls would be placed for each race and some of the special characteristics of the course. He said that the course was slightly undulating with a relatively short straight of under three furlongs which meant that it was difficult for a horse to make up a great deal of ground in the final quarter of a mile; the finish was all slightly uphill. I was also shown the straight mile course which is used for all the shorter races and for a few carefully selected one-mile races.

It is also used for the royal procession which takes place every day before the racing, and I was in a perfect position with a marvellous aerial view to see this magnificent traditional spectacle. With the temperature in the eighties and a bright blue cloudless sky overhead, it was the ideal setting for this most English of occasions. The royal party left Windsor Castle in a convoy of cars at half past one and arrived at the racecourse in time for the procession to head down the straight mile at two o'clock. There were five open carriages, each drawn by four superbly groomed horses and the whole vibrant scenario was a striking splash of colour set against the lush, green manicured racecourse.

In the first carriage were the Queen and the Duke of Edinburgh along with the Prince of Wales and the Duke of Marlborough. In the second carriage, on which most eyes in the crowd were feasted, came the Princess of Wales and Queen Elizabeth, the Queen Mother along with the Duke of Roxburghe and Major Raymond Seymour. They were followed by Princess Margaret,

the Duchess of Marlborough, the Marquess of Worcester and Mr Simon Scrope. With more peers of the realm, royalty and distinguished personalities in the final two carriages, the flotilla swept up the straight, turned sharp left through the royal enclosure and halted at the foot of the back of the grandstand where the party were escorted to the Royal Box.

At that stage I bumped into Mrs Shilling, one of the legendary figures of Royal Ascot, who intrigues and outrages the female sense of taste with her bizarre and eccentric choice of hats each year. On the Wednesday, she was wearing an amazing creation which was based on a giant dart board with three darts stuck in it. I must confess that, as a humble lad from Lancashire, I found it quite grotesque but I thoroughly enjoyed chatting to her and I am all in favour of people being allowed to express their individuality in any reasonable way they like! Whilst Mrs Shilling's hats are not my idea of *haute couture*, they have certainly become one of the sights

to watch out for every June.

Ian Balding was fortunate that, early on in his training career, he had had a royal winner at Royal Ascot and every year, he told me, he desperately likes to have the royal runners good enough to take their chance at the royal meeting. A full month before Ascot, he discusses his probable royal runners with the Queen's racing manager, Lord Porchester, and between them they decide which horses will run. I soon appreciated the extra pressure on them because the huge crowd love nothing better than to cheer home a winner in the Queen's colours and, with so much public money likely to be invested with the bookmakers, the trainer wants to be pretty confident the horses will run really well. Ian Balding had two runners for the Queen that day – Castle Rising in the Queen's Vase and Insular in the Bessborough Stakes, and I discussed their prospects standing in the weighing-room after the first race. Lord Porchester seemed to think the ground might be too firm for

The Queen and the Duke of Edinburgh arrive at Royal Ascot in traditional style

Castle Rising but the trainer was sure this four-year-old would go very close to winning.

Just before Ian and I left to go to the paddock to see the runners' parade for the big handicap of the day, I was fascinated to hear Lord Porchester explain how Her Majesty the Queen had been very excited at the winner coming home a length clear in the Queen Mary Stakes, the race we had all just watched. He said she was cheering and waving as Hi-Tech Girl hit the front at the furlong pole and held on to win from Tumble Dale and Cameron. She showed enough excitement to suggest it might have been one of her own horses, but it transpired that her enthusiasm and interest were sparked off by the fact that her dressmaker had been the underbidder for the filly at the yearling sales; she was delighted because the win proved that her dressmaker had a good eye for a horse.

The conversation then touched briefly on rugby and I was interested to learn that Lord Porchester had been a keen rugby player in his time and had thoroughly enjoyed his playing career, much of which had taken place in the Middle East. He confided that he would have done much better if referees had not felt he was permanently off-side. I sympathized with him and told him I knew the feeling exactly. On our way out of the weighing-room, I saw my old adversary on a 'Question of Sport', Willie Carson, and I asked rather tentatively if he could point me in the direction of a winner. He replied that I would be well advised to have a fiver on Baynoun which he felt would take an enormous amount of beating. That did not best please Ian Balding, Baynoun being in the same race as Castle Rising, but he readily admitted his anxiety.

We crossed the paddock to see the horses for the next race paraded and Ian then took me off to the special stable block owned exclusively by the Queen. All royal runners at the meeting are kept in the royal stable and we had to be specially signed in by the security guard before we could see Castle Rising and Insular. They both looked in superb condition and remarkably cool con-

sidering the oppressive heat and humidity. On leaving this royal yard I was lucky enough to stumble upon the chance meeting of a lifetime with a very select group of people standing isolated in the upper paddock area. The royal trainer took me across and introduced me to the Prince and Princess of Wales and, the man who trained National Hunt horses for the Prince, Nick Gaselee and his wife Judith. We stood chatting for quite a while but the early exchanges were lost on me because, not only was I aware of the stunning radiant appearance of the Princess, I was damned if I knew what to do with my top hat. On being introduced to the royal group, I followed suit when Ian Balding took off his top hat and shook hands with everyone. Like Ian, I then put my top hat back on and engaged in conversation with the Princess. I was feeling relaxed and having a great time when, out of the corner of my eye, I spotted that Ian was holding his hat in his right hand. I tried not to panic but worked out that perhaps when addressing royalty maybe one has to doff one's hat. Or was it, maybe, only when royalty happened to be addressing me? No sooner had I taken my hat off and resumed the discussion about 'Question of Sport' on BBC Television, than I noticed Ian Balding had his top hat on again. (Apparently he had only taken off the hat the second time to wipe his forehead in the burning heat and, afterwards, he said he could not even remember doing it.) It turned out that my intricate analysis of royal etiquette was all in vain. With my hat back on I inquired if the Princess found the high temperature that day (in the eighties) a little uncomfortable in her present condition. As I had anticipated, it was not a bundle of laughs. She had declined to make the pilgrimage from the Royal Box to the paddock to look at the horses because, quite rightly, she wanted to avoid the trek through a jostling throng of people who would mostly be looking at *her*.

Ian told the Prince that he thought the Queen's two horses would run well, especially Castle Rising, and he was rather surprised when Prince Charles said that unfortunately he would not see them as he was leaving after the fourth race to go back to Windsor to play polo. With that, Ian and I returned to the grandstand to watch the Hunt Cup, noticing several ladies looking extremely well dressed with stunning hats but agreeing there was no one at Ascot who was smarter, more attractive or more elegant than the Princess of Wales.

Needless to say, one of the features of Royal Ascot is the annual fashion parade and there were a staggering number of beautiful women dressed in really glamorous clothes and wearing some striking hats. Given complete freedom of choice, I would have been a lot more comfortable in a lightweight suit with a bare head but I have great respect for tradition and, though the Ascot scene is a long way removed from a day out in Chorley, I was delighted to be part of the establishment world of Ascot for a day. Of course, the trappings which go hand in hand with such an unique social occasion have expensive drawbacks. I was able to resist champagne at £30 a bottle and smoked salmon at slightly less but I could not resist the strawberries and cream and was asked to part with over £5 for three very small plates which supported about a handful of strawberries each. The basic diet at Royal Ascot seems to be smoked salmon, lobsters, crabs, oysters, rich meats and strawberries, all washed down liberally with champagne, fine wines and Pimm's. These delicacies are consumed in breathtaking proportions – literally tons and tons and tons of gourmet food are consumed every day and hundreds of gallons of alcohol are swallowed.

Not surprisingly, everyone seemed to be enjoying themselves hugely. This mood was epitomized after the final race of the day when large sections of the crowd congregated round the bandstand and joined in a sing-song for a good hour until the band were exhausted in the heat. It was a smashing way to round off the day and I suspect for a considerable number of the 45,000-strong crowd the best memories of the day would have been the food, the drink, the clothes and fashions, the array of ladies' hats, the music and singing at the bandstand and the generally relaxed bonhomie and camaraderie of a great social occasion.

But as my friend Willie Carson was at great pains to point out, it remains in his book and that of every student of horse racing, the foremost racing week of the year anywhere in the world. With great conviction he affirmed:

Royal Ascot is the very best racing in the world, and it has to be a peak and a real highlight every

Baynoun, ridden by Willie Carson, spreadeagles the field in the Queen's Vase at Royal Ascot

summer. For four days, Ascot provides the best racehorses at every conceivable distance and age group, racing for colossal prize money and tremendous prestige which will be translated at a later date by the fees these horses will attract as stallions and brood-mares. The Derby at Epsom may be a bigger, more spectacular, one-off, simple race but at Ascot you can see the fastest two-year-olds and three-year-olds at five furlongs and six furlongs, you can see the best three-year-olds and older horses at seven furlongs, one mile, a mile and a quarter and a mile and a half. You can see each year the classic winning three-year-olds from England, Ireland and France meeting for the first time to settle, for example, the best miler, in the Coronation Stakes. Three horses in this race, Katies, Pebbles and So Fine had all been sold in the previous two months for a total of over four million pounds, and this race showed Katies, the cheapest at half a million pounds, to be clearly the best.

Royal Ascot is simply about meritocracy taken to its ultimate conclusion, its about the créme de la créme *and every jockey relishes the prospect of sitting on the fastest horses in the world and riding in the very best races. Just think of it — this year about two hundred thousand people will watch three hundred top thoroughbreds chasing over three quarters of a million pounds.*

I'm delighted to report that Willie Carson finished the top jockey at Royal Ascot in 1984, riding brilliantly to win on Morcon, Head for Heights, Habibti and, allowing me the luxury of a rare and much appreciated visit to the Tote pay-out window, on Baynoun. He was at his scintillating best on Habibti in the five-furlong King Stand Stakes on the Friday but he was a trifle unlucky not to win the Bessborough Stakes, the last race on the Wednesday. He was hampered as he began his challenge on Forward in the final two furlongs and he finished second, beaten by half a length by Sikorsky.

This last result provided a first Royal Ascot winner for the most famous American jockey of recent times, Willie Shoemaker. Now in his early fifties, this was his first visit to Ascot and he said afterwards it was a rare experience and everything it was cracked up to be. Curiously enough, three other famous

American jockeys were in action at Royal Ascot: Steve Cauthen, who rode three winners, Darrel McHargue, who had one winner, and Cash Asmussen, who had a second and a fourth from his three mounts on the Tuesday.

Steve Cauthen finished second top jockey at Ascot and this delightful, classically stylish yet immensely strong and powerful rider looked back on the four-day meeting with satisfaction and pleasure:

There is nothing remotely like Royal Ascot in the United States, and I can't think of anywhere else where there would be the same fantastic concentration of outstanding racing over four successive days. The nearest in concept would be the Breeders' Cup at Hollywood Park in Los Angeles each November, where all seven races on the one day are worth over a million dollars each and the trainers and owners are chasing a grand total of around eleven million dollars for one day's racing. But there is nothing in America that is sustained over four days like Ascot. Certainly, even though racing attracts equally big crowds at the weekend in America, they are never dressed up like Royal Ascot and I think there is a lot to be said for the very special atmosphere and flavour of the Royal meeting.

It was reassuring to hear this modest, very likeable and highly talented jockey share our joy at wallowing in fine old British tradition and it was also reassuring to know that England has been doing something better than anyone else in the world for over 270 years. My only regret, as I began the journey home, was the thought that there must have been a very long list of royal winners at Royal Ascot dating back to the eighteenth century, but there was not one in 1984. Nevertheless, I consoled myself with the fact that Castle Rising had run an excellent race to finish a close third in the Queen's Vase and would surely win a big race soon for Her Majesty; and, when all is said and done, I did have £5 on the winner of that particular race – Baynoun – at odds of 2 to 1. I had won just enough to celebrate with a small glass of champagne and a few strawberries and still had some small change left to phone home and tell Hilary I had met the Prince and Princess of Wales.

THE DERBY

The Greyhound Derby, first held in 1927, is the premier event in the dog-racing calendar, attracting at least 15,000 people to White City every fourth Saturday in June. Six qualifiers go like bats out of hell round a 500-metre track in the attempt to make their masters £25,000 in prizemoney. Attendance is well down on the first post-war final when 58,000 people cheered them on, but then a government levy hit the greyhound racing boom hard. 'Going to the dogs' nevertheless has wide appeal. Most races take place conveniently at night, tracks are local and, in theory at least, anyone can own and train the Greyhound Derby winner (although in practice 10 per cent of UK dogs' home inmates are bony greyhounds discarded from unlicensed amateur flapper tracks up and down the country). There is more to training a racing dog than whistling and letting it out of a box.

The well-sprung ribs and muscular physique of the greyhound, who hauls its hind paws in front of its extended forepaws like the cheetah and the hare, is typical of the 'gazehound' or sight-hunting (as distinct from scent-hunting) dog. Although the ancient origins of the greyhound are in dispute, dogs *resembling* the modern greyhound have been depicted on Egyptian tombs, and bones excavated in Mesopotamia dating to 5000 BC look remarkably like greyhound skeletons. Some authorities say they came from the Levantine deserts; some believe 'greyhound' is a corruption of 'Greekhound'. Others say British greyhounds are a separate race. The medieval word was 'gre-hounde', and 'gre' meant simply 'highborn', 'gentle', which they undoubtedly were. In AD 948 British greyhounds were worth six score pence, a tidy sum, and they soon became exclusive to kings and nobles because Game Laws of 1016 ordered greyhounds of low degree to be maimed to prevent them from hunting in His Majesty's forests. The 1486 *Boke of St Albans* included a description of hare-hunting dogs: 'The gre-hounde should be headed like a snake and necked like a drake, Footed like a cat, Tailed like a rat, Ribbed like a beam, Glossy like a bream ...'

Modern greyhound racing with a mechanical hare is a stylized and commercially packaged version of coursing, in which a pair of dogs are 'slipped' to live quarry. Sentimentality about the hare has nothing to do with it; many racing greyhounds today are still trained on the real thing and coursing is perfectly legal in the UK. On the racetrack though, the mechanical hare begins its rail 'run' from behind the starting traps and these automatically fly open when the hare is 12 yards in front – making it more convenient as a spectator sport. A timing device is set going and when the winning greyhound's nose breaks a beam projected across the finish line the timer is stopped. Greyhounds run at 35–40 m.p.h. and there are often collisions and lamings on bends which add excitements for the punters.

At the end of World War I an American farmer, Owen Patrick Smith, was fined for coursing hare on his Oklahoma paddock, and responded by opening a circular track nearby, as well as others at Salt Lake City and in California. The oval-racetrack craze took off in America. In England meanwhile, on a field near the Welsh Harp in Hendon, straightline greyhound racing was afoot. *The Times* of 11 September 1876 carried a report of 'simulated hare coursing' with a mechanical hare propelled by a windlass along a rail – a straight test of speed. The oval track, requiring brainier dogs to brave the bends, arrived courtesy of a Brigadier General Critchley, the Greyhound Racing Association and an American businessman, and opened at Belle Vue, Manchester in July 1926. Greyhounds came to London's White City the following year, and soon there were 40 British tracks, with lighting, seating and all the latest in synthetic hares.

Old bruisers and tacklers like those in the Greyhound Hall of Fame, Kansas, Tring Museum and the British Museum of Natural History (where Mick the Miller, the greatest of them all, stands today) are rougher cut and shaggier than modern racing sylphs; they'd had to manage without centrally heated kennels or recuperative medicines. But all successful racing dogs are smart and intelligent, capable of pacing themselves and spotting the main chance. Some are so competitive that they will look to avenge themselves on a rival for a previous defeat. They are all different, and the punters and trainers know which are the extroverts, wide-runners and sprint-finishers. Races are over in a flash but there's a lengthy check-in beforehand to ensure the dog's identity, weight and fitness are what they seem. The animals have to urinate in a bowl for chromotography testing and their ears are tattooed with registration numbers. 'Nobbling' is deterred by tight security and the use of muzzles because there's a lot of money rolling on the tote and the tick-tack. A giant totalizator shines forth across the stadium, clicking up the odds with every bet placed. This shows the punters where the cash is flowing, and many a shirt is lost on Derby night.

The 1984 Greyhound Derby was one of the few events of this book to which I was able to take my wife, so the two of us set out at lunchtime from Preston to London. Hilary packed her long evening dress and I made sure I had my bow tie and cufflinks to go with my dinner jacket because, thanks to the generous hospitality of the sponsors, the *Daily Mirror*, we were invited to cover the event in style. Hopefully we would be able to hang onto our shirts.

The journey from north London, where we stopped for tea, to the White City took far longer than we anticipated and we missed the first three races. The reason for our late arrival was long traffic delays between central London and the White City – caused by two other conflicting attractions on the same night. As we drove past Earls Court we spotted crowds flocking to a Neil Diamond concert and a little further along we saw a steady stream of cars and coaches turn off at Shepherd's Bush en route for the Queen Park Rangers soccer ground where the evangelist, Luis Palau, was preaching to a huge, open-air crowd.

We arrived in time for the fourth of the evening's 13 races and settled down to dinner in the luxurious surroundings of the main restaurant. There were over 70 tables in this restaurant, neatly laid out and all with a perfect view through massive windows of the track beneath and the enormous totalizator boards at each end of the stadium which gave the approximate odds of each dog before every race, and the result and starting price immediately after it. The room was already bustling with waitresses and wine waiters rushing in every direction, trying hard not to crash into the young girls who came to every table to collect everybody's bet for the next race. It was like a scene from an old Keystone Cops movie, but it seemed to work and to the best of my knowledge there were no major catastrophes during the evening.

It was an extremely civilized way in which to watch greyhound racing and it was evident the regular spectators had made a huge effort to treat their blue-riband event of the year, the Greyhound Derby, as a very special occasion. The cost of the tickets for entrance and dinner was £40 a head but, although not cheap, this included all the trappings and did not seem an outrageous price. The meal was first class. Hilary and I started with potted shrimps on a bed of smoked salmon and had fillet steak in mushroom sauce to follow. We enjoyed an excellent French white and a red wine with the meal, and finished with strawberries and cream, coffee and liqueurs.

While we were dining the lights in the restaurant dimmed every 20 minutes or so, the floodlights drenched the track and we watched the greyhounds ping round after the hare, covering a lap in just under 30 seconds. The races were exciting with dogs hurtling round the bends and flashing down the short straights at speeds in excess of 40 m.p.h. but, none the less, there was disappointment for me on two counts. Firstly, I cannot think of any great sporting events which last, *in toto*, for less than 30 seconds. A Test Match at Lord's lasts five days, the Open Golf lasts four days, the FA Cup Final an hour and a half. I can understand why the population of Preston decided not to join me in an 8-hour round trip of over 400 miles to make the pilgrimage to London to watch an annual ritual which lasts less than 30 seconds!

Secondly, I was very disappointed at the size of the crowd. It was estimated that approximately 20,000 were there for the final, which is nearly 10 times more than most of Britain's greyhound tracks muster for a normal evening's racing but still 60,000 or so short of capacity. As a consequence, the whole evening lacked a little atmosphere in exactly the same way as the men's singles final at Wimbledon or the FA Cup Final at Wembley would if these two famous sporting arenas were three-quarters empty for their most important sporting event of the year. I found it rather sad and depressing to see vast deserted areas all round the track with most spectators huddled around the middle.

This situation was brought home forcibly when I chatted to Harry Carpenter, who has been covering the event for BBC television for 30 years and has witnessed the gradual decline in attendances. I was intrigued to learn he began his working life in 1941 as a sub-editor on the now-defunct newspaper the *Greyhound Express*, and he used to go dog-racing regularly 43 years ago. 'My old man used to bet a bit,' he explained, 'and he used to follow the form in the *Greyhound Express*. I looked at the paper occasionally and noticed an advert for an editorial assistant, applied, got the job and began my working life.' Harry worked for two years before joining the Navy and, on being demobbed, he joined another newspaper, the *Greyhound Owner*. He hit the dizzy heights there of assistant editor but was quick to point out in all modesty that the entire staff of the paper numbered two – the editor and himself. None the less, Harry has clearly known one end of a greyhound from the other for a very considerable time and it is interesting that his love affair with the sport has lasted so long.

He confessed that recently the sport has been in decline generally, with many tracks forced to close, and he was nostalgic in recalling how capacity crowds of 80,000 packed into the White City for the Derby final in the late forties and early fifties. If only 15,000 turned up at Twickenham for the Calcutta Cup rugby union International I would be desperately worried about the future of the sport and this is the sort of plight greyhound racing is in right now. The race has been held at the White City for 57 years but the 1984 Greyhound Derby may well have brought the curtain down on the end of an era. The ultimate fate of the White City stadium has still to be decided, but the likelihood is that the Derby will be moved in 1985 to a different site. Harry Carpenter thought this would be a shame. It is always hard, often unpleasant and sometimes unpalatable to break with tradition and sever the umbilical cord linking the whole glorious history of an event with the modern day. Harry put it in perspective:

This could well be the last year at the White City and, if you take it away from its roots, from this extraordinary and unique amphitheatre, this huge stadium with all its associations from the past and memories of all the great dogs who have run and won on this particular track from Mick the Miller through Pigalle Wonder right up to tonight, you rob the event of part of its soul, its history and its tradition. You may well have another, different sort of event in its place and it may still be called the Greyhound Derby, but it won't be the White City Derby.

The White City was a magnificent stadium when it hosted the Olympic Games in 1908, and it was capable in those days of holding 100,000. In its heyday in the thirties and forties it attracted tremendous crowds to the big athletic meetings and, of course, to the Greyhound Derby. The Derby then, as now, appealed to a wide cross-section of society and it never was the great cloth-cap sport of the working man as it has so often been portrayed. In many ways, it can be compared to Royal Ascot where every class of society is involved. In the earliest years – the late twenties – the then Prince of Wales was a regular attender and royalty turned up at the White City in the thirties.

Sadly, those heady days have long since gone. The decline in interest in greyhound racing is linked directly to the introduction and spread of betting shops. In the old days, people had to go to the track to have a bet but now they simply go to their nearest licensed betting office and there is no need to go to the track. Mingling with the crowd between races I had the distinct feeling that the majority of punters on the terraces were there in the drizzling rain just for the gambling. They seemed the sort of people who would stand on a street corner and lay bets on the colour or the make of the first car to come round the corner.

The actual spectacle somehow needs the betting element to bring it alive and, when I went down to talk to the bookies, they were being swamped by punters indecently keen to be parted from their money. I chatted to Tom Stanley, a bookie on the rails at greyhound tracks for over 20 years, and he confirmed that people came nowadays mainly to have a bet and try to get better value than they could in a betting shop. He reckoned he would take between £5000 and

Whisper Wishes leads Moran's Beef round the final bend of the Greyhound Derby

£6000 on the Derby alone, and around £30,000 for the whole 13-race card on the night of the Derby.

Nevertheless, the Derby only takes place once a year and he regretted that, on a normal night at the dogs, he would be happy to take £5000 altogether. The interest in the Derby is so intense that he began taking ante-post bets the previous October, and the British public would have invested five or six million pounds by the time the hare set off at 22.22 hours on 23 June. Tom Stanley blamed the dramatic decline in attendances on the betting tax, which is crucifying bookies and punters alike, and on the various alternative attractions of the late twentieth century, including television and video.

The Derby was the tenth race on the card and in the 40 minutes prior to the hare being unleashed there was near pandemonium in the ring as the 20,000-strong crowd swarmed all over the place in a feverish flurry of activity trying to place a bet. After my losses at Cheltenham I had resisted the temptation to back any dog in the earlier races, but Alan Kinghorn, the Managing Director of the big London firm of bookmakers, Kinghorns, very kindly offered me a free £50 bet. Without showing any dash of originality I stuck the £50 on the favourite, Whisper Wishes, with the agreement that if by some miracle the dog won, the money would be presented to charity.

In the late spring, 200 greyhounds had fought in the heats for the right to advance to the Derby final. The first round proper took place at the White City on 2 June and 5 June with 12 races involving six dogs per race on each of those nights. On 9 June there were another 12 races in the second round with the four quarter-finals on 14 June. Nippy Law won the first quarter-final,

The proud owner, John Duffy, holds the trophy; the trainer, Charlie Coyle, is in the middle; and I am holding Whisper Wishes, winner of the Greyhound Derby at the White City

Whisper Wishes the second, Glenbrien Champ the third and Proud Dodger the fourth. The first three finishers in each of the quarter-finals advanced to the semifinals two days later, and the first three in each of these races went through to the final a week later. The first semifinal was won by Moran's Beef from The Jolly Norman and the other semifinal was won by Whisper Wishes from House of Hope and Proud Dodger.

The White City tried to recapture some of its past glory in the presentation of the final but, to me, it rang a little hollow and lacked some of the glamour I had always associated with the event when I had watched it in previous years on television.

The lights dimmed in the restaurant leaving the lush bright green grass of the track highlighted in its glory as a fanfare of eight trumpets greeted the parade of the six finalists. They did a complete lap of honour to give everyone an opportunity of seeing the state and condition of each dog before they were loaded into the traps. The hare whizzed past, the traps opened, the dogs exploded round the first bend and, to my delight and surprise, Whisper Wishes was up with the leaders. He hit the final bend in the lead and just held on from Moran's Beef in a pulsating finish to win the first prize of £25,000 and the *Daily Mirror* Greyhound Derby Trophy. I had won my bet and

Kinghorns generously presented me with a cheque for £87.50 which I handed over to the charity of my choice – Research into Muscular Dystrophy.

The dog then mounted the winner's podium surrounded by his delighted owner, John Duffy, and his trainer, Charlie Coyle. A posse of flash bulbs captured the magic moment on celluloid and the trainer led his hero on a lap of honour to acknowledge the ecstatic squeals of delight from the army of punters who love to see a favourite win. As he left the track to return to the kennels, I met up with the dog and discussed at some length his racing prowess with Charlie Coyle.

He became involved in training greyhounds when he was still a teenager and has been involved in the racing game for 30 years. He was wearing a dapper brown suit which had brought him lots of luck and he decided not to tempt fate by discarding it on the most important night of his life. In a lilting Irish brogue, not diminished by 20 years training in England, he announced proudly that he had won over 1000 races in England, Scotland and Wales and now had achieved the pinnacle of any greyhound trainer's career. He described the whole adventure as a fairytale come true and the way half the world came up to wring him warmly by the hand, I gathered he was a very popular man.

I should point out that the usual prize for winning a run-of-the-mill race is a mere £55, which means a trainer or an owner either has to win a lot of races every year or else he has to hit the bookies with a vengeance from time to time. Whisper Wishes only joined Coyle's kennel in December and, since then, he had been treated in much the same way as the other 24 inmates who thrive near Lingfield in Surrey. I was amazed to learn from Charlie that walking plays a large role in the training of a greyhound and he will spend far more time each day walking than running. The dogs would walk for a good hour every morning and then return to the kennel for breakfast.

That meal consists of brown toasted bread with honey and glucose and a drink of milk. In the afternoon, the dogs would gallop 300 or 400 yards, sprinting to

someone and not chasing a hare or anything else. Charlie explained that if the traps opened on a race track and there was no hare, the dogs would still sprint round the track flat out. In the evening the dogs are fed their main meal of the day – chunks of chicken or a pound of the best red meat plus a few extra titbits including, sometimes, a bowl of soup. It was stressed quite forcibly that no tinned dog food would be used to train a thoroughbred greyhound.

Charlie loves his life and revels in the most successful period of his career as a trainer. He regrets that the sport is either in a recession or a gradual decline. He used to have an average of 10 dogs in his kennel every year but now he has 25 and admits that, although he can earn a living out of training greyhounds, the basic economics of the sport dictate that he will never be a rich man. He looked remarkably relaxed and happy when I left him, and also pretty fresh for someone who claimed he had recently only had a few hours' sleep each night with the worry and pressure of the Derby hanging over him.

There is no doubt that greyhound racing dips into a slight trough for the 11 months after the Derby and, whilst I enjoyed my night at the White City, I doubt I would ever go to watch greyhound racing again. Having said that, I appreciate the Greyhound Derby is the biggest night of the year for the dwindling army of greyhound supporters and fanatics, and they are fully entitled to their annual bonanza. It may have left me cold, but to the BBC's greyhound expert, Harry Carpenter, it was still a highly significant night in the sporting calendar. He claimed:

I look on it every year as one of my favourite television highlights. I believe that any sport at the very highest level is well worth watching. Anything that is the supreme event in a particular sport is worth watching, be it a men's singles final at Wimbledon, the last round of the British Open Golf Championship or a world heavyweight boxing title fight. On that basis, the Greyhound Derby is the supreme test of a dog, the pinnacle of its achievement and well worth its place in a list of great sporting events.

LORD'S TEST MATCH

The mecca and administrative home of cricket was founded by a Yorkshireman, Thomas Lord, who opened his first ground near Marylebone Station in 1787 (more sensibly placed for public transport than now). When the lease ran out in 1810 he was obliged to uproot to a new site at North Bank, only to find the Regent's Canal about to pass through his precincts. So in 1814 he moved Lord's yet again, a few hundred yards down the road. And apart from one serious disruption in 1888 when the Great Central Railway threatened to steam through the Nursery End, Lord's has rested secure on its present site ever since.

Lord himself was eventually bought out by a very fine MCC batsman, William Ward, who paid £5000 for the privilege. Ward only really made the ground his own in 1820, however, when he scored 278 against Norfolk on it, the highest score made there for over a century.

MCC, which evolved from the White Conduit Club, became owners of the freehold in 1866. In 1870 the heavy roller was dragged out for the first time, in the attempt to ensure the safety of players and gentlemen from uncertain bounces and facefuls of 'cherry'. Tragically, in June that year, there was an accident nevertheless. An MCC side which included W. G. Grace was being outplayed by Nottinghamshire, and Notts were set 157 to win in their second innings. A wicket fell and in came George Summers, a slender young man of 25, to face the bowling of nippy John Platts from Derbyshire. The ball got up sharply and struck the batsman in the face. Grace said of the bowler, 'I shall never forget his mental distraction,' because Platts broke down altogether when he saw what he had done. Four days after the match, Summers was dead. The ball is believed to have pitched on a tiny pebble.

In 1877, Middlesex became tenants of MCC and began playing 'at home' at Lord's. In 1890 the present pavilion, housing the famous Long Room, was built. Ironically, the cricketing administration presiding there, which objects so strongly to apartheid in South African sport, sees nothing amiss with the fact that women are banned from this and several other pavilions throughout the country, female cricketers notwithstanding.

The ground has many historic features, such as the Mound Stand, Grace Gates, Warner Stand and Grand Stand – with Father Time surveying play from the weathervane. Few spectators notice that the old boy is actually removing the bails, a *memento mori*. He has seen some memorable innings. The first century was made at Lord's by E. H. Budd, in 1816, but this was eclipsed by William Ward's 278, and in 1925 by Percy Holmes' 315 not out for Yorks against Middlesex. A year later the great Jack Hobbs went one better, with 316 not out. These are the only two triple-centuries ever scored at Lord's.

The first Test here began on 21 July 1884, making 1984 the centenary. The original match was a triumph for England by an innings and 5 runs. The Australians' first innings ended in some disarray with E. Peate having taken 6 for 85 and the Aussies totalling 229 (H. J. Scott 75, G. Giffen 63). England, helped by a towering 148 – the first Lord's Test ton – from A. G. Steele, put on 379 and then bowled Australia out for 145, G. Ulyett taking 7 for 36.

In every subsequent Test series held in England, at least one match has been played at Lord's. These have produced some electrifying performances. Don Bradman's 254 in 234 minutes in 1930 still brings tears to grown men's eyes, and Hedley Verity's 15-wicket haul in 1934 was much referred to in 1972, when Aussie seamer Bob Massie scuppered the England batting, taking 16 wickets in his début Test. Pictures appeared in the press of lip salve with suggestions that Massie might have applied it to the ball, though his real weapon was undoubtedly the vertical seam, leaving the batsmen in two minds. Even Hutton in his heyday was afraid of the vertical seam.

Other astonishing feats have included England's prodigious 503 runs in one day's play v. South Africa in 1924, and Bradman's Australians' record score of 729 for 6 declared in 1930. Altogether there have been 75 Lord's Tests. Bradman's 254 and Wally Hammond's 240 in 1938 remain landmarks among Test innings, and the 137,915 people who saw the 1953 England v. Australia Test set a record too.

The seventy-sixth Test Match at Lord's gave England a welcome chance to recover from the disasters of the previous six months, which had included Test defeats in New Zealand and Pakistan and an embarrassing annihilation in the First Test against the West Indies at Edgbaston. I spent most of Thursday, 28 June listening to the ball-by-ball commentary on BBC Radio Three to learn that England's batsmen were showing stiffer resistance against the fearsome West Indies pace attack of Joel Garner and Malcolm Marshall than they had done at Edgbaston.

Unfortunately, the weather disrupted play on the first day but England, despite losing 95 minutes through rain and bad light, had made a useful start. At the close of play, they were 167 for 2 with the red rose of Lancashire in the shape of Graeme Fowler very much to the fore. Fowler was 70 not out and Lamb 13 not out.

On the Friday morning, I arrived at Lord's at half past nine and went to the nets to watch the West Indies limber up and to chat with their captain, Clive Lloyd. I saw them indulge in a series of stretching exercises and do some running; it was easy to understand Clive's confidence in his team because their bowlers all display an incredible combination of athleticism and power and it was a great thrill to meet them and see them close up.

I have played and loved cricket from my early schooldays and, whenever my brother-in-law comes round to the house, we rustle up one or two friends and organize an impromptu game in the garden. I used to play league cricket for Chorley in the Northern League in Lancashire and I enjoyed it as much as our wicket-keeper, one Paul Mariner, the England international soccer player. The game is in my blood: my grandfather was a keen cricketer and became Chairman of the Northern League and my uncle was captain of Lancashire in 1962. Although I enjoy playing tennis and golf, I think that, after rugby, cricket is my favourite sport.

After leaving the nets on the Friday morning, I made my way to the box of a good friend of mine, Charles Robbins, the Chairman of the Middlesex Cricket Committee, and I spent much of a marvellous day out watching the cricket from there. The box was side-on to the pitch and I was staggered at the phenomenal speed of the ball through the air as Malcolm Marshall and Joel Garner ripped into the English middle-order batting. People may think rugby is a

rough, tough game but I would rather face the entire All Black pack on my own at Twickenham, or up a dark alley, than bat against these two black tornadoes. Up to that point, I had always fancied myself as a bit of a batsman but if I had been in the middle facing those bowlers I think the square-leg umpire would have found my backside in his face and he would have had to push me back towards the stumps. In future, I shall have to temper my criticism of batsmen who are out to lose shots against the West Indies pace attack because, watching them face the might of the West Indies attack, I reckoned television could have made a nice programme for their series called 'Survival'. Everything happens so quickly. I came to the conclusion that, somehow, watching at home, I have never fully appreciated the frightening delivery and speed of the great fast bowlers.

Live at Lord's, the impact was inescapable.

With the West Indian supporters tending to be less introverted than the typical MCC member, their appreciation of anything accomplished by their countrymen can usually be measured on the Richter scale; the banter and noise from the West Indian fans added greatly to the excitement of the occasion. With just over 26,000 crammed into Lord's on the Friday morning, the atmosphere was fantastic.

Having suffered on behalf of Fowler, Botham and the others for the whole of the morning session, I was very pleased to be invited up to the BBC Radio commentary box by the producer and the mastermind behind the ball-by-ball commentary team, Peter Baxter.

From their position, directly behind the bowler's arm straight down the pitch, I was

Lord's cricket ground in all its glory viewed from the nursery end during the Second Test

able to watch the afternoon session from a completely different angle and though the pace man still looked horrifically menacing, the effect was not quite as overpowering as it had been from the side. It was a pleasure to watch and listen to the radio team in action and, as I have always known, being an ardent member of their world-wide audience, their wit, repartee and critical analysis greatly enhance my enjoyment and understanding of the occasion. The doyen of broadcasters is undoubtedly Brian Johnston and I was delighted during the afternoon to have a long conversation with him about the Test series and Lord's as a venue.

With the sparkle and twinkle in his eyes clearly recapturing at once a thousand wonderful memories witnessed over the last 50 years, he said:

A Lord's Test Match is a unique experience for everyone. It is always a marvellous five days for me, from the moment I walk in through the Grace Gates and meet a quorum of old England cricketers standing chatting in the shadow of the stand to the moment when stumps are drawn at the close on the final day. I know where all my old chums will be having their refreshments or picnics and I love every day, when I'm not doing the commentary for a session, to stroll right round the ground. It takes me about an hour and everybody greets me and asks me how I am and what I think about this batsman or that bowler, earnestly seeking my opinion and then, like as not, telling me I'm a hundred per cent wrong. But the people are kind and friendly and generous and I meet so many old chums in the most unlikely circumstances, either queuing at the souvenir shop, or the hamburger van or the loo, or the sweet shop or trying to buy a scorecard or a lottery ticket or sneaking in or out of the Ladbroke's betting

Ian Botham
celebrates as
Mike Gatting
catches Gomes

tent or the Tavern bar. It's all action and all full of interest.

Of course, the pitch itself is unique because of its famous slope and sometimes I immerse myself in its history by standing in the Long Room which lies between the players' changing rooms and the pitch and through which and along which all the great cricketers of the world, right through the whole history of the game, have strode on their way to the crease, or crawled along on their way back. It evokes hundreds and hundreds of wonderful memories and it is mind-boggling to think of all the great moments of cricketing folklore that have been seen by the MCC member standing in the Long Room in the last hundred years. The place simply buzzes with history, tradition and marvellous memories.

The atmosphere is so overwhelming that David Steele, the England batsman, in his first Test at Lord's, left the England changing-room to go in to bat, walked down one flight of stairs to the entrance of the Long Room but, instead of entering, he continued down one other flight of stairs straight into the gents loo where he prepared to take guard. Poor chap was hopelessly lost and nearly broke the two-minute rule before someone found him and pointed him in the right direction. The sense of history in the Long Room is all round you and, when a batsman comes back like Fowler after his Test century today, you get a feeling staring at the countless portraits round the wall of the past great men of England, the Lord Hawkes, the Plum Warners, and the others all looking down, that they have given their approval of the successful player's great deeds. But when poor Mike Gatting came in after his duck, the eyes on the paintings somehow all seemed to be looking in another direction.

Brian first covered a Test at Lord's for the BBC in 1946 when India were the visitors, and he hasn't missed a Lord's Test since. Brian reckoned that watching Garner, who seems about nine feet tall rocketing in to bowl, must rate as one of the most formidable and intimidating sights he has ever seen. From his skyscraper height, he injects not only blistering speed but sharp, wicked bounce, as well. He compares Garner's ferocity with that of Wes Hall 20 years ago. He feels Marshall is equally lethal and facing Michael Holding is not his idea of a Sunday-afternoon picnic. He reveres the

West Indies skipper Clive Lloyd steers the ball through the close field at Lord's

incredible batting skills of Richards but implores schoolboys not to try to follow suit, because only an undiluted genius could do what the unorthodox Richards does so brilliantly. Brian has great respect for Don Bradman as an amazing accumulator of runs but concludes that the South African Barry Richards is probably the best batsman he has ever seen. Unfortunately, he has been precluded from playing Test cricket, but there have been enough other highlights to keep Brian Johnston purring endlessly with satisfaction. He said with conviction:

The best match I ever saw was the 1963 game against the West Indies which ended in a draw. Colin Cowdrey broke his arm in that match but came in to bat to join David Allen who was

facing, with two balls to go, as the last man in and six runs needed for victory. It was classic, enthralling stuff. In that final, pulsating climax everything was possible – an England win, a West Indies win, a tie, a draw. On each of the five days the match seesawed with both teams constantly experiencing contrasting fortunes, and that match remains etched on my memory for eternity.

The best innings I ever saw is an impossible question but, if pushed, I would settle for Wally Hammond's two hundred and forty against Australia at Lord's in 1938. There again, I saw Percy Chapman in 1930 make a brilliant hundred and twenty-one against Australia, also at Lord's, hitting twelve fours and Charlie Grimmett's flighted deliveries for four sixes; and I marvelled at Everton Weekes, covered in bruises and in some pain making over ninety for the West Indies against England. And Dexter's knock in that 1963 Test wasn't a bad little innings. Crikey, I could go on all day, I've seen so many great innings.

Little did we know it on the Friday, but we were soon to see yet another, on the Tuesday, when Gordon Greenidge hit his double century at a run a minute to win the Test; on the second day, however, the talk was confined to Marshall and Garner. That fine England all-rounder Trevor Bailey was also in the BBC commentary box and he supported the general view that the West Indies opening attack has had few equals:

Marshall is probably the quickest bowler in the world, and Garner is probably the best. Holding is still a fine bowler but no longer the menace he was on the last tour while Baptiste and Small are not yet quite Test Match class. There is no doubt that this is a very strong West Indian pace attack but I believe England have had to face slightly better balanced attacks in the past fifty years. I think the last West Indies tour was better with Holding, Roberts and Daniels and, going back further, Hall, Griffiths and Sobers were a dangerous threesome. I would also have to mention the great Australian trio of Ray Lindwall, Keith Miller and Bill Johnston, which was extremely strong. The strength of these teams was that they each had at least a three-pronged attack with one outstanding spin bowler lurking in the background. This West Indies team rely almost exclusively on just their two opening bowlers.

As a quick bowler himself, I asked Trevor to sum up the threat the current England batsmen faced. 'Garner is the major threat because his unusual height means the ball is being delivered at fierce pace from an unaccustomed height and trajectory. In consequence, he extracts tremendous bounce out of even a good length delivery and, to all these advantages, he adds control and discipline. Marshall and Holding are more straightforward; they are just fast – very, very fast.'

I also spoke to another outstanding former England Test star, Tom Graveney, about the best way to play Garner and Marshall, and he said they would have presented him with terrible problems because he preferred to play off his front foot and these two tearaways should probably be played off the back foot. At lunch on the Saturday, it was the turn of one of England's best opening batsmen, Sir Len Hutton, to put Garner and Marshall in perspective:

I would definitely put them into the best ten fast bowlers of all time but not, I think, in the top six, although I have to confess that Garner might just squeeze into that illustrious company. I would put Keith Miller in his day and in the mood at the top of the list with Ray Lindwall and Dennis Lillee not far behind. I think Brian Statham would deserve a place in the top ten for his incredible consistency and accuracy and Fred Trueman might just make it as well. At their best, Michael Holding and Charlie Griffiths were worthy of inclusion too, although whether they would be better than Joel Garner I am not convinced. My one criticism of the current West Indies pace men is the number of short-pitched deliveries they bowl. In my view, a good batsman should never get out to a short-pitched ball because he has the opportunity to see it through the air and off the pitch, whereas a good length up to the bat he can only see through the air.

Warming to his theme, he confessed he would love to be out in the middle, squaring up to Garner and Marshall because, as he said, 'There's no future in getting old.'

By lunch on that Saturday, the match was delicately poised. England had ended their first innings midway through Friday at 286 with Fowler making 106, Chris Broad in his first Test a highly commendable 55 and Ian Botham a useful 30. By the close of play the West Indies, who lost Gordon Greenidge, Desmond Haynes and Larry Gomes for 35, recovered well to finish at 119 for 3 with Viv Richards 60 not out and Clive Lloyd 32 not out. The morning session on the Saturday was highlighted by the controversial dismissal of Richards, lbw to Botham for 72. The umpire who made that decision, Barry Mayer, admitted in private to Viv Richards during the weekend that, on reflection, he was probably wrong and he apologized for his mistake. Unfortunately, the story leaked out and made newspaper headlines on the Monday. I think it was brave and honourable of Mayer to admit his error and apologize because we are all fallible and can make mistakes and there is nothing to be ashamed of afterwards. I wonder how many soccer or rugby referees or tennis umpires would admit, after watching a video re-run, that perhaps they were wrong. At any ratc by lunch, with Richards and Lloyd both out, the odds were tilting slightly in England's favour.

By mid-afternoon, they were all out for 245 – 41 behind England with Ian Botham returning the superb figures of 27 overs, 8 wickets for 103 runs. England ended the day at 114 for 4 in the second innings and the fifty-seventh wicket stand between Alan Lamb and Ian Botham continued to flourish on the Monday. By the time they had taken the score from 88 for 4 late on Saturday to 216 for 5 on Monday, they had steered England into a winning position on which they failed to capitalize. After Botham was lbw to Garner for a magnificent 81, England seemed to lose a little faith in their ability to actually beat the apparently unbeatable West Indies.

It is easy to be an armchair critic but I have to question the decision of Alan Lamb, in full flow, and Derek Pringle to appeal successfully against the bad light on the Monday evening. A critical hour's play was lost and England would surely have been better to bat on in the gathering gloom. If a wicket had fallen, that would have been the time for Gower to consider encouraging the new batsman to appeal against the light.

A flurry of activity on the final morning led Gower to declare at 300 for 9, leaving the West Indies to chase a mammoth task of 343 in five and a half hours. England were soon deluded into a fool's paradise when Haynes was run out for 17 with the score at 57. But that was to prove England's solitary moment of ecstasy. The rest of the day was a story of uninterrupted agony. Gordon Greenidge was in rampant, dynamic form and carved the England bowlers, Botham and Willis especially, to shreds as he raced to a scintillating 214 not out. Larry Gomes ended the match on 92 not out and the West Indies won by 9 wickets with time to spare. For England's players the final day, which promised so much, must have been very

dispiriting, depressing and soul-destroying and I have every sympathy for them. On the other hand, the play of the West Indies and their bold aggressive policy of attack will linger in the memory for many a long day.

The following week I met up with Clive Lloyd and we looked back together on the Lord's game. He told me:

I have played cricket on every Test ground in the world but at the end of the day, Lord's is the true home of cricket. It is the dream of every cricketer in the world with any ambition, be he English or West Indian, New Zealander or Australian, Pakistani or Indian, to play at Lord's, and I know that the special, magical atmosphere there brings out the very best in everyone. I know that I have always done well there, leading the West Indies to World Cup triumphs in the final, once against England and once against Australia, to a Test Match win over England and also for Lancashire in the Gillette Cup Final.

As Wembley is to football and Twickenham is to rugby, so Lord's is the home of cricket. Just like the 1963 game at Lord's, the 1984 match was one of the greatest that has ever been played. It had all the ingredients of an epic encounter with the pendulum swinging non-stop until lunch on the final day. I felt England played really well for four days but then, when it mattered most, their bowling let them down. Ian Botham had a fantastic match and, up until the last day, gave the performance of a lifetime, but he finished the final day with bowling figures of twenty overs, no wickets for a hundred and seventeen runs. But there was nothing anyone could have done to stop Gordon Greenidge. He produced one of the all-time great innings, especially when you remember it came on a well-worn pitch in the fourth innings on the fifth day. He attacked incessantly, played a huge range of audacious strokes and yet, in nearly five hours, hardly gave a chance, such was his control and skill.

Funnily enough, I was always confident we would get the runs at the time though, in retrospect, I realize what a tremendous challenge it was. No side in history has done as well in the fourth innings of a Test Match and the credit must go to Greenidge and Larry Gomes for rewriting the record books, rather than blaming the England bowlers for a substandard effort. Having said that, if I had been the England captain, I would have been bitterly upset and annoyed at the way his bowlers fell apart and failed to produce a good line or length for most of the final day. I would have demanded that they kept the ball up and made it as hard as possible to score runs without taking real risks. But the truth is that England are short of top-class Test bowlers at the moment and this West Indian side is clearly the best in the world at the present time. We have beaten Australia handsomely and now England and, although it is arguable the 1963 West Indies side was as good or even better, it has been a thrill for me to lead the 1984 side and to win such a fabulous game in my last Test appearance at Lord's.

Clive felt that England probably ought to have batted on during Monday evening even in the failing light, but somehow I got the idea that he thought his lads were going to win whatever England did. However, that was not the impression I got from Ian Botham when we looked back over the game. He said he thought at the time that England were wrong to declare on the Tuesday morning, and they should have prolonged their innings until lunch to ensure the match could not conceivably have ended in a West Indian win. He argued that the psychological fillip an honourable draw would have given England was exactly what was desperately needed. The last thing they needed was another defeat, particularly one so exquisitely fashioned by two outstanding batsmen at the peak of their powers.

What I think a lot of people don't understand is that the English were always going to struggle on the final day because the wicket was playing as well as ever and the West Indian batsmen, having failed in the first innings, were going to make damn certain they didn't fail again. In fairness, too, it should be stressed that we had fought against the odds to a standstill, to reach a position of equality on the final morning, but our bowlers were in no state, physically or mentally, to bowl the West Indies out. I know I was feeling tired and jaded from two important innings which I had played on the Friday, on the Saturday evening and most of Monday, and I had bowled twenty-seven overs flat out on the Friday and Saturday. I bowled another twenty overs on the Tuesday but, hard though I concentrated, it was a losing battle trying to find the line and length to contain, let alone dismiss, Greenidge in full flight. Once he had played himself in it was impossible to know where to pitch the ball to force him to defend and, by midafternoon, even if I had known precisely where I wanted to pitch the ball, I doubt honestly that I was capable of accomplishing such a feat six times every over. You have to remember that one or two wayward deliveries each over and four excellent deliveries still meant 8 runs an over to Greenidge, or possibly 4 runs an over to Gomes. It was a dreadful, insoluble predicament. It is all too easy to sit in an ivory tower and criticize the English bowlers for an appalling display, but first it is important to

Gordon Greenidge, the West Indian match winner in the Second Test flays the England bowling on his way to 214 not out and a remarkable victory

examine the background.

I share Ian Botham's view that he and his colleaues were on a hiding to nothing. He told me that he knows bowlers who have sleepless nights wondering how they are going to bowl, where they are going to pitch the ball to try to dismiss or, at least, contain, Greenidge, Viv Richards, Clive Lloyd and Larry Gomes. It is like saying to John Lloyd: Why did you not keep breaking McEnroe's serve if you wanted to win? Or telling Nick Faldo if Tom Watson shoots a round of 66: you should do a 65.

Ian continued:

Some things in life are easier said than done. The main problem was that early on we probably tried too hard to bowl them out on the Tuesday and, by the time we wanted to slow them down, Greenidge and Gomes were unstoppable. I know it sounds negative but by the start of the afternoon session we should have been thinking solely of survival, rather than harbouring hopes of an elusive victory. By the time we came to terms with reality, it was too late. It is also easy to say we should have made more runs, but when you have three of the fastest bowlers in the world hurling the ball at you at over ninety miles an hour you have about four-tenths of a second to react and you end up playing more or less by instinct. I think the Second Test was a very exciting match but, inevitably, from our team's point of view it was frustrating to see the game finally slipping out of our reach. I reckon our two Tests against the last Australian team at Old Trafford and Headingley were even better matches, but this Lord's Test was still a great game of cricket.

I was amazed after the final day's play how the pundits had the gall to criticize Botham and I hate to think how England would have fared in this match without him. I don't think people appreciate just what a superb cricketer he is and how he is the backbone of English cricket in the eighties. His workload in a five-day Test is astronomic and I have always admired him greatly for his incredible natural talent and fierce determination. Those critics without a quarter of his ability would be well advised to keep a diplomatic silence. There are no better all-rounders in world cricket just now.

Nevertheless, there was one 27 years ago in 1957 on the last occasion England beat the West Indies at Lord's in a Test Match. Trevor Bailey was the hero of the hour, mesmerizing the visitors in the first innings with some destructive pace bowling taking 7 for 44 as the West Indies collapsed to 127 all out. In reply, England made 424 with Colin Cowdrey making 152 and Godfrey Evans 82. England went on to win by an innings and 36 runs as they dismissed the West Indies for 261 with Bailey the best bowler, taking 4 for 54. I asked Trevor what he remembered of that game and he replied that he knew England had won but that was all. He could not recall a single one of the 11 wickets he had taken, although he had a hunch Cowdrey made some runs. I wonder if I'll remember anything about England's rugby Grand Slam in 1980 in 27 years time – an English rugby triumph about as frequent as Test wins against the West Indies at Lord's.

Consequently, I wondered if it was a bit depressing for Brian Johnston, watching England's cricketers fail so often. 'No, not really, at least not any more. When you get old like me, after fifty years following the game, you really learn to love the game for its own sake and nowadays I just love watching great players playing well. I used to mind terribly, of course, and I used to blub a bit when England lost, but now I just accept it and instead I admire and respect the likes of Garner bowling or Greenidge or Richards batting or whoever it happens to be.'

Finally, I wondered, to a man steeped in a lifetime of cricket and one who obviously loves and savours every moment of it, I popped a hypothetical question. I asked Brian: What would he do if the secretary of the MCC came up to him and said, 'It's been lovely seeing you at Lord's for the last fifty years but I'm afraid we've had a complaint and we can't let you into this ground ever again'? Without a moment's hesitation Brian replied, 'If for some obscure reason I was forbidden to enter the Grace Gates, then I would simply have to climb over the wall which would be a trifle undignified at my age but I couldn't possibly miss a Test Match at Lord's while there's breath left in my body. It's quite unthinkable, isn't it?'

The sight English batsmen feared most this summer – Joel Garner thundering in to bowl

THE WIMBLEDON CHAMPIONSHIPS

'Anyone for croquet?' was what members of the All-England Club used to say when it was formed in 1870 at its old Worple Road site. They had heard about the new-fangled lawn game 'Sphairistike', popularized by Major Walter Wingfield and derived from the ancient indoor game of 'real' or royal tennis, but considered it a flash in the pan. Still, they did need to raise cash for their croquet and the All-England Club decided to hold a lawn tennis championship for this purpose.

The first final was staged on Thursday, 19 July 1877, at 4.30 p.m. The weather was filthy, but 200 spectators paid one shilling to watch the 'Men's Single-Handed Championship of the World'. This is still inscribed on the trophy, though nobody disqualified Swede Björn Borg for winning it with a double-handed backhand. Old Harrovian Spencer Gore, using the then-orthodox sliced underarm side service and reaching over the net to volley, beat William Marshall for the first title 6–1, 6–2, 6–4. The net was 3 feet 3 inches at the centre and rose to 5 feet at the posts, so all Gore had to do was to patrol the sagging middle. The new champion thought tennis boring, and wrote that it wouldn't catch on for 'want of variety'.

In 1878, another Old Harrovian, P. F. Hadow, thought he'd have a go at the Championships whilst on leave from the coffee plantations in Ceylon. Every time Gore approached the net to take his volleying position, Hadow simply lobbed the ball over his head. Hadow won 7–5, 6–1, 9–7 and returned to Ceylon without giving another thought to tennis. It was a spectacular year, though. A. T. Myers had shocked everybody by using an overarm service in the Championships for the first time.

The following year was even more exciting: the final was won by a man of the cloth, in the person of Canon J. T. Hartley, who trounced 'St Leger' 6–2, 6–4, 6–2. The losing finalist, on closer inspection, turned out to be Vere Thomas St Leger Goold. He and his wife were later arrested for humping two trunks around Europe containing the dismembered remains of a Madame Levin, and were charged with murder.

Next came the reign of the Renshaws. Twins William and Ernest really stirred things up playing each other in the challenge round of 1882 because, apart from giving spectators double vision, they also brought to tennis all the elements of the 'modern' game: fierce volleying, speed, elegance and the smash. William fairly blasted poor Canon Hartley off the lawn in record time – 37 minutes – to win the 1881 title. William went on to win seven times in all; Ernest won it once, in 1888. Good as he was, Willie

Renshaw did enjoy the advantage of a challenge system, which operated until 1922, whereby the previous year's winner went straight into the final to meet the winner of the challenge tournament.

Women first took part in 1884, the year the men's doubles was introduced. Maud Watson beat her sister Lilian in the final, 6–8, 6–3, 6–3. In 1887 the title went to Charlotte 'Lottie' Dod, at the age of 15. Lottie wouldn't be allowed to compete under current rules, the minimum age now being 16, but at all events she was bored with pat-ball tennis and said the best women players were 'learning to volley more'.

The age of the Doherty Brothers, 1897–1906, made tennis famous at home and abroad. Reggie (R.F.) and Laurie (H.L.) won the doubles eight times, and the singles four and five times respectively. They had been the game's first great ambassadors, and in 1907 all the Wimbledon titles went overseas. In 1913 the 'Californian Comet' Maurice McLoughlin lost the final to Anthony Wilding, but the Comet brought to Wimbledon a power service that was to change the game forever.

The Championships were becoming a crowd-puller. In 1919 the annual ballot for tickets had to be introduced and on 26 June 1922 the All-England Lawn Tennis and Croquet Club moved to larger premises at Church Road – its home today. In 1924 seeding was necessary for the overseas entries and in 1927 full seeding was introduced. The Championships even had a royal competitor, with the future King George VI playing in the doubles in 1926. The superstars of the day, though, were Mlle Suzanne Lenglen and 'Big Bill' Tatem Tilden.

Lenglen moved acrobatically, like a ballerina, and wore a wide bandeau. She had beaten seven–times champion Dorothea Lambert Chambers 10–8, 4–6, 9–7, saving a couple of match points and she caused a sensation whenever she played. So did American Tilden, who virtually owned men's tennis in the 1920s and whose stage presence and all-court command frightened his opponents half to death. From France came the 'Musketeers' – René Lacoste,

Henri Cochet and Jean Borotra, christened the 'Bounding Basque' because he was always leaping up to the net to volley in his black beret.

The pre-World War II era ushered in Ellsworth Vines, with his terrific 128 m.p.h. service, Don Budge, also of America, and Jack Crawford of Australia. One Briton, though, had the measure of them, and 1984 happens to be the fiftieth anniversary of the first of his three consecutive men's singles titles – Fred Perry. A bronze statue commemorating Fred's reign now stands in Wimbledon's grounds (Fred wanted it overlooking the ladies' dressing-room if possible) – a testimony to the last great British man of tennis, who might have strung together many more Wimbledon titles had he not been obliged to turn professional.

The post-War years have seen many changes and many champions. Jack Kramer, the American player who made a million; Maureen 'Little Mo' Connolly, whose brilliant career was cut short by a riding accident; the Harry Hopman-coached Australians, Rod Laver, Ken Rosewall and Lew Hoad, who turned toughness into an art. John Newcombe, the last of the Aussie conquerors, won in 1970 and 1971, with Margaret Court lifting weights and devastating opponents in the sheilas' game. Women's tennis has seen startling variations of style, from Evonne Cawley's athletic grace to Chris Evert-Lloyd's precision and Martina Navratilova's all-court power. But the record for most women's titles – 20 between 1961 and 1979 – is held by Billie Jean King, an entrepreneur who made women's tennis big business.

The modern era had really dawned in 1968, the year of the first Wimbledon 'open' Championships for amateurs and professionals which swept away under-the-counter payments and years of 'shamateurism'. In 1969 pro Pancho Gonzales beat non-pro Charlie Pasarell, 16 years his junior, 22–24, 1–6, 16–14, 6–3, 11–9, 112 games in 312 minutes – the longest match ever. The tie-break was introduced in 1971. The following year saw one of the greatest finals of them all: between ramrod-straight serve-and-volley

A study in the explosive power of John McEnroe

American Stan Smith, and Romanian genius Ilie Nastase, whose eloquence with a racket and fractious on-court behaviour set something of a precedent. Nastase became at once an idol and a villain, and Wimbledon's traditional gentility has never fully recovered from his passions.

The role of hero and villain has now been taken over by John McEnroe – the brilliantly, almost indecently, gifted but sadly undisciplined current world number one. In June 1984 he had been unable to conceal his disappointment and anguish at losing to Ivan Lendl in the final of the French championships in Paris:

That final definitely took something out of me, mentally and physically. Mentally, I really wanted to win that match and I'm really frustrated because a lot of things went wrong and everything went in the opposite way to what I had planned. I had so many opportunities to win, that makes it even harder. If I'd lost easily it might have been easier to bounce back, but knowing that I really should have won and feeling I lost because I just choked a little bit and the heat got to me was upsetting. I just got anxious and then I started getting a bit uptight.

In England he began the build-up to the Wimbledon Championships by capturing all the headlines on both the front and back pages of the daily papers for his behaviour, outrageous even by his standards, at the Stella Artois tournament at Queen's Club on the day of the final. The trouble erupted when his opponent, fellow American Leif Shiras, was 4-2 ahead in the second set. McEnroe had a chance to break back in the next game but on game point the umpire, Roger Smith, overruled a lineswoman's call in McEnroe's favour. McEnroe exploded to provide the large crowd with one of the most disgraceful scenes I can recall at a major sporting event in recent times. First, he called the umpire a 'moron' and initially he refused to play on. He demanded, and got, an audience with the referee Jim Moore and Grand Prix supervisor Kurt Neilsen, and when they declined to instruct the umpire to change his decision he lost his cool completely. 'You guys sit here like two bums

on a log and say nothing because some idiot in the chair sits there and does nothing,' exclaimed the enraged McEnroe. He later directed a four-letter obscenity directly at his opponent, made some unworthy retorts to hecklers in the crowd and summed up his feelings towards the umpire when he complained, 'There's a thousand officials to choose from, and I get a moron like you.' McEnroe lost that set but won the match comfortably enough in the end. With typical lack of gallantry, he refused to shake hands with the umpire.

I suspect that even McEnroe was surprised and possibly taken aback at the reaction of the national papers, radio and television. Quite rightly, they lambasted him and, miraculously, the message seemed to penetrate his thicker than average skin. If he had been a rugby player at international level and carried on the way he did at Queen's, he would probably have been suspended for a season or, with a bad track record, even banned for life and I think it is essential that no player ever becomes too big for a sport. I'm afraid I found his behaviour quite unforgivable and inexcusable.

His ultimate victory at Wimbledon exactly three weeks later, cheered on by the great British public and admired and respected by the whole world, has to be seen against the background of turmoil at Queen's Club and his defeat by Lendl. The complete transformation in his character and behaviour and his uncanny ability to reach sheer perfection in the men's singles final at Wimbledon encapsulate the remarkable story of a remarkable man.

It is a pleasure to record that at Wimbledon he conformed and, furthermore, up to the final he produced some top-class tennis. He swept aside all comers with apparently effortless ease and, when the occasional doubtful call was given against him, he reacted with perfect decorum. In the other half of the draw the number three seed, Jimmy Connors, emerged victorious over the second seed Ivan Lendl, a man more suited to clay courts than the grass of Wimbledon. The public then had the head-to-head confrontation they wanted – John McEnroe against Jimmy Connors. By the

Martina Navratilova, all power, poise and timing

time the battle-hardened combatants had walked onto Centre Court shortly before two o'clock on Sunday 8 July, there had been a cluster of highlights which I feel are worth recording.

Not just because of George Orwell's forebodings, but also because the ladies were celebrating their Wimbledon Centenary, 1984 was a very special year. In 1884 Henry Jones persuaded the fellow members of the committee of the All-England Club to allow ladies to compete in their own championship. The game is a lot faster today than it was then, but the skills are the same, and it was a rare treat on the second Monday of the Championships to have a parade of lady champions on Centre Court. This moving ceremony was conducted by the 'voice of tennis', BBC television commentator Dan Maskell, who introduced each of the 17 former champions in attendance. They then trod a path across the famous Centre Court where, down through history, they had recorded their great moment or moments of triumph, to be introduced to the Duke of Kent, President of the All-England Club, accompanied by the Duchess of Kent, and to be presented with a unique Waterford crystal glass to mark the occasion. Martina Navratilova was the first called forward as the most recent winner and, in reverse order, the crowd gave a warm response to Chris Lloyd, Evonne Cawley, Billie Jean King and Margaret Court, with more prolonged applause for the three post-War English winners, Virginia Wade, Ann Jones and Angela Mortimer. With the imagination winging back on a time machine, there were several nostalgic moments as Maria Bueno and Althea Gibson strode boldly forward, followed by Doris Hart and the legendary Louise Brough, and further back still to the pre-War days of the 1939 champion Alice Marble. Finally, saving the best moment to last, Dan Maskell summoned forth the grand old lady of women's tennis, the English girl who won Wimbledon 60 years ago, in 1924 and again in 1926, Kitty Godfree. To the resounding cheers and applause of everyone present this sprightly, fit 88-year-old who still plays tennis regularly at the Queen's Club, marched up to receive her memento.

The ceremony over, with a final flourish these 17 champions did a lap of honour before departing from the most celebrated tennis arena in the world, almost all of them for the very last time.

Happily, I was able to catch up with Kitty Godfree and chat to her briefly about the Wimbledon Championships over the years. She was the most delightful and charming lady and the possessor of a lively mind and an excellent memory. When she won the Wimbledon titles in 1924 and 1926, she received a voucher worth a few pounds to be exchanged for goods at Mappin and Webb the famous jewellers still going strong today. However, she does not grudge the colossal money which the top players earn nowadays:

The biggest single difference between 1924 and 1984 is the prize money – I received five pounds and Martina Navratilova will receive eighty-nine thousand, nine hundred and ninety-five pounds more than that. The game is still more or less the same. The strokes, the forehand and backhand, down the line or cross-court, the lob, the volley and the half-volley, the serve, the basic style are all just the same sixty years on, although I must admit the modern players are bigger, stronger and faster than we were, producing more powerful tennis. But the technique is the same and the good players of the twenties like the good players of the eighties all had a sound technique.

Kitty is glad she played in the era she did because she doubts she would have had the patience and inclination to have been a full-time professional. 'I think the players, men and women, take the sport too seriously now, and a lot of the enormous fun we had and the pure enjoyment we got from tennis has disappeared from the sport. I feel the game nowadays is measured by the stars in the dollars they earn rather than the fun and satisfaction they receive and that is a pity, isn't it?'

Looking back through the years and making allowances for the vastly improved equipment the modern players use – better racquets, balls, shoes – she felt three players are on a pedestal out of reach of mere mortals.

Martina Navratilova is absolutely brilliant and a phenomenally powerful player. For

**The world's
number one
player with the
world's number
one prize**

*sheer grace, style and artistry I would single
out Maria Bueno who just seemed to glide
across a court. And from my own playing era
I would suggest that Suzanne Lenglen, a born
entertainer, a real prima donna, a magical
director and a wonderfully athletic, aesthetic
player, the darling of the Roaring Twenties,
would have been as good as any of the modern stars.*

Kitty could find little fault with the play
of Navratilova on her way to the final. She
overpowered and overwhelmed everyone in
double-quick time and it was easy to
understand why she was red-hot favourite to
win the title for the third successive year, a
rare feat achieved by only three players in the
last 50 years – Louise Brough, Maureen
Connolly and Billie Jean King. In the final
she met Chris Lloyd and had to play her very
best tennis for the first time in the
Championships to take the opening set to a
tie-breaker. Mrs Lloyd had hit her best form
and stretched the champion to the limit
before succumbing 7-6. The intense effort
and concentration required for that supreme
but unsuccessful battle for domination
seemed to drain her emotionally and

physically, and her resistance was broken.
The second set was a formality – 6–2 in barely
half an hour.

Martina Navratilova, the queen of world
tennis, had retained her crown with another
majestic performance. At the moment she is
the best in the world and seemingly
invincible – just as John McEnroe totally
dominates men's tennis. His clash with
Jimmy Connors promised to be a hard-
fought classic but it turned out to be a one-
sided romp.

This was my third visit to Wimbledon in
the past four years but, at the risk of being
accused of name-dropping, this was the first
year I hadn't been invited to the Royal Box.
However, I managed to secure an excellent
seat at the back of the court, high-up, with an
excellent view, right under the BBC box.
The atmosphere is like the old Roman amphitheatre with 14,000 people packed round the
court, all within earshot of the two gladiators.

Just two years before, Connors had won
Wimbledon, beating McEnroe in the final;
for a man whose reputation has been built
on his tremendous fighting qualities, his
total capitulation was completely unexpected. The opening game was an ominous
portent of what was to follow. McEnroe won
it without conceding a point and produced
blistering aces of such awesome speed and
power, and so skilfully angled, that Connors
must have been trembling in his shoes. I was
staggered by the speed and depth of the
McEnroe service. Apart from McEnroe's ten
clean aces, Connors was often at full stretch
just to return the ball, allowing McEnroe to
storm to the net and ruthlessly, mercilessly
punch away winning volleys. Connors was
hopelessly outgunned, and lost in only 1
hour, 20 minutes to the most comprehensive defeat in a men's final at Wimbledon
since Donald Budge beat Bunny Austin in
1938. And it may well be another 46 years
before the Centre Court at Wimbledon
witnesses another performance of such
brilliant artistry and total domination as this
genius McEnroe provided in 1984. It was a
totally captivating and breathtaking display
which will live in people's memory for a very,
very long time. Dan Maskell rated it the best
single performance he had ever seen, and

Chatting to Lord Scarman at Wimbledon before he spent the afternoon in the Royal Box

great former champions like Fred Perry and the Frenchman Jean Barota were not disposed to disagree. The general feeling among punters and experts alike, was that no one had ever come closer to tennis perfection on Centre Court than John McEnroe in the 1984 final.

Afterwards, I suppose typically, McEnroe was not inclined to underestimate his own achievement, claiming:

I think this was perhaps the greatest match I ever played. I served about seventy-five per cent of first serves in and I just felt real good from the back of the court and at the net. I got a few breaks, a few let calls and I thought Jimmy looked a bit slow out there. My game plan was to be aggressive and to come in on his serve if he stayed back, and it looked as if he knew that was going to happen because he was serving and volleying quite a bit more than he normally would have. It was really unbelievable, I can't put it into words, everything just worked out wonderfully.

Whilst the public simply accept his all-round genius on court, the player himself explained that he had analysed his game and made considerable improvement since he lost to Connors at Wimbledon in 1982:

I have recaptured some of the aggression which was missing, worked hard on my serve and volley, and I started a couple of years back to play a little too much in the back court and certainly, against Jimmy, that is not the best way to play. I think I'm getting better all the time and that is my aim – to get as close to my potential as I can possibly get. This year I went out there and really played well but if I had had an off day and Jimmy had started getting into it then anything could have happened.

The fact was he played almost as well in winning the first two sets against Ivan Lendl in the final of the French championships in Paris four weeks earlier, but then hit a bad patch and could merely tread water as Lendl recovered to win the next three sets and the title.

Had that haunting memory been on his mind during the Wimbledon final? McEnroe admitted:

It definitely crossed my mind. I didn't feel as if I was playing quite so well in Paris and certainly my serve was not going so well, and on clay it is

I wonder how many more times the name of McEnroe will appear on the Wimbledon Trophy

harder to stay in the groove when you feel everything is going right. But here Connors and I knew it was a different surface, grass is very different and, unlike Paris, I never thought I would feel tired if the game went to four sets. In fact, I believe that when I'm playing well grass could be my best surface though personally I like to play indoors in a supreme court. But the thing is when I get my serve working as I did here, grass really suits me. I mean Jimmy is the best returner of serve in the game, and he never really came close to breaking me.

It seemed to me that the manner and style of McEnroe's victory was what pleased him. 'What surprised me most was the fact that it seemed as if I overpowered Connors, which is something I haven't done that often. I hit the ball harder than he did in the rallies, I served a lot harder than he did and, in all the times we've played, that could be the first or, at most, second time I've hit the ball consistently harder than him, and I completely overpowered him.' Oddly enough, even when playing such regal tennis, McEnroe was still aware it could all slip away as it had done in Paris:

It was a nice feeling to be out there, to be playing well and to be two sets up, but I was still worried that I might relax and that, if he could get back into the match at any time, he is one of the greatest fighters of all time and who knows what would have happened. The fact is I continued the momentum in the third set and that made me feel terrific. Wimbledon is a great forum if you are playing well, and it is great being out there when you are playing great tennis, but I also know it is a nightmare when you are playing badly.

It is an awesome thought that McEnroe believes there is more improvement in him yet and, although with his third Wimbledon win he is catching up fast on Bjorn Borg's five titles in the late seventies, he realizes it will get harder not easier to keep his grip on the trophy. 'There are good young players coming through now, and I think that it is good for the game when new names appear and new young guys emerge to challenge the established players. I think it could get ineresting in the next couple of years if guys like Pat Cash the Australian, and Mats Wilander of Sweden continue to fulfil their potential.'

Perhaps, for me, the most gratifying

aspect of the whole fortnight was the fact that John McEnroe behaved impeccably throughout, not just on his way to winning the singles but also en route to his men's doubles victory with Peter Fleming. After his various tantrums and outbursts in England during the last three or four years it was a pleasure to see him in control of his emotions and so perfectly disciplined. It was fascinating to hear him afterwards talking about his behaviour. He explained:

I felt a bit bad about winning that easily because people are going to say, 'Well, because he won that easily that is the reason he was able to control himself.' So there's no way I can win in a situation like that. I played the greatest match I have ever played and there were a couple of debatable decisions I felt, but certainly the way I was playing there was no reason to get angry and I wasn't going to anyway. However, in a way, I wanted to have a close match and show that in a close match as well as one that isn't close, I could keep control. I felt pretty relaxed out there on Centre Court, as relaxed as I have ever felt in a tournament. I felt when I got out there on court, that was the one place that nobody could really do anything to me any more and that, if I didn't say anything, they would just have to watch the way I played tennis and it worked out well, because it was a nightmare the previous couple of weeks.

Not surprisingly, the furious reaction to his behaviour at Queen's Club in the papers affected him, but he was not prepared to give any credit to the media or anyone else for his disciplined performance at Wimbledon. Whatever the reasons, long may the improvement continue because, in that sort of mood and playing at his best, there is no finer and more thrilling sight on a tennis court anywhere in the world. One thing is for sure, Jimmy Connors will not dispute that contention. He was blown off court by a whirlwind display like a leaf in a tornado. The fact is he beat everyone else who mattered, and yet he was obliterated in the final. Both Navratilova and McEnroe are so superior, when they are at their best, to the rest of the players on the circuit that it must feel like sitting on the top of Everest looking for the nearest challengers at ground level through the wrong end of a telescope.

Connors was in philosophical mood afterwards. He asked plaintively:

Hell, what can you do? You go out there and give it your best shots all the time, but he was playing incredibly well and I, on the other hand, was struggling a bit. Tennis players, like entertainers in show business, have their up days and their down days, and I'm afraid McEnroe had an up day and I had a downer. It was rough out there, and I would have liked to have played a whole lot better and had a different result but life is going to go on, there'll be a new day tomorrow and I'm going to continue to play tennis and I'm going to go on enjoying playing and hope that next time it will all be a bit different. I've been in Wimbledon finals before and I've won and I've lost. I've been on both sides of the fence, and if you can handle them both the same, then I guess you are pretty lucky; but that's what you must try to do. Days like this do happen and the less they happen in my career the happier I'll be. But no matter what, my head never goes down. There is one thing I would like to make perfectly clear that, once the tennis is over, it's over. Once we leave the court it's finished, whether I win or I lose. There is no point in worrying about it because I may not like the result but there is nothing I can do about it. I can't change the score, I can't replay the match the next day, the result will be in the record books for ever and I must just accept it.

Jimmy Connors arrived at the after-match press conference sporting a smart bow tie and looking chirpy, and he conducted himself with great dignity. He paid tribute to McEnroe and put a remarkably brave face on what must have been a bitterly disappointing day. I left the sweltering centre court – temperatures had been over 80°F in the shade and over 100°F out in the middle of the court – content in the knowledge that in the space of 24 hours I had seen two of the greatest tennis players of all time, John McEnroe and Martina Navratilova, play the most scintillating tennis to retain their titles. It had been a tremendous thrill to be there and I shall always remember the dynamic triumph of McEnroe.

In the end it turned out to be a year of records because it was the first time in history that the defending champions in all five competitions successfully retained their titles; it was also the first time ever that the top seeds in all five competitions were victorious. This meant that the top seeds and defending champions in the mixed doubles, John Lloyd of England and Wendy Turnbull of Australia, held their title with a straight sets win over Steve Denton and Kathy Jordan. There was more encouraging news for British tennis too, when young Annabel Croft won the girls' singles title to become the first home-bred winner for 27 years. In the final she beat the South African Elna Reinach after dropping the first set.

There is no doubt, though, that the abiding memories of Wimbledon 1984 will be the precision, power tennis of the winners of the singles titles, McEnroe and Navratilova. I shall also remember the new, reformed, born-again McEnroe leaving the court after his victory in the final. He bowed to the Duke and Duchess of Kent in the Royal Box in such an exaggerated style he almost smacked his head on the turf in front of him. When on court to receive the trophy from the royal couple, they said that they thought it was the best they had ever seen him play. He concurred, and rounded off a great fortnight in his life by saying he looked forward to seeing them at the same time, same place in the same circumstances next year.

THE OPEN

The oldest Open Championship in the world was first contested on Wednesday, 17 October 1860. That was it – one day. Willie Park (Senior) won, with a score of 174, by two strokes over 'Old' Tom Morris of Prestwick. If the scores sound strange, this is because the Championship was over three rounds of Prestwick Golf Club's own 12-hole course on the Ayrshire coast. By tradition only seaside courses have been used for the Open – 14 since its inception – and in the old days golf balls were made of feathers (perhaps from seagulls), soaked in brine, tightly bound and called 'featheries'.

In 1857 Prestwick had organized a foursomes knockout contest for eight clubs and in 1858 it had held an individual tournament for amateurs. 1860 was the first Championship for professionals, and is generally referred to as the first 'Open'. The real thing was not in fact staged until 1861, but only three amateurs have won the event since: John Ball, double-winner Harold Hilton and triple-winner Bobby Jones.

The Open has been contested every year since then, apart from during wartime and in 1871. The reason for the latter hiatus was that 'Young' Tom Harris, Old Tom's son, had won the first prize, the 'belt', for three years running, whereupon it became his personal property. The replacement trophy, a silver claret jug, is the one presented today. In 1892 the tournament doubled its length to 72 holes, and there were three venues considered suitable at the time: Prestwick itself, Musselburgh and St Andrews. St Andrews offered the most fearsome test.

The seventeenth, the loathed 'Road Hole', has been described by Bobby Jones as 'one of the most terrifying experiences the game has to offer'.

The first English professional to win was J. H. Taylor in 1894. Taylor, Harry Vardon and James Braid shared 16 titles between them and six of those were Vardon's record haul. Prior to 1920 the event was organized jointly by the Royal and Ancient Golf Club, Prestwick Golf Club and the Honourable Company of Edinburgh Golfers. Then the R and A took over, and the Open went international. The Americans arrived in strength and stormed the title – Walter Hagen, Bobby Jones, Gene Sarazen. Henry Cotton kept the home fires burning with three wins over 11 years and, when the Americans stayed away on their own rich circuit after World War II, Peter Thomson and Bobby Locke ruled the roost. But then, in 1960, another American stirred things up – Arnold Palmer. He was runner-up to Kel Nagle at his first attempt, but went on to win in 1961 and 1962, bringing his own 'Arnie's army' with him.

It takes a lot of guts to win the Open and few who saw the courage of Britain's Tony Jacklin holing out to win in 1969 will forget it. Nor will they forget Lee Trevino, SuperMex, carving and chattering his way to victory in 1971 and 1972. South Africa's Gary Player became, in 1974, the first man to win the title using the large American ball, and Tom Watson belied his early reputation as a 'choker' to take the Jug five times. Spaniard Severiano Ballesteros had trouble tailoring his immense power to the fairways at Royal Lytham; he took an alternative route to victory, down the rough and through the car park.

But for nerve-racking Opens it would be hard to beat 1970, when 'the Golden Bear', Jack Nicklaus, defeated Doug Sanders in a play-off at St Andrews – 'the home of golf', as Jack called it in his post-victory euphoria. Nicklaus had sat in the scorers' caravan with his head in his hands thinking he'd blown his chances because Sanders had only to hole a 3-foot putt for the Championship. Sanders missed, slithered into a play-off and then sank out of sight. Victory meant more than usual to Nicklaus, hitherto considered an overweight upstart with a crewcut followed over the greens by Arnie's army muttering insults. As Jack holed out in 1970 he tossed his putter high in the air and wept. That was the moment the British public took him to their hearts.

Until 1965 the British public didn't actually get much chance to see the golf because the Open traditionally finished on a Friday. Television has been a major influence in attracting not only more viewers but more money. Between 1970 and 1980, total prize-money rocketed from £40,000 to £200,000.

The 1984 winner was due to collect £50,000 for himself – that is 50 times what Peter Thomson received in 1955. As it transpired the crowds were so vast throughout the week of the tournament, surpassing all previous records by a considerable margin, that the R and A generously decided to use the unexpectedly large gate receipts to increase the prize-money by 10 per cent. The winner duly received a cheque for £55,000.

I turned up at half past eight in the morning for the start of the first day's play; I would have been even earlier if I had managed to find a parking space within two miles of the clubhouse. I spent the morning trying to acquaint myself with the layout of the course and the peculiar problems of each hole. I discovered quite quickly that the difficulties for the golfers begin at the very first hole, and do not end until they leave the eighteenth green. I play golf with unbounded enthusiasm but not a great deal of skill and boast a handicap of between 20 and 24 depending on the direction of the wind and the stakes involved. I reckoned every hole was damnably difficult, and I think the eighteenth was about the only one I would have felt reasonably confident of negotiating respectably.

The first looks deceptively straightforward but, when play commenced I witnessed Sandy Lyle drive over 300 yards straight into the Swillycan burn which meanders menacingly in front of the green. He had to pick his ball out and drop it on the far side of the green for a penalty of one shot. Not a great start to his Championship challenge, and his misfortune was repeated by the legendary Jack Nicklaus half an hour later. He drove into the perfect position in the middle of the fairway, well short of the burn, but he then underclubbed with his approach shot and landed in the burn with the same disastrous consequences as Lyle. He dropped a shot and, from that moment on, never threatened to take a hand in the tournament. It was this first hole which also destroyed the joint overnight leader, Ian Baker-Finch, on the last day of the Championship. He did exactly what Nicklaus had done, hit his second shot into the burn and, after 54 holes of immaculate golf on the first three days, he proceeded to disintegrate.

Interestingly enough, the day after the Open ended, I played in a pro-am golf tournament with the professional Peter Tupling and he told me that the most important single factor in determining the complexities of playing the Old Course was the placement of the pin on each hole. For example, the Swillycan burn runs along the front of the green and, if the pin is placed at the front of the green near the burn, it is impossible to play a second shot which will leave the ball anywhere near the flag. However, if it is put in the middle of the green, then there is a fair chance for the top golfers of pitching over the water and on to the green and stopping the ball quickly to have a good chance of a birdie putt. If the flag is placed at the back of the green – some 25 yards from the water – then even the good club golfer would fancy his chances of a par or even a birdie. Similarly, Peter confirmed, on all 18 holes it was possible to make the going relatively easy or infuriatingly difficult for the players, and during the Open Championship the authorities tended to err on the side of difficulty.

Every hole was full of interest and character but, with the wind generally blowing behind the players on the first nine holes, and the handful of holes round the loop providing the best chance of birdies, the real crunch came during the inward nine which were played, on all four days, into the wind. Here the tournament was won and lost and, early on that first morning, I selected four holes which I thought would play a significant role in the final destiny of the trophy. The par-three eleventh was only 172 yards but the players were confronted by an elevated green surrounded by bunkers of the most gruesome kind. They were nothing like the bunkers on my local course at home but deep craters from which, for a rookie like me, there would be no escape. The wretched victim in the middle of these bunkers has to play the ball out almost vertically and would inevitably drop a stroke. The hole demanded a precision tee shot, and nothing less would do. The long par-five fourteenth of 567 yards against the wind, with rough lining the fairway and a few bunkers strategically placed, was another marvellous hole and it took really good woods to get anywhere near the green. The sixteenth – known as 'the Corner of the Dyke' – was a short 382-yard par four but again a hole where any deviation of a true line would invariably be punished. If, perchance, players survived this far intact, they then faced the daddy of them all – the seventeenth, the famous 'Road Hole', one of the greatest holes of golf anywhere in the world and the graveyard of many championship hopes.

It is a 461-yard dogleg to the right which brings alarm bells and red flashing lights to mind the moment the player sets foot on the tee. He is faced with a drive over the protruding one-storey building of the 'Old Course Golf and Country Club' which completely camouflages the fairway at which he is aiming. The title of the building is printed right along the near side and, for the perfect shot, the ball should be hit over the word 'Country' with a slight fade. That would leave the ball on the right-hand side of the fairway with the best approach to the green. However, if the ball is driven straight over, or to the left of, the words 'Old Course' then it will end up in the rough and, even worse, it will be impossible to aim for the flag because a terrifying bunker guards the whole of the green from that side. If the ball is driven from the tee over the word 'Club', or to the right of it, or hit with too big a fade, it will land in the garden of the hotel, which is out of bounds, and a two-stroke penalty will be inflicted on the poor player who has to start all over again, playing his third shot off the tee. This happened to Severiano Ballesteros when he was leading the Open in 1978.

Once on the fairway, even in the perfect position, there is no time to relax. The hole is jealously guarded by bunkers at the front and side, and by the road and a wall a few feet past the green at the back. Having arrived safely on the green in two which, I hasten to add, not many people do, the way to the flag is typical of every St Andrews' green – full of pitfalls. The greens are sloping, undulating and very fast, giving a lot of good putters sleepless nights before the tournament and nightmares after it. But, for most people, just reaching the green in two is the biggest problem and many of the world's greatest players have come to grief here with a resounding thud. No one had any worse fate, though, than the Japanese player Tommy Nakajima. In 1978, he hit the back of the green in two but hit his putt too hard and watched helplessly as it sped across the green into the bunker. He took four more shots to extricate himself from the bunker and, with another two putts, he was down in nine. From going for a birdie, he finished five over par for the hole. The Old Course can do that at any time. In 1978, out of 150 starters only one player, the American Ben Crenshaw, beat par at the seventeenth over four days – he had one birdie three, and three par fours. It is hardly surprising then that this hole ultimately decided the fate of the 1984 Open.

I left it that Thursday morning concluding it was a wickedly difficult test of skill and nerve and appreciating how it could so easily put an ugly dent in a hitherto pleasing scorecard. I adjourned to the massive tented village which is so much a part of big golf tournaments, and was pleasantly surprised at the fare on offer. I had read Brian Barnes earlier in the week attacking the over-commercialization of the Open and claiming the world's greatest golf tournament had been turned into a jamboree on a par with social events like Henley and Royal Ascot, littered with hospitality tents. But I must say I found it all perfectly orderly and well presented and not in the least offensive. In fact, I bought a new pair of golf shoes and was sorely tempted to buy a new set of golf clubs, so enticing was the range wherever I looked.

After a snack lunch, I arrived on the first tee in time to watch Nick Faldo drive off, and I spent the next five hours following him around. The sun was out and it was very warm, although the breeze of the morning was blowing stronger all the time and by mid afternoon it made life much tougher as the golfers played into it on the back nine holes. Nick made a good start with a splendid drive down the middle, a perfect pitch to the heart of the green and a beautifully struck putt for a birdie three. Unfortunately he dropped a shot at the long par-four fourth but recovered instantly with a superb eagle three at the 564-yard par fifth. Level par for the rest of the outward nine gave him a score of 34. He started back in rare style with magnificent pitch shots and a single putt for birdies at the tenth and eleventh and managed a par at all the remaining holes except the seventeenth where he succumbed to the pressure and took five. He was back in 35 for a total of 69 which left him in joint fifth place, along with Severiano Ballesteros and the American Tom Kite, one behind a little-known Australian who was to become a household name come Saturday night, Ian Baker-Finch, and two shots adrift of the three leaders, Bill Longmuir of Scotland, Greg Norman of Australia and the American Peter Jacobsen.

It is probably worth recording that, of the

élite leading group, only Bill Longmuir managed a par at the seventeenth. Norman, Jacobsen, Kite, Faldo and Ballesteros all took five. Tom Watson, the defending champion, also had a five, the Welshman Ian Woosnam and the American Bob Gilder each took seven and, by the end of the long hot day, more people had dropped shots at the seventeenth than any other hole on the course, and more people were over par than level par at it. But one man had a story to tell and something to celebrate. The 26-year-old Scot, Brian Marchbank, helped himself

Severiano Ballesteros driving over the horizon

to a birdie and, by the late afternoon, he was still the one and only man to achieve that notable distinction. At the other end of the spectrum, former Open champion Bill Rogers was afflicted with an apparent death wish at the par-five fourteenth. He suffered a lifetime's torment by slicing his drive out of bounds from the tee. He put down a second ball and did the same thing again. He put down a third and, like a good darts player, landed it beside the first two, out of bounds. He kept his fourth drive off the tee in play and five shots later he rattled in a putt for a twelve. The man who won the Open at Royal St George's, Sandwich, just three years ago in 1981 was going to win nothing this year. He left the final green a broken man claiming, *'I shall be very surprised if I turn up to play tomorrow.'*

However, after a good night's sleep Bill Rogers was on the first tee at five to nine the next morning to fulfil his obligations; suffice it to say he never troubled the leaderboard. He added a 77 to his 82 and failed by 11 shots to survive the cut to play the final two rounds. He was joined at the wrong end of the table by four other very distinguished

Open champions who failed to finish in the top 80 of the 156 starters and so failed to qualify for the final two rounds – Gary Player, Arnold Palmer, Tony Jacklin and Kel Nagle. At the right end of the leaderboard, the second day ended with the 23-year-old Australian rookie, Ian Baker-Finch, sitting perched on top of the world, three strokes ahead of Nick Faldo, Severiano Ballesteros and Lee Trevino. One stroke behind came Bill Longmuir and a further shot away came a group which included Tom Watson and Bernard Langer. Of these leading seven players, only Baker-Finch managed a par four at the seventeenth. The others each dropped one shot to par except Bill Longmuir who had a seven, from which mentally he never recovered.

Nick Faldo had another excellent round with only one bad shot to spoil his string of seven birdies comprised of four on the outward half and three on the inward half. At the par-five fifth he drove into a bunker and, perhaps being a trifle over-ambitious, he went for length and failed to come out cleanly. The ball hit the lip of the bunker and rebounded behind him. He took a six there,

Nick Faldo appreciating just how small the hole is during his troubled third round

but played so well otherwise that there were high hopes of a first British victory since Tony Jacklin in 1969. The problem is, though, that the extra pressure on Faldo, as the only British golfer with a realistic chance of winning our Open, means that he finds himself the centre of media and crowd attention every waking moment during the four days of play. The crowds in 1984 smashed all records, beating the previous highest attendance by an incredible 45,000. On these first two days, over 70,000 people covered the course, but the thickest concentration round a British player was the bustling group following and encouraging Nick Faldo.

He spotted me on the first day as he set off from the second tee and we had a pleasant little chat. He seemed relaxed and confident, tucked in on the heels of the leader. When the third round commenced, things started to go wrong and carrying the hope of a whole nation does not help.

He suggested:

There's too much talk about me really. I don't mind taking the burden of being British favourite to win the Open, that's fine, but I wish everyone would stop talking about it. I'll talk to the media for a month afterwards if I win it. They can talk to me every single day if they want, as long as they give me a free run before and during it and don't ask stupid questions such as 'Are you going to win?' They are just silly questions and I don't want to waste my time even trying to answer them. I am sure, though, that the press will always want to build it up. The thing that is difficult for me is that I have to be so protective of what I say because if I say, 'Oh, yes, I am playing well this week, I feel I have got a great chance,' I know that tomorrow's two-inch banner headlines are going to read: 'I'm Going to Win'. It makes me look a right Charlie. This is the toughest event in the world, even without the added pressure of being the British favourite and, as soon as you feel that the round is starting to go nicely for you, there is pressure all around you. You have to play the golf course and the Old Course is a great course so you have to get over that pressure first. Then you have the pressure of the Open itself and the pressure of a great international field, and there is a lot of heat on you all the time.

The third round was not kind to Nick Faldo. He missed a short putt on the first green and that seemed to unsettle him. He dropped three more strokes on the easier outward nine to turn in 40 and, although he came back in a commendable 36, his total of 76 ended his title challenge for another year. It is interesting to note that this really likeable, utterly dedicated and fiercely competitive young man hit back on the last day with a round of 69 to finish joint sixth with Greg Norman, and leave Scotland £16,390 better off. It is even more interesting to note that of the 156 players who lined up on the Thursday, only two broke 70 in three of their four rounds – Ballesteros and Faldo. Saturday was a bitter disappointment for Nick, but his time will surely come.

The highlight of the Saturday was the spectacular round of Tom Watson who was trying to win the British Open for the sixth time to equal the long-standing record of Harry Vardon. Five shots off the lead at the end of the second round, he attacked the course in the most aggressive style right through the afternoon, ignoring the gusting wind and destroying the course. With the adrenaline pumping through him, he produced an unforgettable round which included seven birdies and only on one hole did he drop a shot to par. He even managed a par four at the seventeenth – the only time in four rounds that he did. Incredibly, he had three or four putts which just lipped the hole or he might have had a 62 or 63 – he was certainly playing well enough for that to have happened. This was the best individual round of the Championship. The cheering, appreciative, ecstatic crowd knew it, and Tom Watson knew it.

That was my best round of the year and one of the best of my whole career. I know I mustn't be greedy but I hope I can improve tomorrow. There is still room for improvement because I missed four putts for birdies on greens that are getting really fast. I went out feeling confident today and my touch was very good. I had particularly good pitch shots at the third, sixth and seventh holes which are not easy approaches, and I was able as a result to pick up birdies at all three. And for the first time, I played the

Tom Watson, in the final round, playing from the wall at the seventeenth where he failed to make par

Ballesteros sinks the crucial birdie putt on the final green

seventeenth the way I wanted to. After a five on Thursday and a six on Friday, I hit a good drive onto the fairway, put a two-iron onto the front edge of the green and I was able to two-putt from about 80 foot across the green. It is exactly what I tried to do yesterday and the day before and it gave me particular satisfaction. I got it today, but it'll get me more times than I'll get it. However, I was pleased with this round. I was very aggressive and positive and if I can play like this again tomorrow, I may have a good chance of winning.

Sadly for Watson, he could not produce his form three days in a row. He had 14 birdies during his second and third rounds which is outstanding golf by any standards, but it was asking too much to repeat it on the final day. The same applied to Ian Baker-Finch who finished the third round joint top

with Watson on 205, two strokes ahead of Ballesteros and Langer. They were a further five shots ahead of the field, which meant of the 60 golfers that qualified for the final round only the top four had any real chance of winning.

Predictably, though disappointingly, Baker-Finch fell away rather abruptly, ending the day with a 79 in joint eleventh position. None the less, he can be proud of his bold effort and, with a good technique and relaxed, yet confident approach to the game, this young man, winner already of the New Zealand Open, is sure to become a major force in the years to come. His heroic deeds on the first three days will not easily be forgotten. Bernard Langer was always just off the pace, guaranteed third place but never really threatening to win the Championship. In the end, he squeezed into joint second by taking seven shots for the last two holes (a four and a three) as against nine by Tom Watson.

But the final round was really a head-to-head battle between Ballesteros and Watson. Ballesteros, playing with Langer, was at his brilliant, unpredictable best often looking his most dangerous when buried in the rough, on the wrong fairway or in the occasional bunker. Houdini was a mere amateur when it came to executing daring escapes from impossible situations; Ballesteros has long since perfected the art. While Langer's putting betrayed him, Ballesteros was quietly chipping away at Watson's lead. He knocked in a putt of 14 feet for a birdie four at the fifth and hit a deadly tee-shot to within six feet of the pin at the short eighth for a second birdie.

Meanwhile Watson, whose pitching to the green had been an object lesson to one and all during the third round, found the lethal accuracy deserted him when he most needed it. He was, after all, contrary to most people's expectations, merely mortal. He three-putted the second green, the fourth green and the fifth green and, instead of giving himself a cushion against his nearest challengers, he found himself one behind Ballesteros with nine holes to play. By this stage he had shaken off his playing partner Ian Baker-Finch and he was able to

concentrate on the two Europeans in the penultimate match, immediately ahead. By the fourteenth tee, Watson was one stroke ahead. Playing inspired golf, he grabbed three birdie threes at the tenth, eleventh and thirteenth but he took a five at the fourteenth to Ballesteros's four. This left the best two golfers in the world level with four holes to play in the greatest tournament in the world, on the most famous of all courses. Par fours at fifteenth and sixteenth left the two golfing giants locked together with two holes remaining.

In my view, it was only fitting that the seventeenth should decide the winner. Ballesteros hit his drive over the fairway and into the rough on the left. From there he hit a six-iron an almighty crack to the heart of the green, and he proceeded to two-putt for a par four. This was the only time all week he secured his par at the seventeenth and it could not have come at a more dramatic moment.

As Ballesteros strode to the eighteenth tee, Watson was analysing his ball, perfectly positioned in the middle of the seventeenth fairway. 'I had the perfect angle to not only approach the green, but to attack the flag,' he recalled afterwards, 'but I wasn't sure which club to use. At first, I thought it was a three-iron, then I went for a two-iron, but I knew as soon as I hit it that it was a bad shot.'

In point of fact, it was the worst shot he hit all week. It went through the green at a fair lick across the famous road, and hit the wall at the back. The ball finished about 18 inches from the wall, which made an accurate chip impossible. He hacked the ball cleverly onto the green and two-putted for a five. While all this was going on, a tremendous roar went up from the eighteenth green. Ballesteros had birdied the last, which meant that Watson had to finish with a two to force a play-off. He had a mammoth drive and a solid approach but still needed two putts for a 73 and a total of 278 to share second place with Bernard Langer. With a four-round total of 276, Ballesteros had beaten by two shots the Open Championship record at the Old Course, set by Kel Nagle in 1960. It was the end of a wonderful week's entertainment and excitement,

watched by 188,000 people on the course and countless millions live on television right round the world, principally in Japan, New Zealand, Australia, Canada, America and Europe.

For his reward, Ballesteros received a cheque for £55,000; but that, nowadays, is just the tip of a very lucrative iceberg. As Open champion for the second time, he will command high fees in personal appearances in what has become a highly marketable sport. The day after the Open, he played golf at The Belfry. It was a well-known company's golf outing, and they pay generous appearance money to a famous celebrity to join them for the day. With two British Opens behind him, it is estimated that Severiano Ballesteros can command fees of between £15,000 and £25,000 a day and he may be involved in around 25 such days each year. In the next 12 months he will earn the best part of half a million pounds from various personal appearances away from the tournament circuit in the high-powered and extremely lucrative commercial world. Over and above this, his brand-name clubs will bring him in a considerable sum and the prize money will ensure his annual earnings will comfortably top three-quarters of a million pounds a year in the foreseeable future. Not a bad reward for a former boy caddie from Pedrana in Spain, with outsize and outrageous ambition and the skill and temperament to match.

And yet the funny thing is that if the first prize at St Andrews had been a £5 note and there had been none of the vast riches available from the extra-curricular and peripheral activities of the game, I am certain Severiano Ballesteros and Tom Watson would still have been fighting out the finish of the hundred-and-thirteenth British Open. I firmly believe, and so do they, that the game is about winning the title, being the Open champion. The tournament revolves around not only the inherent skills of each player but around their will to win. It mirrors their whole attitude to the sport and to life; it is about pride and honour and prestige, and not even a million pounds can buy or change that.

FIFTEEN

MOTOR RACING

THE BRITISH GRAND PRIX

The first British Grand Prix was held at Brooklands in Surrey, in 1926. GP racing had begun 20 years before, in France, though continental Grand Prix races were virtually part of the tourist industry and could be staged on the streets of almost any town. In England, racing on the roads was illegal. The Brooklands GP was sparsely attended; the following year it was tried once more and then abandoned until 1937, when it was staged at Donington Park on a new road circuit on private land. Here the Nazis had a field day, showing off their superior Mercedes and Auto Union cars. The 1937 race was won by Bernd Rosemeyer and the 1938 one by Italian ace Nuvolari – both in Auto Union cars.

In 1948 the British Grand Prix was tried once more, this time at Silverstone, and this time was a success with the public. On 2 October 120,000 spectators were there to witness a remarkable display by two Italian drivers, Villoresi and Ascari, who had been relegated to the back of the starting grid after turning up late for official practice. The Italians came from behind, Villoresi winning in a Maserati. From then until 1954 Italian cars like the Maserati and the great Ferrari dominated Grand Prix racing. In 1955 the British GP was switched to Aintree, venue of four subsequent Grand Prix, and in that year Stirling Moss became the first victorious

British driver to win his home GP, in a Mercedes. Two years later he won in a British car, a Vanwall, though it was actually fellow-Briton Tony Brooks' vehicle and Stirling hopped into it in the pits, mid-race. Such swops are now forbidden.

These days the British GP alternates between Silverstone (odd years) and Brands Hatch (even years). Silverstone has been used 21 times to date and Brands only 10 times, but the latter has seen some historic races. About 20 miles south-east of London, Brands was first used for grass-tracking in the 1920s and the first four-wheel affair was in 1949, when 500-c.c. Midgets raced there. The 2.65 mile-long course, with its famous Clearways, Paddock Bend and Druids Corner, was the scene of a legendary victory by Jim Clark in 1964. Only 3 seconds separated Clark from his nearest rival, fellow-Briton Graham Hill, after 212 miles of racing. The winning car was also British – a Lotus. Until 1969, when Scot Jackie Stewart won in a French Mantra, the Lotus and the Brabham were the toast of the British GP.

Not until 1950 were the World Championships introduced, and the first race of these Championships was – the British Grand Prix, run at Silverstone on 13 May 1950. Guiseppe Farina won in an Alfa and went on to become the first world champion. In all, 87 different makes of car have entered world championship races, but only 23 have actually won a Grand Prix (up until the end of the 1983 season). Ferrari have entered 359 cars and won 88 races – both are records. These are the drivers' honours. Most GP wins: Jackie Stewart, with 27. Most British GP wins: Jim Clark, with five (1962–5 and 1967). Most races: Graham Hill with 176. Most World Championships: Juan Manuel Fangio, with 5. The lap records are pushed back with frightening frequency. Didier Pironi, in a Ligier, set the lap best at Brands with 130.02 m.p.h. in 1980.

Safety is a major concern, especially of the drivers. In 1961, the GP Drivers' Association was formed, not as a trade union so much as a track-inspection committee. In 1969 they had the Belgian GP cancelled because they disapproved of the track and in 1970 they insisted the German GP be switched from the Nürburgring to Hockenheim. Alberto Ascari, Jim Clark, Jochen Rindt, François Cevert and Ronnie Peterson are among those who have died on the track; many have perished in practice and testing. Ex-world champion, South African Jody Scheckter says, 'You have a 13–1 chance of coming out alive, which is pathetic.'

One of the most dreadful crashes in recent years occurred in 1976 on the Nürburgring, when defending world champion, Austrian Niki Lauda, was going flat out in fourth gear in his Ferrari at about 140 m.p.h. halfway round the second lap at a corner called the Bergwerk. Suddenly his car turned sharp right, skidded across the track and slammed up the sloping bank into the crash barrier. The car came down backwards onto the road with its left side torn away and the fuel tanks ignited. Lauda, trapped in the burning wreckage, was given the last rites at a Mannheim hospital but, incredibly, recovered to win the Grand Prix World Championship in 1982. Only savage scars remain of the near-tragedy six years before.

Certainly, judging by his outstanding performances this year, Lauda does not seem to be suffering any residual mental scars from his horrifying crash and, equipped with the fastest car, he and his team-mate Alain Prost were always going to be the two drivers

everyone had to catch at Brands Hatch. Much as I admire Lauda for his unquestionable courage and determination, I was desperately hoping that the John Player Special British Grand Prix would be won by a British driver and, in particular, Derek Warwick.

I first met Warwick when he appeared with me in the special FA Cup Final edition of 'Question of Sport' on BBC television in May, and I found him an exceptionally likeable, down-to-earth guy who had the ability to reach the top in the fiercely competitive and highly dangerous world of motor-racing. He told me that his interest in cars started at a very early age indeed.

My family were heavily involved in cars and wagons, and when I was still knee-high to the proverbial grasshopper, running around in nappies, I was already fascinated by cars. They've always been in the family blood and even now I work, along with my father and uncle, in the family business making trailers, known as the Warwick trailers. This was actually how I got started because the family were interested in stock-car racing, and in 1969 at the age of fifteen I became the world stock-car champion. All the hours spent as a youngster driving wagons and trailers at home had helped me enormously, and I proceeded to follow the logical profession. I competed in Formula Four racing, generously sponsored by Warwick trailers, and in 1975 and 1976 I won the British and the European championships. In 1977 and 1978 I moved into Formula Three racing, sponsored by BP and in 1980 I was signed by the powerful Toleman team to drive for them in Formula Two racing. I was runner-up in the European championships that year and at the end of the season, although I had a few offers from elsewhere, I signed with Toleman to drive in the Formula One Grand Prix championship in 1981.

His first Grand Prix was at Las Vegas, and since then he has driven in another 35 over four years up to the 1984 British Grand Prix. He is still a long way behind vastly experienced drivers like Niki Lauda (151), Jacques Laffite (145), Riccardo Patrese (103), René Arnoux (88) and Nelson Piquet (85) but he is now an established Grand Prix driver, having shaken off the rookie image a

The Brands Hatch circuit

long time ago. He had four enjoyable years with Toleman before switching in 1984 to the ambitious and more generously financed Renault team.

I had a wonderful time with Toleman and had a great working relationship with them, especially the chief engineer John Gentry who is god-father to one of my children, but the sad fact is that, compared to Renault, they are underfinanced and though it was a terrific wrench to leave them, I know it was the right decision and we have remained on very friendly terms. My first drive for Renault was at the end of March, where I was leading the Brazilian Grand Prix and had a wonderful chance of winning when my suspension broke just ten laps from home and I was forced to drop out of the race. Two weeks later I finished third in the South African Grand Prix and at the end of April in the next race, the Belgian Grand Prix, I achieved my best result to date when I came second behind Michele Alboreto. In the fourth event of the year, the San Marino Grand Prix the following week, I finished fourth behind Alain Prost, René Arnoux and Elio de Angelis. This meant that in the first four Grand Prix races of 1984, the car had performed superbly and I had actually caught a glimpse of the 'promised land'.

However, since the first week of May we have been plagued by disaster after disaster, in which we have had a series of minor mechanical problems that have resulted in a string of four Grand Prix in a row – France, Monaco, Canada and Detroit – where the car has been retired during the race. The blame for the failure to finish the Dallas Grand Prix at the beginning of July lay not with the car but with me. I was dicing for the lead with Nigel Mansell and went to overtake him when my car veered off line. Unfortunately the tyres were sticky which means that if, when cornering at speeds approaching ninety miles per hour, the car deviates at all from the racing line, the probability is loss of control. That is what happened, and I careered into the crash barrier. It was the end of the race for me and the first time I have ever had to walk back to the pits. I wished a big hole in the ground had opened in front of me and swallowed me up. When I reached the pits I could see nothing but very long faces, and I knew the huge team of mechanics, backers and

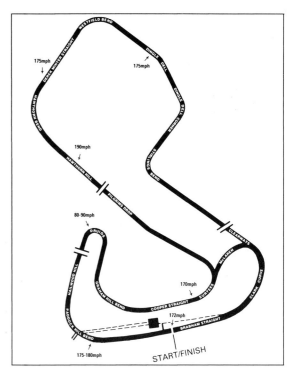

supporters would all be moaning and groaning with good cause and, although they were all very sympathetic, I knew it was doubly important to do well in the British Grand Prix.

There are only four British drivers in Formula One racing at the moment, not through lack of ability, stresses Derek Warwick, but through lack of sponsorship. Of the four, prior to Brands Hatch, Warwick with his early success in April was doing best with 13 points in the World Championship table. Martin Brundle was close behind with 8 points, Nigel Mansell had 6 points and Jonathan Palmer had yet to be finished in the first six to earn any points. At the top of the table Alain Prost in a McLaren had opened up a big lead with 34½ points, followed by Niki Lauda also in a McLaren with 24, Elio de Angelis with 23½ in a Lotus, René Arnoux with 22½ in a Ferrari, Keke Rosberg with 20 in a Williams and Nelson Piquet with 18 in a Brabham.

On the day of the race I drove down to Epping and then completed the journey to Brands Hatch by helicopter in 15 minutes instead of crawling along by car in mammoth traffic jams and taking about three hours. Not that I was the only person to think of this method of transport. Around 1800 helicopters landed and took off on a field about three times the size of a rugby pitch. The sky was swarming with choppers for a couple of hours. It was a spectacular way to travel and my first trip in a helicopter was one of the highlights of a tremendous day out. The crowds were flocking in all morning and a record 120,000 were waiting in the stands and lining the circuit by the time the race was due to start.

The focal points on the circuit were full of nostalgic memories for followers of the sport because, apart from the well-known landmarks such as 'Clearways', 'Druids' and 'Paddock Hill Bend', they have in order 'Clark Curve', 'Stirlings Bend', 'Derek Minter Straight', 'Hawthorn Bend', 'Surtees', 'Cooper Straight', 'Graham Hill Bend', 'Hailwood Hill' and 'Brabham Straight' where the race starts and ends.

Derek Warwick said it is one of the best Grand Prix circuits in the world and, unlike Dallas which is just like a giant Scalectrix track, Brands Hatch is a real drivers' circuit with subtle bends and curves, a whole range of gear changes and straights for overtaking. He pointed out how important it was to do a fast qualifying time in practice to earn a good position on the grid on the day of the race, because any car not in the front three or four rows would have very little chance of winning. He admitted that this year the McLarens have proved themselves far and away the fastest and most reliable cars, and they are in a first division all of their own. He reckons there is not much to choose between the Renault, Ferrari and Lotus teams, and he was confident that he would do really well in the British Grand Prix. He did the sixth fastest time in practice and was well placed for the race proper on the third row of the grid alongside Keke Rosberg.

Before the racing began the spectators were treated to a magnificent air display from the Red Arrows aerobatic team, also the Army's new helicopter display team, the Eagles. Other famous aircraft winged their way across the skies including, from the past, Lancaster bombers, Hurricanes and Spitfires from the Battle of Britain Memorial Flight, and from the present day, the super-impressive shape of Concorde.

But fascinating though the display overhead was, the 120,000 people at Brands Hatch and the worldwide television audience of over 900 million were there for the display on the ground. The razzmatazz is an integral part of the total experience and I must say on this, my first visit to a motor-racing Grand Prix, there was an incredible number of glamorous-looking ladies. As the race got under way the atmosphere was tremendous, and I was struck at once by the deafening noise as the field of 27 starters roared by on the first of the scheduled 75 laps covering 196 miles. Once my eardrums had recovered from that initial unexpected battering I was able to concentrate on the blistering speed of the cars, not only rocketing down the straights, at between 170 m.p.h. on the Brabham straight and the Derek Minter straight, and 190 m.p.h. along Hawthorn Hill, but also cornering round the 180-degree bends of Druids at 90 m.p.h. As with other events I was attending for the first time, I was surprised by the blinding speed of the action, which is far greater in real life than I had appreciated hitherto on television.

I had learned from listening to the television in the past that every Grand Prix is 'packed full of incredible, remarkable drama and sensation' and, sure enough, on the first lap of the 1984 Grand Prix, the long list of superlatives was in evidence at the opening skirmish. The cars of Phillipe Alliot and Jo

Derek Warwick preparing for the countdown at Brand's Hatch

Gartner seemed to touch each other and took out of the race Eddie Cheever in his Alfa Romeo and Stefan Johansson in his Tyrrell. The British driver Jonathan Palmer in a Ram appeared to lose control of the steering coming into the bend at Clearways 11 laps later, and he crashed into the barrier. He scrambled clear as his car caught fire but, with the smoke billowing across the track, the stewards waved the red flag to stop the race. It was a critical juncture as Lauda and his team-mate Prost had both overtaken the early leader Piquet while the other drama was unfolding.

The race was restarted 50 minutes later with the placings on the grid the same as they had been on the eleventh lap and not as they had been when the red flag appeared to halt the race. This did not best please the McLaren team because Prost and Lauda were in positions two and three behind Piquet whom they had overtaken. It mattered little. The officials decided to count the time for the first 11 completed laps and the next stage – 60 laps – and add them together to determine the final result of a race reduced in total to 71 laps from 75. From the outset of the second race of 60 laps, Piquet, in pole position for the thirteenth time in his career, was beaten to the draw by Prost who snatched the lead with Lauda in third and Derek Warwick not far behind. Only 19 of the original 27 cars took part in the second stage, and only four of

Warwick in action in his Renault during the British Grand Prix

these ever threatened to win.

Lauda slipped past Piquet at Druids and on lap 27 he overtook the leader Prost who was having mechanical problems. Piquet and Warwick also roared past Prost and soon the World Championship leader was forced to drop out of the race with gearbox trouble leaving Lauda, Piquet and Warwick to fight out the finish. The order from lap 34 of the 60 laps to lap 55 stayed constant with Lauda leading from Piquet, Warwick, De Angelis and Senna. Lauda built up a useful lead, clocking the fastest lap of the day in the process. He did lap 43 in 1 minute, 13.19 seconds which is an average speed of 127 m.p.h. although still 1.6 seconds slower than the lap record set by Didier Pironi in 1980.

The result, assuming his car survived, became a formality for Lauda and interest lay mainly in the battles behind him towards the end of the race. Andrea de Cesaris and René Arnoux had a rare old ding-dong battle for seventh position before Arnoux asserted his superiority. It was also interesting to see the newcomer to Formula One racing, 24-year-old Brazilian Ayrton Senna, threading his way through the field to go third in the closing stages. He was helped at this stage by Nelson Piquet and Elio de Angelis suffering engine problems in the last few laps, and this meant the final order as the cars flashed past the chequered flag was Niki Lauda first, with Derek Warwick second, Senna third, De Angelis fourth, Michele Alboreto fifth,

Arnoux sixth and Piquet seventh. Only 13 cars finished the race, less than half the field, and of these it should be pointed out that both Piquet and De Angelis ended the race at cruising rather than Grand Prix racing speed.

The crowd had given Warwick a marvellous response throughout the race and in the later stages, as he moved up the field and held on to second place in determined style, they were on their feet cheering and yelling every time he went past. A few days after the race I spoke to Derek again and he was clearly delighted with his performance and a haul of 6 points to push him back up the championship table to 19 points. Prost still held the lead with 34½ points followed by Lauda on 33, De Angelis on 26½, Arnoux on 23½, Rosberg on 20 and then, in sixth place, Warwick. He was delighted the car performed so well and added, it was also an enormous relief to finish a Grand Prix when you consider that he had had to retire in all the previous five races. His great faith in the Renault car was justified and he had driven as well as either of the two drivers he most admired in racing, Jim Clark and Jochen Rindt would have done.

He has now become an established star in his own right and Renault are going to be a considerable force in the future. He said:

At the moment nobody can compete with the McLarens but I believe the Renault is the next fastest and we'll be working hard to make improvements for next season. This was my fourth British Grand Prix and it is a great thrill to drive in front of the British people because they gave masses of encouragement with their ecstatic support. I must admit all that cheering and waving brought a lump to my throat and, of all the crowds all over the world, only the Italians show more enthusiasm.

The reason for that is understandable because, from what I hear about drivers on the roads in Italy, every one of them sees himself as a future Grand Prix driver. I was interested to hear about the dangers of a sport in which a significant number of the drivers suffer fatal accidents. Derek explained:

To me, the important thing is to feel one hundred per cent confident about the car, not just in general terms but on the day of the race. I have to know it has been fully tested and that everything is in perfect condition. If I am even a trifle concerned about anything from brakes to clutch to gear box to tyres then I can't concentrate properly during the race. But as long as the mechanics have done their job and are satisfied then I have a hundred per cent faith in my ability to complete the race and I think it is fair to say all Grand Prix drivers have plenty of self-confidence. This is not to say that I am unaware of the dangers and consequences of a nasty accident. In the last fifteen years, half a dozen top racing drivers have lost their lives on the track so it is pointless denying the grave risks involved, and I wish if I was going to reach the top in sport that I had been John McEnroe or Tony Jacklin but, all in all, I'm contented with my lot.

I enjoyed my conversations with Derek both before and after the race at Brands Hatch and this down-to-earth, happy family man is very much my kind of man. Off the track he is a pleasant, friendly sportsman – on the track he is a fierce but fair competitor. I can honestly say that if ever a man deserves to succeed and reach the top it is Derek Warwick, and no one in the whole of Britain would be more delighted if that comes to pass than I. I believe he is the star of the future but he would join me in saying that, brilliantly though he did to achieve his best Grand Prix placing in finishing second at Brands Hatch, the day and the race belonged to the two times former world champion, Niki Lauda.

The Austrian, at 35, the third eldest driver in the race, rewrote the record books in July with the promise of more to follow. In winning the British Grand Prix for the third time – only Jim Clark, with five victories, has won the race more often – he was winning his twenty-second Grand Prix. That is just five behind Jackie Stewart's record of 27 wins and, in collecting 9 points at Brands Hatch, Lauda became the top points scorer in Grand Prix history. In his career stretching 13 years from 1971, he has accumulated in his first 152 races the massive total of 367½ points, beating the old record held by Jackie Stewart by 7½ points. Some record, some driver and, as far as I was concerned looking back at the Grand Prix, some race, some day out!

**The face of a
champion: Niki
Lauda, the man
who came back to
triumph**

SIXTEEN

THE OLYMPICS

The Ancient Greek Olympics were held in honour of Zeus at Olympus in the Peloponnese. The festivals, held every four years then as now, were not simply sporting: they included competitions in art, literature, music, rhetoric and drama and continued, with some interruptions, from 776 BC until AD 394, when Roman Emperor Theodosius abolished them. They had by then lapsed from their original purpose – the single-minded pursuit of excellence – and there was a lot of corruption and cheating, with contestants after more than just laurel wreaths. There would be no more fun and Games for 1500 years. Odd attempts at revival, such as the Cotswolds Olympics of the seventeenth century, were doomed to failure.

The modern *sporting* Olympic movement began in 1896, the inspiration of Pierre de Fredi, Baron de Coubertin, who considered the important thing was not the winning so much as the taking part – the amateur, as distinct from the professional, ethic. A crowd of 80,000, which included George I, watched the sports – cycling, fencing, gymnastics, shooting, swimming and water-sports, track and field sports, wrestling and weightlifting. The King promised a horse and cart to the winner of the marathon, the first departure from the 'taking part' ideal. The following couple of Games were something of a shambles, being organized as part of a World Exhibition and a World Fair. Boxing was added to the sporting menu, along with archery, equestrianism, yachting, rowing and football. Better success was had

with the 1908 London Olympics at White City, though there was an almighty row when somebody forgot to run the American Stars and Stripes up the flagpole and an American 400-metre runner was disqualified for obstruction. Team-mates walked out in protest. They missed the hockey, introduced that year.

The Stockholm Games of 1912, introducing the modern pentathlon to the programme, were memorable chiefly for American Indian Jim Thorpe, who won the pentathlon and the decathlon, and was then disqualified for having played basketball for cash – 'professionalism', the authorities ruled. The 1920 Games in Antwerp were devalued by the political exclusion of defeated nations Germany, Austria, Hungrary and Turkey and the absence of the Russians who declined the invitation. But in Paris in 1924, the future Hollywood Tarzan, Johnny Weissmuller, made his mark, winning three golds and a bronze in the water. This was also the year of *Chariots of Fire* athletes Eric Liddell and Harold Abrahams, gold medallists for Britain.

The 1932 Olympics were held, like the 1984 Games, in Los Angeles and the organizing committee made a million from the Olympic Village and other money-spinners. The British Olympic Association likewise made a profit from the 1948 Wembley Games – in stark contrast to the 1976 Montreal Olympics which bankrupted the city. Hitler staged the Berlin Games of 1936 in a brand-new 100,000-capacity stadium. All was going well at the Propaganda

Daley Thompson, all strength, power and explosive speed as he wins the 100 metres in the decathlon in a personal-best time

Ministry until black American J.C. 'Jesse' Owens stormed to victory in the 100 metres, 200 metres, 4 × 100-metre relay and long jump. Basketball and canoeing had been added to the Olympic fare, and Leni Riefenstahl's monumental film of the Games immortalized them for posterity.

The 1952 Helsinki Games are recaptured in two words: Emil Zatopek. His treble of gold-medal records 5000 metres, 10,000 metres and the marathon were augmented by Mrs Dana Zatopek in the javelin, where she won the gold with a record as well. Scarcely less exciting was British Chris Brasher's performance in the steeplechase in Melbourne, 1956. He was at first awarded the gold, then disqualified, then reinstated. And in the Roman Games of 1960, one of the greatest athletes who ever lived emerged to take the light heavyweight boxing title – Cassius Clay.

1968 signalled the beginning of the end of Olympic credibility, as black American athletes Tommie Smith and John Carlos stuck their fists in the air on the podium in a 'black-power' salute. Subsequently the Games degenerated into the punchbag of the politically aggrieved. Munich 1972: Palestinian terrorists killed 11 Israeli competitors and officials. Montreal 1976: 22 black African nations showed off over a rugby tour of South Africa and stayed away. They missed Rumanian genius Nadia Comaneci on the bars taking the first perfect 10 in Olympic history. Moscow 1980: America, West Germany, Japan and assorted others stayed away in protest at the Russian invasion of Afghanistan. *They* missed Britain's Daley Thompson, Allan Wells, Steve Ovett and Seb Coe collecting four track and field gold medals.

ICE DANCE AT THE WINTER GAMES

Ice dancing was only included in the Olympic programme in 1976, though couples have been performing on ice ever since Samuel Pepys made traces with Nell Gwynn during the great freeze-up of 1683. In those days they used to hold bull baits on the frozen Thames anyway, so a quick minuet might have gone unnoticed. A set-pattern ice dance seems to have come

originally from Vienna, where formal dancing reached its height of elegance and expertise in the waltz ballrooms of the 1880s. The Vienna Skating Club merely adapted their love of Strauss and rhythmic precision to floating on ice. There was an ice waltz in faraway Halifax, Nova Scotia in 1885, and an exhibition of ice-waltzing in 1894 in Paris, but nothing that could be classed as competitive ice-dancing until the 1939 British Championships, when Reg Wilkie and Daphne Wallis skated to victory at Westminster. After the War, the United States followed Britain's lead and held their own event in Washington.

Ice dancing differs from pair skating (from which it derives) in that lifts are restricted – both feet should never actually leave the ice simultaneously – and the emphasis is on interpretation of rhythm and tempo, and on technical perfection. Championship events are divided into two halves. The first of these covers compulsory dances – traditionally three – and includes an original set-pattern dance of the competitors' choice. The first organized set-pattern routine was the lively Ten Step or Schöller March, named after its Viennese inventor Franz Schöller. The chassé is repeated in the modern version, making it a 14-step rather than a 10-step. The second formal dance was the European Waltz, followed in 1909 by the Kilian, again of Viennese choreography.

British dancers spent a lot of time in the ballrooms during the Depression to keep their peckers up and showed their inventiveness on ice in the 1930s, beginning with the tango of Paul Kreckow and Trudi Harris, and then a string of dances from Erik van der Weyden and Eva Keats – the foxtrot, Rocker foxtrot, Viennese waltz and Westminster waltz. The threat of war didn't daunt the keen, local ice-rink dancers; in fact they escaped into a world of new patterns and routines inspired by popular music – the blues, the Argentine tango, the quickstep, the fast circular *paso doble* and the rumba. The flood of invention in the American waltz, the Starlight waltz and the 'Gregory Rumba' added new dimensions.

The second half of championship events, though, is for many spectators the most

Jayne Torvill and Christopher Dean dance in the shadow of their five rings of confidence

The strain shows on the faces but nothing conceals the supreme artistry of the greatest skaters in the world

exhilarating – the freestyle. This is a new piece of poetry in motion, with novel interpretation of known dance movements, and it carries two sets of marks: one for technical merit, and one for artistic impression. Poetic licence is permitted – separations, pivots, spins etc. – but these movements are carefully supervised for artistic relevance and anything not strictly integrated into the dance as a whole is penalized, however skilful.

The first World Championships were held in 1952 in Paris and the first champions were British: Lawrence Demmy and Jean Westwood, who went on to win four in a row. British ice dancers have continued to set the standard ever since, with Bernard Ford and Diane Fowler in the 1960s and latterly Jayne Torvill and Christopher Dean. Torvill and Dean have pushed back the frontiers of ice dance with their originality, passion and wit, but they have not done so without upsetting the die-hards. The Russian coach Natalia Bestemianova waggled the rulebook over their magnificent Bolero, which begins with a long preamble to set the scene of two doomed lovers about to hurl themselves into a volcano. The preamble contains no actual skating at all, but much kneeling, swaying and snake-slithering of Torvill down her partner's body. Bestemianova said it should be penalized, but few who saw the pair lying 'dead' on the ice at the end of their four minutes would agree.

The Winter Olympics in Sarajevo dominated international sport in February, and the Games themselves were totally dominated by the superb performances of the gold-medal champions, Torvill and Dean. Not the ideal build for the sport myself, I have yet to master ice-skating, but I was as thrilled, excited and moved as any other blue-blooded Briton by the stunning routines which these two conjured up in 1984. Their captivating displays had gripped the imagination of the public long before the Olympics, with handsome victories verging on perfection in the British Championships (six years in succession), European Championships (three times in three attempts) and World Championships in 1981, 1982 and

1983. They set new standards which no one in the world could emulate, and these two brilliantly gifted and utterly dedicated sports personalities have, over a period of four years, left the Russians and the Americans trailing in their wake.

The European title was safely collected once again in January 1984, and their fourth successive world title was to follow in March in Canada, but had they failed in either of those competitions it would not have been too disastrous because they had already scaled those particular mountains. However, 1984 in Sarajevo was to be their one and only opportunity of Olympic Gold. The pressure on them was enormous; their response was majestic.

Instead of the typical chic ski resort, the Winter Olympics were being held for the first time in an industrial city. The ice-dance competition took place in a brand-new sports complex which had taken two years to build and was only completed a fortnight before the Games began. Sarajevo is like any other industrial town – Birmingham or Sheffield for example – full of high-rise flats and a surfeit of smoke. The weather was equally depressing with a steady rainfall, a host of hanging, grey clouds and a distinct lack of snow. Nestling in a basin surrounded by mountains, it is a curious town where the East meets the West. There is a strange blend of the oriental and the occidental. The Olympic village was comprised of about 50 high-rise flats and there were very few extra-curricular social distractions like pubs and nightclubs. It lacked the amenities associated normally with a top-class ski resort.

After three days of rain, high winds and fog, during which the blue-riband event of the slopes – the downhill skiing – had to be postponed three times, the snow came to save Sarajevo's reputation. Against this uneasy background towards the end of the first week the ice dancing commenced with the compulsory dances, followed by the set-pattern dance routine two days later and the free skating – with the now famous Bolero – another two days after that. The world champions arrived in Sarajevo late as they had completed their training preparations in Germany but, as soon as they appeared in

A portrait in majestic elegance and grace

The Olympic title to add to the European and World crowns already won

the stadium to practise, they attracted huge crowds. Most of the other competitors regard Torvill and Dean as superhuman creatures from another planet who are in a different class and quite invincible. Their reputation is worldwide and their popularity is immense. In the same way that Carl Lewis was the star attraction of the Games in the summer, so Torvill and Dean were the centrifugal point in Sarajevo.

When they first appeared on the ice in the competition proper the atmosphere was quite special. A hush fell around the whole stadium and, despite the deafening silence, the crisp air was filled with a tingling anticipation and an almost unbearable mixture of tension, apprehension and excitement. We had seen the Russians, the Americans and the Canadians and they had all been dazzling. Torvill and Dean were quite simply vastly superior. They were perfection. On each of the three nights of competition they attained the unattainable. They proved the impossible was possible after all, and they did it with grace and elegance and seemingly effortless ease.

Nobody could fault the faultless exhibition of the breathtaking Bolero in the free skating on the final night of competition. They achieved an unprecedented collection of 12 maximum marks for artistry, along with three maximum marks for technical merit; this made Olympic history. The crowd, and some of the judges, rose to accord the champions a well-deserved, prolonged, standing ovation. With the adrenaline still pumping furiously, the anxiety was over; they had notched up yet another dynamic personal triumph.

I discussed the Olympics with both in early August, six months after their win and shortly after their return from the enormously successful professional tour of Australia. They admitted the pressure had been pretty acute, but agreed that:

In a sense it helped us, being favourites, because it meant even in training and practice with huge crowds, fellow competitors and television cameras permanently focused on us, we had to always do our very best. This gave us a wonderful competitive edge. Admittedly, we did make a couple of slips, literally, early on, falling in practice, but that happened after a seventeen-hour train journey from Germany to Sarajevo and after our luggage was late in arriving in our rooms. We then had to dash to the rink to train and were not at our sharpest. But after that initial hiccup we settled down. Fortunately, we don't tend to make too many mistakes in competition.

They do not watch other competitors in practice, preferring to concentrate on their own programme, and this is something they make a point of in all major competitions.

They also talked about the town and the life there:

After training each day, it was rather boring in Sarajevo. It was quite monotonous because there was nothing to do except watch television, listen to music, hang around the camp or stay in our rooms. But once we reached the stadium for the first event – the compulsory dance – we were in the perfect frame of mind to respond to the very special atmosphere. A surprisingly large number of British supporters had made the trip over and it was a tremendous boost to see so many Union Jacks in the crowd. It all helped to bring out the best in us and we reckon that the Winter Olympics was probably the best we have ever skated, especially in the free dancing section. Everything came just right and all the timing was precisely correct.

I wondered, had they been confident of taking the gold? 'No,' they said, 'we never really discussed or considered that question. Obviously, the previous years of training and competing had all been geared towards our ultimate goal – the Olympic gold – but we never talked about winning the gold so much as just making sure we always did our absolute best every time we were on the ice.'

They agreed that they preferred the free dancing to the compulsory and set-pattern routines but, by the time they had come to the last section and their Bolero, they were already in pole position. 'The Bolero would probably be the most outstanding highlight as we look back on Sarajevo. We still both get excited reflecting on the nostalgia of that whole night, the Bolero, all the sixes for artistic impression, the gold medal – the only one we had not previously won – and the national anthem. It was quite a night.'

It certainly was and we all enjoyed watching them at the peak of a marvellous career in which they won every major title and fulfilled every conceivable dream and ambition. Approaching midnight on 14 February – St Valentine's Day, which Dean had earlier celebrated by giving Torvill an orchid – the undisputed king and queen of ice dance were duly crowned Olympic champions. Amongst a barrage of telegrams was one from Her Majesty the Queen. It read: 'Many congratulations on a superb performance which we watched with great pleasure.' Along with about 55 million other appreciative British fans, I can only echo those sentiments. We had all seen and enjoyed something we would never see again. Torvill and Dean are unique.

THE SUMMER OLYMPICS

Regrettably, I was unable to take three week off work to travel to Los Angeles for the duration of the Summer Olympics, but night after night I did enjoy a very good grandstand seat in my lounge at home in front of the television, and often into the early hours of the morning. I am grateful to

Desmond Lynam each night and Frank Bough every morning for their excellent presentation on BBC television. It was easy in my office to see who had been watching through to three o'clock every morning. Instead of the usual rings round their eyes they had all developed *five* rings around their eyes; but it was all in a worthwhile cause.

Just after midnight on Sunday 29 July British Summer Time, the lavish and ostentatiously spectacular opening ceremony got under way to signal the start of the 1984 Olympics. Organized in the very best (or worst, depending on your standpoint) Hollywood, tinsel-town tradition, the ceremony was just like a major Cecil B. de Mille extravaganza, only more so, if that is possible. They say 'there is no business like show business' and America, especially Los Angeles, is the living proof and embodiment of that cliché. They had even taken the trouble in Olympic year to ensure that the President of America was a former employee of the Hollywood film industry. The niece of Jesse Owens ran with the Olympic torch before handing it over to the great decathlete Rafer Johnson who lit the flame which was to burn for the next fortnight. The ceremony, seemingly staged with an unlimited budget, was quite sensational; 84 grand pianos appeared at one point. Ronald Reagan gave the Games the official blessing: 'Celebrating the twenty-third Olympiad of the modern era, I declare open the Olympic Games.' But, although I think the choreographer and director of this outrageously glorious event, one David Wolper, deserved the first gold medal and an Oscar, the scars behind the façade were impossible to conceal.

Politics and sport are inevitably intertwined at this level and, following the American boycott of the Moscow Olympics in 1980, it was not the biggest surprise in the world that the Eastern bloc had chosen to boycott the Los Angeles games. The deafening cheers for the Rumanians, the Yugoslavs and the Chinese at the march past were slightly incongruous. Clearly the Americans were expressing relief that some Communist countries had turned up, but it was clear to one and all that the absence of the competitors who were assured of

**The fastest man
in the world and
the hero of the
American
Olympics – Carl
Lewis**

approximately half the medals available greatly debased the currency. Without the Russians and East Germans a lot of people would win gold medals and know full well that they were still, probably, not the best in the world, just as it had been in Moscow. This meant Britain would win far more medals than they had in Montreal in 1976 or Munich in 1972, but at what cost and of what real value? I must say I find the increasing political involvement in sport abhorrent, and the Los Angeles Games were spoilt, if not actually ruined, in the same way that Moscow had been. By the end of the first week people tuning into the television coverage could have been excused for wondering if the American national anthem was actually the theme music for the Games, because it was played so often.

None the less, although the Americans won the most medals of every kind, they did not win the first. That honour befell China – competing at the Olympics for the first time since 1952 – in the shape of 27-year-old Haifeng Xu who took the gold in the free pistol shooting. The best British news on the opening day of competition centred round our two main individual hopes in the swimming; both June Croft in the 100-metres freestyle and Adrian Moorhouse in 100-metres breaststroke qualified for the final. But the joy was short-lived because neither collected a medal in either the 100 metres or the 200 metres. In the latter Miss Croft, who has devoted her life to swimming, started favourite but finished sixth.

Britain did not have to wait long to pick up her first medal. On the second day of competition Michael Sullivan, a 41-year-old bank manager from Surrey, won the bronze medal in the small-bore rifle shooting behind an American Edward Etzel. At this stage we were also lying third in the Equestrian Three Day Event in the team competition and, by the time the cross-country section and the Showjumping had followed the Dressage there were double celebrations. The team, Virginia Holgate, Lucinda Green, Diane Clapham and Ian Stark took the silver medal behind the United States, and Virginia Holgate captured the individual bronze. In stifling muggy heat,

quite alien to the British squad, this was an excellent result at the end of a hard week of competition. To prove, if proof was needed, that our horses were as good as the riders, the showjumping team of John and Michael Whitaker, Steven Smith and Tim Grubb defied the oppressive conditions to win the silver medal on the second Tuesday of competition.

I shared the typical British optimism that we would be laden down with medals won in the swimming pool, and I was delighted that some medals were collected after the early disappointments. The British quartet of Neil Cochran, Paul Easter, Paul Howe and Andrew Astbury led the way with a courageous bronze medal in the 4 × 200-metres freestyle. The women's 400-metres freestyle produced a mini bonanza with a bronze for June Croft, richly deserved for 10 years of selfless dedication to the sport, and a silver for Sarah Hardcastle, who went on to win the bronze in the 800-metres freestyle. Neil Cochran also won a second medal when he finished third.

The five swimming medals were almost matched by our shooting squad. Following Michael Sullivan's bronze, Malcolm Cooper won our first gold medal in the small-bore rifle three-position event and Alastair Allan took the bronze. Barry Dagger also won a bronze in the air-rifle event. Along with our two equestrian medals, British pot-hunters had collected a tidy little bag of 11 medals by the end of the first week of competition.

The final week began well as the swimming ended and the athletics began. Keith Connor claimed the bronze in the triple jump and there was a bronze for Neil Eckersley and a silver for Neil Adams in the judo, with another well-deserved bronze for Kerrith Brown to follow. The highlight though, at the end of the second weekend, was the gold medal for the coxed fours in the rowing. At eight o'clock in the morning on Lake Casitas, with fog and thick mist hanging over the water and obscuring the tops of the neighbouring mountains, the British crew of Steven Redgrave, Andy Holmes, Richard Budgett and Martin Cross under the guidance of their cox, Adrian Ellison, made a little bit of history when they

The British coxed four, exhausted but elated as they cross the line and strike gold on Lake Casitas

Britain's Neil Adams sits disconsolately after being beaten by 'ippon' – judo's equivalent of a knock-out – for the first time in 10 years, by West German Frank Wieneke. Adams took the silver medal

became the first British rowing gold-medal winners since 1948. Displaying a calm, controlled confidence they eased ahead of the powerful American crew in the last quarter of the race to win impressively.

A couple of hours later, on that eventful Sunday morning, the redoubtable American Joan Benoit, just a few weeks after a knee operation, won the women's marathon from the Norwegian Greta Waitz with the winner of the London Marathon, Ingrid Kristiansen, fourth. The picture which will linger longest in most people's memory of the marathon will be, not Joan Benoit crossing the line but the 39-year-old Swiss athlete Gabriella Andersen-Schiess, walking, staggering, stumbling, semi-conscious, her face and body distorted and racked in anguish as she waved officials away and falteringly lurched round the track to finish 24 minutes behind the winner. To rapturous applause she finished thirty-seventh out of 50 runners, a performance full of pride and courage, before she was whisked off in an ambulance.

The athletics is the most interesting of all the Olympic competitions for me and I was delighted to stay up watching television into the early hours of the morning and see Britain, having often done well on the track

in recent Olympics, actually collect three medals in the javelin. David Ottley won the silver in the men's competition with his very first throw of 85.74 metres. Ranked out of the first 10 before the competition began, he celebrated his twenty-ninth birthday in good style, showing grim determination and discipline in difficult conditions, with a strong sun upsetting some of the more fancied contestants.

The women's javelin was expected to be a straight fight between the reigning world champion Tiina Lillak of Finland and Britain's Fatima Whitbread, with Tessa Sanderson the best of the rest. All three qualified with ease and, in her first throw in the final, Tessa Sanderson set the target for everyone to chase with a superb throw of 69.56 metres. As the drama unfolded that throw was never bettered, although Lillak came closest with a throw of 69 metres to take the silver. Fatima Whitbread held third position early on, dropped back to fourth but, showing plenty of character and resolution, came again with a throw of 67.14 metres to clinch the bronze.

For those like myself who remember watching Tessa Sanderson break down in Moscow when, unaccountably, she failed to

qualify for the final of the javelin, and who
recall her bitter disappointment then and in
Helsinki last year when she narrowly failed
to win a medal in the World Championships,
her moment of triumph was indeed a
moment to savour. Tears of despair had
turned to tears of joy and the heartbreak of
Moscow was well and truly buried. Tessa has
shown admirable resilience and strength of
character to overcome a series of injuries, a
loss of form and the haunting memory of
Moscow. I was absolutely delighted to see
her standing on the rostrum, clutching her
gold medal, to become the first British girl in
the history of the modern Olympics (since
1896) to win an outright field medal in a
throwing event. This triumph by a British
girl in Los Angeles stands out as the most
memorable single moment for me. I was also
most impressed and relieved, after the ill-
informed press reports about excessive
needle amongst the British trio, to see
Fatima and Tessa hugging each other at the
end of the competition and speaking so
generously about the other in the televised
interviews. These two girls did themselves
and Britain proud, and we should be proud
of them.

On the same day, Kathy Cook ran her

Tessa Sanderson, a model of concentration as she prepares to make her first throw – the one that won her the gold

heart out to win the bronze in the 400 metres, and Seb Coe took the silver in the 800 metres, although it should be pointed out he was comprehensively outgunned by the strapping Brazilian Joaquim Cruz. Britain had been expected to dominate the event and it was not the result I had anticipated. But, with Peter Elliot missing the race altogether with an injured ankle, and Steve Ovett suffering from a breathing problem and finishing the race gasping for air, I suppose it was gratifying that Coe salvaged some honour.

On the credit side, for the first time in 20 years we won a medal in weightlifting when David Mercer finished third in the middle-heavyweight division. Also included in my list of marvellous achievements are: bronzes in the women's long jump (Sue Hearnshaw), yachting (Jo Richards and Peter Allan), boxing (Bobby Wells), wrestling (Noel Loban), the women's 4 × 100-metres relay (Simone Jacobs, Kathy Cook, Beverley Callender and Heather Oakes), the marathon (Charlie Spedding) and the men's hockey (a

team which defied all odds and expectations); and a silver in the men's 4 × 100-metres relay (Kriss Akabussi, Gary Cook, Todd Bennett and Phil Brown) in a new British and European record time. I was delighted for all these British winners, particularly Kathy Cook who was winning her second bronze in Los Angeles and her nineteenth major international medal altogether – more than any other British girl and a just reward for this wonderful athlete.

But now, as the Olympics entered the final four days, my attention was riveted to the athletics stadium and five events in particular – the decathlon featuring our one world-class superstar Daley Thomson, the 1500 metres, the 5000 metres, the women's 3000 metres, and Shirley Strong in the 100-metres hurdles. The zenith came in the decathlon; the nadir in the 3000 metres.

No praise can be too high really for Daley Thompson, who proved he is the finest all-round athlete of this and probably any other generation. It was fabulous to watch this brilliant superstar in action and I was pleased to see not only did he achieve personal best-ever performances in the first three events – the 100 metres, the long jump and the shot – but smiling and waving unlike the vast majority of athletes in Los Angeles, he committed the sin of actually being seen hugely enjoying himself. He is a great competitor and relishes every second of top competition and this attitude shifted the pressure onto his main rival, Jurgen Hingsen of West Germany. Thompson's fierce competitive instincts shone through in the discus where he had two disastrous throws. With his third and final throw, he rose superbly to the challenge and the occasion with another personal best to break Hingsen's heart. What little resistance Hingsen had left evaporated completely in the pole vault when Daley cleared 5 metres to beat the West German at one of his prime events. After finishing the first day 114 points ahead he was never in danger of being overtaken, and this British version of Superman duly collected the gold, although he failed by one miserable point to equal Hingsen's world record total for a decathlon of 8,798 points.

He is, without any doubt, the greatest athlete of his kind, and he is the supreme master of 10 vastly different disciplines. Press conferences demand an extraordinary sort of self-control and discipline however. It seems to me that the flippant remarks Daley made during his press conference were simply a reaction to the stupidity of some of the questions. His response was misunderstood and thought by many to have been unnecessarily arrogant, which was a shame.

The attractive Shirley Strong was also a marvellous competitor. She was even delightful and pleasant in defeat when she failed by a couple of inches to win the gold medal in the 100-metres hurdles. She had looked mighty impressive in the heats and semifinal, even though she started slowly on the last occasion, and she ran a fabulous race in the final to take the silver medal after finishing four-hundredths of a second behind the American Benita Fitzgerald-Brown. She came over as a really lovely lady, magnanimous in defeat and smiling bravely though admitting her tremendous dis-

The dashing Shirley Strong going for gold in the 100-metres hurdles, only to be touched off on the line by Benita Fitzgerald-Brown of America

Kathy Cook collecting one of her two bronze medals to cap a great week in her life

appointment. There was a note of real determination when she said she had four years to prepare for the next Olympics in Seoul in 1988.

Tragically, there will probably be no more Olympics for the first lady of American athletics, their 1500- and 3000-metres star, Mary Decker. For her, Los Angeles was a cataclysmic disaster. She opted out of the 1500 metres to concentrate all her efforts on the 3000 metres and she reached the final relatively effortlessly for the media showdown with Zola Budd. She led for most of the final until, three laps from the end, Zola Budd hit the front just in front of her. Twice Budd and Decker seemed to touch and, on the second occasion, the American tripped and crashed off the track onto the grass where she lay prone, with an injured leg and injured pride. To leave the Olympic scene without a medal of any description was unthinkable and, in retrospect, tragic. I have every sympathy for Miss Decker but Budd most certainly did not trip her deliberately. The incident affected Zola badly; in the next few seconds she faltered before wilting visibly and dropping right back through the field to finish a very disappointing seventh. After all the publicity prior to her selection, and the subsequent publicity regarding Mary Decker, I wonder whether Zola Budd thinks she might have done better to have stayed in South Africa away from the hounding press.

The exit of Mary Decker in the 3000 metres left the way clear for Maricica Puica of Rumania to take the gold from Britain's Wendy Sly who ran aggressively to win the silver and confirm her status as Britain's top female middle-distance athlete.

The 5000 metres was also an anticlimax for Britain with David Moorcroft, overcome by the oppressive conditions and cruelly fast pace, folding up in the second half of the race to finish a long way down the field. Tim Hutchings was a courageous but well-beaten fourth and one could only admire the blistering run of the tiny Moroccan, Said Aouita, who stormed through to take the gold.

Nevertheless, half an hour earlier at three o'clock on the Sunday morning in Britain, I was leaping up from my armchair in front of my television set, screaming home Seb Coe and Steve Cram in the 1500 metres. This was Britain's finest hour on the track, and the British athletes ran a perfect tactical race. Coe was never out of the first three, yet he never made the running, allowing a variety of athletes to give him a good lead. On the

The favourite from America, Mary Decker, leads the 3000-metres field round the bend, moments from disaster, followed by Zola Budd (151) and Wendy Sly (175), with the eventual winner, the blond Rumanian Maricica Puica, right behind Decker

The most controversial moment and incident of the Games – Mary Decker stretched out beside the track and out of the Olympics

last lap he cruised to the front pursued by Cram and they sprinted clear of the field. Just as in Moscow, Coe had taken the silver in the 800 metres and the gold in the 1500 metres. He has fully justified all the superlatives heaped on him during the past few years. There is also little doubt that in the near future the redoubtable Steve Cram will be ready to take over as the world's top 1500-metres athlete. The two saddest moments though, for me, were seeing Steve Ovett, suffering from a virus which inflicted breathing problems on him, leaving the track by ambulance after the 800-metres final to spend two days in hospital and then being stretchered off after dropping out of the 1500-metres final on the last lap when in fourth position. In the most important week of his life, he was too ill to reproduce his best form, and that was heartbreaking for him and very sad for his legion of fans.

For the final postscript it is hats off to all our 35 medal winners, especially the five gold-medal champions, and also a special word of praise for the two outstanding medal winners from America. The top women's athlete was Valerie Brisco-Hooks who won three gold medals – the 200 metres, 400 metres and 4 × 400 metres relay – and became the first athlete to complete the Olympic double of the 200 and 400 metres. But pride of place at the top of the Olympic tree must go to the 23-year-old sprinter extraordinaire, Carl Lewis, who emulated the legendary Jesse Owens' 1936 haul of gold. Carl Lewis rewrote the post-War record books with four gold medals – the 100 metres, 200 metres, long jump and the 4 × 100-metres relay – and his margin and style of winning could scarcely have been more impressive and conclusive. In my eyes, and most people's eyes come to that, he was the star of a fabulous two weeks of competition at the 1984 Los Angeles Olympics.

Seb Coe points an accusing finger towards his critics in the press box and says, 'I told you so' as he wins the gold medal in the 1500 metres in Los Angeles

A distraught Steve Ovett during the worst week of his career as breathing problems force him out of the 1500-metres final

Steve Cram tucked in nicely in mid-division en route to the silver medal in the 1500 metres

SEVENTEEN

POTPOURRI

I would like to round off my sporting year with a brief look at half a dozen other major sporting occasions which took place during 1984 and which I feel very strongly ought to be included or I would risk devaluing the book. Three of these events I was able to watch live and the other three I have seen on video recordings. Whilst for one reason or another I am not able to devote more space to them, I believe it is very important to make generous reference to each of them.

The reason I was unable to watch the Grand National live at Aintree was quite simply that I spent the last weekend of March in Hong Kong for the Cathay Pacific Hong Kong Bank World Seven-a-Side Rugby tournament. This is without any shadow of doubt the best rugby tournament of its kind in the world and, spread over two action-packed days, it is a magnificent, extravagant festival of all that is best not only in rugby but in sport in general. For the two days of competition 24 of the top rugby-union playing countries of the world assembled in Hong Kong and the atmosphere, like that of the unique city itself, had an air of magic. It is like a rugby-union Commonwealth Games, and Cathay Pacific, the Hong Kong Bank and the Hong Kong Rugby Union are to be warmly congratulated on producing and organizing a truly magnificent tournament.

Where else in the world would you see the giants of global rugby – New Zealand and Australia with their full international seven-a-side teams, along with the cream of international rugby players from England, Scotland, Ireland, Wales and France – take on the emerging nations such as Fiji, Japan, Western Samoa, Canada, America, Tonga and Korea, as well as the incredibly enthusiastic minnows of the rugby scene including Thailand, Sri Lanka, Papua New Guinea, Singapore and the Solomon Islands. This competition brings together every colour, race, creed, shape and size of rugby player in a joyous celebration of everything that is good about the last of the great amateur sports, and it was a great privilege and pleasure for me to attend for the first time. I was amazed to hear beforehand that rugby was played in many of the countries who were competing and, by the end of the first day, I was even more amazed by the remarkably high standard of skills displayed by some of the lesser-known teams. The tackling of the Western Samoans was about as decisively lethal as any I have seen, and the handling and passing of the Koreans and Japanese was superior to anything in the British Isles at the moment. These two countries, like so many of the Far Eastern teams, are handicapped by their lack of size because they are physically dwarfed by the All Blacks and the Australians, but they won the hearts of the huge crowd with their brave and skilful displays.

It was tremendous for me to watch the national team of Taipei – Kwang Hua – playing Australia and although the Chinese lost they defended with great courage and clearly relished their meeting with the giants of the game, the winners of the tournament for the previous two years. It was exciting to watch Malaysia with a team of 5-foot, 7-inches and 11-stone players give the mighty French Barbarians a decent game until their strength and stamina gave out, or to see Papua New Guinea, after training for six months, give America a fright before capitulating. One of their players five years ago, Lucas Senar, a little leprechaun of a fellow, was voted the player of the tournament, and he still proudly cherishes photos of him tackling the great Scotland and British Lions stars John Rutherford, Roger Baird and Jim Renwick in a memorable match in the 1980 tournament. He became a national folk hero at home when the photos appeared in the local newspaper. There are only eight clubs in Papua New Guinea but the 300 players there are as fanatical and dedicated as any in the world. They watch the televised recorded highlights on video of all the big internationals from Britain, France and Australasia, and the famous stars of rugby are household names not just in the valleys of Wales, the north of England and the borders of Scotland but in Port Moresby and the entire length and breadth of Papua New Guinea. Lucas Senar enthused:

> *Everyone in my country knows of Rutherford, Renwick and Baird and the small rugby-playing community respect them as some of the greatest runners of all time. For the people of Papua New Guinea it was an honour that we shared the same field as those gods of the game, but just imagine how I felt when, during our match, I tackled them. I live twelve months of every year for the Cathay Pacific tournament and in 1981 I played against the Australians with the Ella brothers and Argentina who were captained by Hugo Porta. For all the countries in Asia this is the most important weekend of the year, where we share seventy-two hours with the best players in the world in a wonderful spirit of goodwill, sportsmanship and friendship.*

It will be of great interest to the authorities in Britain that, if they do nothing else to encourage rugby in Papua New Guinea or for that matter in most of the smaller rugby-playing countries of the Pacific basin (and, to the best of my knowledge, they do not), they will be delighted to hear that, by allowing the famous international players of the British Isles to compete in Hong Kong every spring, they are making a huge and worthwhile contribution to spreading the gospel of running rugby in the far outposts of the game. I heartily applaud their involvement. The final this year provided the best game and highest standard of sevens rugby I have seen, and the Fijians, all athletic grace, speed, power and uninhibited skill, genius and outrageous flamboyance, demolished a New Zealand side of raw power packed to the gunnels with outstanding players who were, however, a shade too slow in thought and deed to contain the most gifted runners in the world. The perfect setting of the Government Stadium in Hong Kong, a green oasis in the middle of a concrete jungle, surrounded by hills, on a warm pleasant day with the temperatures in the seventies, was matched by two days of marvellous rugby which has no equal anywhere else, and I am looking forward to visiting this spectacular sporting occasion next year.

I regretted missing the Seagram Grand National at Aintree, but I was able to watch a recording when I landed back in England. The course at Liverpool is not all that far from my home in Preston and there is a special atmosphere and excitement engendered every year by the event, which is generally acknowledged as 'the greatest steeplechase in the world'. I ought to point out that, for sheer class and quality, nothing compares with the Cheltenham Gold Cup but for drama, thrills and spills the Grand National is out on its own. The size and build of some of the fences are terrifying and, with the big drop on the landing side of many of the fences an unusual and dangerous hazard, the miracle to me is not that there are so few bad injuries to man, woman and horse, but that such a good percentage manage to survive the likes of 'Beechers Brook' and the 'Chair' to actually finish the race.

Whilst I would quite enjoy the opportunity to play a round of golf out of the public eye and limelight at St Andrews on the Old Course or play a game of tennis on Centre Court at Wimbledon, nothing, but

Secreto, far side, ridden by Christy Roche getting up to beat El Gran Señor in a photo finish at the Epsom Derby

nothing, would persuade me to sit beside Derek Warwick in his Renault doing 190 m.p.h., stand in the middle of Lord's with Joel Garner in a bad mood thundering up to the wicket to bowl at me, or climb on board on a nine-year-old 4½-mile steeplechaser to tackle Aintree. I may have been a second-row forward not always noted for super intelligence but I firmly believe in *chacun à son goût*, and I see no point in risking life and limb in the pursuit of sport. I admire the National Hunt jockeys for their seemingly inexhaust-

ible supply of bravado, and the 30 or so jockeys who, each year, accept the formidable challenge of Aintree are the unsung and underpaid heroes of the racing game. Probably half of the 40 jockeys who went to post for the 1984 National fully expected to part company with their horses at some stage during the race. As it happened, a record number of 23 finished the race and a crowd of nearly 37,000 watched the four leading market rivals do fierce battle at the business end of the race.

Jumping the fourth last, the Irish challenger Greasepaint was, despite a big weight, hanging on grimly to the lead with Hello Dandy putting in a lively challenge. Gradually, relentlessly, Hello Dandy wore down the opposition and, safely negotiating the final fence, he set sail for home. He drifted tantalizingly across the course towards the stand rails on the long run-in, and Greasepaint drew level with him once again. But, in the closing stages, Hello Dandy, after 4½ gruelling miles and 30 big fences, found greater reserves of energy and, showing rare courage, drew away to win by four length from Greasepaint. The 1983 winner Corbiere, under the crushing top weight of 12 stone, came a very gallant third.

With housewives, grannies and virtually everyone who was not spending the weekend potholing, enjoying a bet on the race, the Grand National is an integral part of the British tradition and our heritage, and it is good to report that, thanks to the recent generosity of Ladbroke's in looking after Aintree for the last seven years and now the new sponsors, Seagram, the race and the racecourse are finally safe. The threat of extinction has, at last, been removed; with the long-term future of the race guaranteed, the Grand National will, happily, remain part of the British way of life for ever and a day.

So, too, will the Derby, and 1984 produced a marvellous finish between two outstanding racehorses, El Gran Señor and Secreto, both trained in Ireland. After his comprehensive victory in the 2000 Guineas at Newmarket, El Gran Señor (trained by Vincent O'Brien, ridden by Pat Eddery and owned by football-pools multi-millionaire Robert Sangster – the most powerful triumvirate in British racing) was the hottest favourite to win the Derby for years. The horse began the race at odds of 11-to-8 on and few of the quarter of a million people at Epsom that day expected the wonder horse to be beaten. The gypsies and fortune tellers on the famous Heath were, by all accounts, unanimous for once, and it had been generally agreed in the incredible world of bloodstock values in the mid-1980s that, if the hot favourite duly won, the colt would immediately be worth somewhere between 60 and 80 million dollars as a stallion at stud. To me it sounds like monopoly money, and it is hard to believe a horse can be worth those sort of figures. However, as Pat Eddery cruised round Tattenham Corner into the straight, going easily in fifth place and poised to pounce, he knew the stakes were high. The 250-to-1 outsider and no-hoper At Talaq swept round the final bend into the straight pursued by Telios (100-to-1), Claude Monet (12-to-1), Elegant Air (50-to-1), El Gran Señor (11-to-8) and Secreto (14-

to-1). Trained by Vincent's son, David O'Brien, Secreto had finished third in the Irish 2000 Guineas, and was quietly fancied by connections to show considerable improvement at Epsom.

As the field of 17 runners charged down the straight the biggest live sporting crowd of the year anywhere in Europe saw El Gran Señor cruise through to take the lead over two furlongs from the winning post, and he looked as if he was going to stride away to win. However, at this point, Secreto burst out of the pack to begin his challenge and, in the final two pulsating furlongs, he began, relentlessly, to wear down the favourite. Suddenly, with the race on in earnest and with the two principals drawing clear of the rest of the field, El Gran Señor's stamina began to give out and, as the horse started to tire, he began to drift across the course to the right with sheer fatigue. In a driving finish, Pat Eddery desperately tried to nurse El Gran Señor home but, hard driven by Christy Roche, Secreto got up right on the line to win a thrilling race by the narrowest possible margin – a short head. It was a fantastic race and will live in the memory for a long time.

So too will the final of the European Cup, the premier soccer Cup for the best club sides in Europe. For several seasons now Liverpool have dominated English football and, under Bill Shankly and Bob Paisley, they enjoyed considerable and well-deserved success. Now a third inspiring manager is in charge – Joe Fagan – and in his first year he was to lead Liverpool to another first-division title and to Rome for the final of the European Cup against AS Roma. It was another nerve-racking sporting occasion which I watched on television in Majorca, where I was on holiday with my wife, Hilary. The bar was mostly filled with Germans and I was glad they had no team through to the most prestigious club final in Europe. A handful of English supporters sat round giving Liverpool all the encouragement we could muster, and we were delighted when Phil Neal, that faithful Merseyside servant, opened the scoring after quarter of an hour when he prodded the ball past the Italian goalkeeper after he had failed to hold a dangerous cross from the wing.

However, just before half-time Pruzzo headed the equalizer and that remained the score at half-time, at full-time and at the end of extra time. For the first time in the 28-year history of the European Cup final the trophy was to be decided on a penalty shoot-out. Each side nominated five players to take penalties, and Liverpool made a disastrous start when Steve Nicol ballooned his shot over the bar. Bartolomei scored for Roma. Neal was successful for Liverpool but Conti failed for Roma. 1-1 with 3 more penalties for each side to follow. Souness, Rush and Kennedy all scored for Liverpool but Francesco Graziani fluffed his kick and, by 4 penalties to 2, the European Cup was on its way to Anfield. England may not be unbeatable at international level, but our top clubs are still as good as any in Europe, as Tottenham Hotspur had proved a week earlier by winning the UEFA Cup, beating Anderlecht, also on penalties after extra time.

These results show there is nothing wrong with the steely nerve of our top soccer players, and that also applies to our top motorcyclists who race on two wheels at breakneck speed in the highly competitive world of Grand Prix racing. The British Grand Prix at Silverstone took place at the beginning of August.

As with the motor racing Grand Prix a huge crowd of over 50,000 turned up to watch the big race – the 500 c.c. event – even though hopes of a British victory were rather forlorn. With the reigning world champion Freddie Spencer on the sidelines, injured and out of title contention, the top of the world championship table had become a straight battle between the two Americans, Eddie Lawson and Randy Mamola, but there was still considerable domestic interest for me in the performances of Ron Haslam and Barry Sheene who have done so much to inspire British youngsters in recent years.

Sheene has shown rare courage in recovering from an horrific crash and dreadful injuries to race again at the highest level, but I was disappointed to discover that his machine at Silverstone lacked the necessary power to give him any chance of winning. The fact that he was able to spend much of the race up with the leading half a dozen competitors speaks volumes for his genius as a rider, and it is fair to reflect that the skills which had helped to win the world title had not deserted him.

However, after the three practice sessions, Barry Sheene found himself in seventh position on the starting grid behind the initial pace-setters Raymond Roche, Didier de Radigues of Belgium, the two Americans Lawson and Mamola and Ron Haslam. At the end of the second lap, the Union Jacks were being furiously waved as Ron Haslam led the field into Abbey Curve at around 140 m.p.h., hotly pursued by Radigues, Mamola and Sheene. By the end of the third lap, Lawson had moved up to fourth place with Sheene slipping back and that was the position at the end of the sixth of the 28 laps of the race, except that Radigues, having briefly taken the lead, dropped out of contention. The superior power of the Honda of Mamola and the Yamaha of Lawson inevitably allowed them to nibble away at Haslam's lead and, during the eighth lap, Mamola hit the front from Lawson with Haslam relegated to third place.

From there to the finish, Mamola dominated the race. It was a dramatic sight to watch him cornering at speeds in excess of 100 m.p.h. with his body straddled across the bike and one knee almost scraping along the track. His manoeuvrability was quite remarkable as he accelerated round the various bends at frightening angles and speeds, and he was quite invincible on the straights, touching 200 m.p.h. Lawson, with such a big lead in the world championship table, was not inclined to take unnecessary risks and seemed perfectly content to follow in Mamola's slipstream, secure in the knowledge that second place would be another giant step on his way to his first world title.

Haslam battled bravely to hold third position and Sheene did particularly well on his outdated Suzuki to finish fifth. The whole 80-mile race was a stirring spectacle. Mamola had only one real moment of anxiety and that was when he was suddenly confronted by an extremely startled rabbit on the track. He hit the wretched creature but kept control of the bike and Lawson, in hot pursuit, was equally surprised when a flying dead rabbit hurtled through the air to ricochet off his knee and land on the side of the track. It was an alarming incident, but it failed to break either the concentration or the dynamic rhythm of Mamola and he went on to win in convincing style.

I have the greatest admiration and respect for these fearless sportsmen who risk life and limb in such a potentially hazardous occupation as motor cycling. It is partly by accepting the high standards set by Grand Prix riders that I decided, in retrospect, the Embassy World Professional Darts Championship, which I visited in January at Stoke-on-Trent, could not justifiably be classed as a great sporting event. I spent a relaxed and pleasant evening at the Jollees Showclub in the company of Jocky Wilson but, much as I enjoyed Jocky's demonstration of skill and the convivial atmosphere of the competition, I felt that this particular event, more than any other, would be nothing without the influence of television.

Jocky was great fun and had an amazing story to tell from humble beginnings living in a council house and playing in the local darts league in Fife in Scotland to scaling the dizzy heights and becoming champion of the world in 1982. I marvelled, as I sat with a pint of beer watching Jocky in his first-round win over Terry O'Dea, not just at the consistent accuracy of his throwing but also at the mathematical facility with which he was able to flick the darts in rapid succession into the appropriate treble, double and single numbers as he approached the finish of a game. The moment he threw a treble 20 to leave himself, say, 85 to win the game, he knew instantly which combination he required. He would throw, in a trice, one dart into the treble 19 and the next without time to blink into the double 14. But, somehow, to elevate the game of darts into a great sporting event would be wrong and, with great respect for the undeniable talents of the men who play at the top level, I am afraid they are no more deserving of the real sporting accolades than domino or croquet players.

I reckon Jocky Wilson would be as good at rugby as I would be at darts; *chacun à son goût*

The participants scarcely struck me as dedicated athletes, with many of the best players showing a tendency to appear overweight and unfit and, whilst I do not for a moment grudge them the extremely lucrative rewards of heavy television sponsorship, I believe it would be wrong to devote any more space to what is, in the final analysis, a very minor sport. The game of darts is put into proper perspective when I look back on a marvellous year; the outstanding sporting highlights for me were not Jocky Wilson and Eric Bristow with their accurate throwing.

My highlights were watching Severiano Ballesteros sinking his final two putts on the Old Course, St Andrews on the seventeenth and eighteenth greens, to win the British Open Golf; John McEnroe proving in the men's singles at Wimbledon that he is probably the best tennis player of all time; Martina Navratilova proving equally majestic in the women's singles; Lucinda Green and Beagle Bay at Badminton demonstrating woman and horse in perfect harmony, sheer poetry in motion; and also the fastest Boat Race of all time. I shall always remember the power and grace and terrifying speed of the West Indian fast bowlers; the guts and determination of Ian Botham; the dignity of boxer Frank Bruno in defeat; and the inspirational glamour and tingling atmosphere of such unique occasions as the Calcutta Cup rugby, the London Marathon and the FA Cup Final. I shall long treasure the memory of the fearless Niki Lauda winning the British Grand Prix for the third time; the heroic performances of all our medal winners at the Olympic Games in Los Angeles, especially our golden girl Tessa Sanderson; and, right at the top of the roll of honour, the mesmeric magic of Torvill and Dean on the ice at the Winter Olympics in Sarajevo. They were simply sensational and, as they stood on the podium to collect their gold medals and the National Anthem was played, it was perhaps the most poignant moment of all. At that moment, as with all the many great British sporting occasions of 1984, I was proud to be British.